Milan since the Miracle

D1527311

Milan since the Miracle

City, Culture and Identity

John Foot

Oxford • New York

First published in 2001 by
Berg
Editorial offices:
150 Cowley Road, Oxford, OX4 1JJ, UK
838 Broadway, Third Floor, New York, NY 10003-4812, USA

Berg is an imprint of Oxford International Publishers Ltd.

Library of Congress Cataloging-in-Publication Data
A catalogue record for this book is available from the Library of Congress.

British Library Cataloguing-in-Publication Data
A catalogue record for this book is available from the British Library.

ISBN 1 85973 545 2 (Cloth)
1 85973 550 9 (Paper)

Typeset by JS Typesetting, Wellingborough, Northants.
Printed in the United Kingdom by Biddles Ltd, Guildford and King's Lynn.

The biggest *grazie* of all goes to Marina and Lorenzo.
Without them, I would never have even tried to
understand Milan, let alone stayed long enough
to study this strange and most enigmatic of cities,
its peripheries and its inhabitants.
This book is dedicated to them, with love.

Contents

List of Maps and Illustrations ix

Acknowledgements xi

1 Milan, City of Fragments 1

2 Mass Cultures and Popular Cultures in Milan: The 'Boom' and After 19

3 City of Movement: Milan and Mass Immigration, 1950–2000 37

4 Divided City: Milan and Cinema, 1945–2000 71

5 Television and the City: The History and Impact of Television in Milan, 1945–2000 85

6 Capital of Design, Capital of Fashion 109

7 The Milanese Urban Periphery: Myth and Reality, 1950–2000 135

8 From Boomtown to Bribesville: The Images of the City, 1980–2000 157

Conclusion: Whose City? Which City? 181

Appendix 1: Films Cited 185

Appendix 2: The History of Milan since 1945 – Society, Culture and Politics, A Personal Chronology 187

Bibliography 201

Index 229

List of Maps and Illustrations

Map 1. Milan. The city centre (Lorenzo Sartori, 2000).

Map 2. Milan. The centre and the periphery (Lorenzo Sartori, 2000).

Figure 1: The Pirelli Tower under construction (Archivio Storico Pirelli).

Figure 2: The Pirelli Tower nearing completion (Archivio Storico Pirelli).

Figure 3: City and countryside. Workers on strike outside the FACE factory in Bovisa, 1964 (S. Loconsolo; Archivio Storico Fiom).

Figure 4: Immigrants. *Rocco and his Brothers*, final scene. The workers return to the Alfa Romeo factory. Ciro and his girlfriend kiss (Luchino Visconti, 1960; BFI Films, Stills, Posters and Designs).

Figure 5: Industrious Milan. Alberto Sordi as a factory foreman, *Il Mafioso* (Film still; A. Lattuada, 1962; BFI Films, Stills, Posters and Designs).

Figure 6: Marcello Mastroianni, with the Pirelli skyscraper in the background (Film still; M. Antonioni, *La Notte*, 1960; BFI Films, Stills, Posters and Designs).

Figure 7: The old periphery. *Miracolo a Milano* (Film still; V. De Sica, 1951; BFI Films, Stills, Posters and Designs).

Figure 8: Clerks. Ermanno Olmi directs *Il Posto* (Film still; Ermanno Olmi, 1960; BFI Films, Stills, Posters and Designs).

Figure 9. Cinema and the City. Luchino Visconti directs *Rocco e i suoi fratelli* from the top of the Duomo, 1960 (Film still, Luchino Visconti, 1960; BFI Films, Stills, Posters and Designs).

Figure 10. The Pirelli Tower on completion, at night (Archivio Storico Pirelli).

Figure 11: Industrial Periphery. Sesto San Giovanni, April 1961. Workers from the Breda company at the factory gates (Archivio Storico Fiom).

Figure 12. Industrial Province. Workers leave a factory in Legnano, 1962 (Archivio Storico Fiom).

Figure 13: Industrial City. Workers leave the Pirelli plant, 1955 (Archivo Storico Pirelli).

Figure 14: Protest. Workers besiege the Pirelli Skyscraper during the 'hot autumn', 1969 (Archivio Storico Pirelli).

Figure 15: Protest. Pirelli workers sit in. *La Galleria*, 1969 (Archivio Storico Pirelli).

Figure 16: The 'old periphery'. Bovisa. Piazza Bausan, 1960s (Postcard Image).

Figure 17: City of Time. The Alarm Clock production line from the Borletti Factory (Milan, 1950s: Archivio Storico Borletti).

Figure 18: Fashion and Design. The *Superleggera* chair, Giò Ponti (Cassina. Model 699. 1957. Photo by Aldo Ballo).

Figure 19: Milan Today. Piazzale Lugano, 22, 2000 (Antonio Conese, Tam Tam Fotografie).

Figure 20: Milan Today. Piazzale Lugano, 22, 2000 (Antonio Conese, Tam Tam Fotografie).

Every effort has been made to obtain permission to use copyright photographs included in this book. I would like to thank Viviana Rocca at the Pirelli Archive, the staff at the Fiom Archive, Antonio Conese, Lorenzo Sartori and the BFI in London for help with obtaining images or the preparation of illustrations.

Acknowledgements

This book would never have appeared without the emotional, moral and financial support of various institutions, friends, family members and colleagues. The early work (especially the research behind Chapter 3) was carried out whilst I was a research fellow at Churchill College, Cambridge. The generosity, flexibility and understanding of Churchill proved invaluable. The remaining research has been completed under the auspices of the British Academy whose Institutional Research Fellow scheme allowed me research time that is denied to most academics. I would also like to thank these other institutions for crucial financial help along the way: the British School at Rome, the Leverhulme Trust, the Nuffield Foundation, the Graduate School, the Dean's Travel Fund and the Italian Department at UCL. Various individuals have read my work and commented upon it, or inspired me to pursue specific projects. Many of these are friends who have helped me in various ways in different countries along the way. Paul Ginsborg has been a constant inspiration despite his own heavy workload and commitments. His influence on all my work has been central from the very beginning. Bob Lumley has often taken on more work to allow me to continue my research. He has been a continual source of constructive ideas, help, advice and criticism since 1996. The same can be said of my colleague and friend, John Dickie. I would also like to thank David Forgacs, Russell King, Jonathan Morris, Stefano Musso, Stephen Gundle, Giulio Sapelli, Gianfranco Petrillo, Sandra Wallman and Salvatore Palidda. The staff at the Feltrinelli, Braidense and Comunale libraries in Milan have always been ready to meet my often bizarre requests for books, newspapers and photocopies. Many anonymous readers and seminar attendees have aided me in big or small ways with queries, analytical lacunae or by pointing out simple factual errors. Illustrator Lorenzo Sartori prepared the maps of Milan used in this book.

Other individuals have kept me sane and sated throughout my various travels, moves and journeys. All of my extended family have been patient with the whims of constant travelling and crossed-out phone numbers: Clare and Kate Fermont and various Foots and Beckinsales – Matt, Mary, two Monicas, Paul, Robert, Rose, Tom, Michael. My mum Monica also compiled the index for this book and sent me a constant stream of cuttings relating to Italy. Paul, my dad, inspired me to write in a readable style and has indoctrinated me with a healthy disrespect for the Academy. My Italian grandmother Silvia, who died in 1986, has always been an inspiration to me. Outside the family, and in no particular order, I would like to

Acknowledgements

thank Simon Parker, Robert Gordon, Lawrence Grasty, John Parker, Alice Angus, Lesley Punton, Barbara Placido, Roberto Maestri, Paolo Natale, Luigi Mazzari, Daniela Fossati, Claudio Uracchi, Daniele Arpini, Daniela Cipolla, Fabio Lazzaretti. Chiara Moretti has provided priceless pastoral help over the last ten years, and has even helped me understand Milanese dialect. I really would never have finished this book without her. Helen Castor and Julian Ferraro were especially supportive during some bad days in 1999. Penny Green and Bill Spence (and Grace) have been the best landparents any tenant could wish for. I also owe a great debt to the staff of Air UK, Alitalia, KLM, Go and now Buzz. Finally, a special thanks goes to Ian Wright and Tony Adams.

Map 1: Milan City Centre.

Key to Maps 1 and 2

1 *Il Duomo di Milan* (Cathedral)
2 *La Rinascente* (Department store)
3 *Palazzo di Giustizia* (Central Law Courts)
4 *Carcere di San Vittore* (San Vittore Prison)
5 *Palazzo dell'arte* (The Art Palace, exhibition space for the *Triennale*)
6 *Fiera* (Trade Fair Zone)
7 *Grattacielo Pirelli* (The Pirelli Skyscraper)
8 *Stazione Centrale* (Central Train Station)
9 *Stazione Garibaldi* (Garibaldi Train Station)
10 *Stadio di San Siro* (San Siro football stadium)
11 *Via Corelli* (Detention centre for immigrants without papers, previously a temporary housing area for homeless immigrants)
12 *Cerchia dei Navigli* (ex-Circle of Canals)
13 *Mura Spagnole* (ex-Spanish walls)
14 *Circonvallazione* (ring road)

Map by Lorenzo Sartori.

Map 2: Milan. City centre and periphery.

–1–

Milan, City of Fragments

A city which has consumed itself again and again (Primo Moroni)

The city is constructed by its gaps (Stephen Barber)

Over the last fifty years, the city of Milan has gone through a series of tumultuous changes. As the 'capital of the miracle', Milan led Italy's extraordinary economic miracle and consolidated its role as the financial and industrial capital of Italy. Hundreds of thousands of immigrants arrived from across the peninsula and the city's periphery began to dominate the historic centre. New estates sprang up around the city, extending the urban area across to Venice to the east and Turin to the west. The hinterland stretched as far as the eye could see. Culturally, the city was the centre of early Italian television production, and produced a series of film-makers whose work went to the very heart of the contradictions of the boom years. Luchino Visconti's *Rocco and his Brothers* (1960) symbolized the miracle in Milan. Luciano Bianciardi's marvellous polemical novel *La vita agra* (1962), set in the Milan of the miracle, depicted a city able to win over even the most incorrigible of potential rebels. Giovanni Testori published an evocative series of novels (with the collective title *The Secrets of Milan*) set amongst the lumpenproletariat of the city and the hinterland, from Giambellino to Roserio to Novate Milanese to Via MacMahon to Bovisa (1961, 1985, 1996, 1998).

Yet, almost as soon as it had begun, the boom came to an end. Industrial production began to shift away from the city itself and the immigrant wave slowed down to a trickle. This process went unnoticed by sociologists and historians with the upheavals of 1968. Workers and students dominated the streets of Milan for over ten years, occupying the central city streets which had been cleared of the city's working classes in the post-war period. The Piazza Fontana bomb of 1969, and the Dreyfus-like cases of Pinelli and Valpreda, radicalized thousands of young people and provided the focus for protest through the 1970s. Milan invented a new date to rank with 1 May and 25 April – 12 December. During the 'years of lead', the struggle turned violent and each side was left with numerous martyrs to mourn and avenge.

With the end of student protest, Milan was faced with a yet more painful process of de-industrialization. Companies that had constructed the city and given work to thousands of Milanese and immigrants began to close, one after the other: Breda, Falck, Alfa Romeo, Innocenti, OM, Pirelli. The characteristic crowds of workers with their bluecoats (*Tuta Blu*, or white, for Pirelli) disappeared almost overnight. Just as the working class reached its peak of institutional bargaining power, it found itself confronted by the *tabula rasa* of globalization. Industrial zones became known as *aree dimesse* (*discharged* or *removed* areas). An eerie silence settled over areas once dominated by noise, smoke and masses of workers at the beginning and end of every shift. Classic working-class areas no longer contained any members of the working class. In ten years, Milan made the painful and traumatic shift from an industrial to a post-industrial city.

Politically, this second great transformation was managed by the party which had governed Milan, in coalition with other political forces, since the end of the second world war – the Socialists. The period of de-industrialization was marked by an embracing of the new values of a new city – service industries of all kinds, stock market investment, the fashion industry, private television and advertising. The spending spree of the *Milano da bere* ('Milan is good enough to drink', an advertising slogan that came to symbolize a whole period of urban life) of the mid to late 1980s came hard on the heels of the national government of Bettino Craxi, Milanese socialist and organizer of his immense political power base in the city. *Milano da bere* both reflected and embraced the new values of the post-industrial city. The 1980s were also characterized by the institutionalization of political and economic corruption. In February 1992, the arrest of a minor Socialist politician began the most far-reaching and dramatic judicial enquiry in Italy's history. Milan became *Tangentopoli* – Bribesville. New political forces entered the fray to fill the huge gaps left by the disappearance of the Socialists and the Christian Democrats and the deep crisis of the traditional left – deprived of its classic social base and unable to adapt to a new epoch of work and investment. The regionalist Northern Leagues took a brief grip on the city in the 1990s, more through a general disgust with political corruption than from any positive regionalism on by the Milanese electorate. In the mid-1990s, other new political forces began to dominate Milanese politics, in particular Silvio Berlusconi's *Forza Italia!* organization. The city where Berlusconi had first re-shaped the urban landscape – with the Milano 2 and Milano 3 housing developments – and then re-moulded the cultural landscape through private television and advertising, became the centre of his political project. Meanwhile the left struggled to make any impact in the city that had been the capital of the Resistance, the capital of 1968, the capital of the union movement and the cultural stronghold of the intellectual left right up until the 1970s (Petrillo 1998a; Lumley 1989).

This book is an attempt to understand, explain and describe the history of these processes which have transformed Milan over the last fifty years. This is not a traditional history. There is no classic *chronology* here. The chapters are not neatly divided under titles such as 'politics', 'culture' and 'economics'. Every chapter deals with all of these areas, and more. Nor is this a history of the whole city. Whole areas are omitted. Others are given disproportionate space. This is a micro-history of a city, and takes as its subject matter certain emblematic neighbourhoods, spaces, places, events, films, television programmes, roads, immigrants, objects of design and desire, and events. These micro-moments and entities will explain the macro-changes that have dominated most of the accounts of the city's history to date. Thus, my book will tell us more about the city and its peoples than we already know – and not just the city of Milan, but The City, not just Milan, but Italy.

All the crucial movements, booms, slumps and moments in twentieth-century Itaiian history have had their epicentre in Milan. The first trade unions took root in Milan, fascism was made in Milan and the socialist reformists made of Milan the jewel in their crown. The resistance was led from Milan and saw its final act there in 1945. The city was the centre of the economic miracle that transformed Italy, and the location of the most popular and successful television programme in Italian history – *Lascia o raddoppia?* – Double or Quit? (1954). Silvio Berlusconi later created the first private television empire in the city. The 'strategy of tension' was to begin in a bank in Milan, and the de-industrialization of the 1980s also hit this city first. Milan was the centre of Italy's creative-industrial design revolution in the 1960s and later became one of the world's fashion capitals. Armani, Prada and Versace replaced Falck, Breda and Pirelli as the economic bosses of the city. Much of Italy's history is bound up with that of Milan, and the story of Milan can be read as the story of a nation.

Certain of these spaces, places, moments and events are evoked and studied throughout this book

Landscapes. Flat City, Ugly City, Grey City, Foggy City

Milan is a flat city, its only hill is artificial – created by war rubble (Monte Stella) or by railway bridges. In theory, you should be able to see for miles, but another characteristic of the city gets in the way – the fog in the winter, the mist, the *afa* (sultry weather) in the summer. The spectacular views of the mountain ranges to the north and west should be available to most Milanese most of the time, but in fact they only 'appear' once a year. Milan is a city intimately connected in the public mind with its weather – the suffocating smog of the summer and above all the wintertime fog – la *nebbia*. True Milanese are said to be born 'with fog in their lungs'. Milan is a city that, often, is invisible – literally. Almost as a consequence of this, Milan is a grey city, a black-and-white city where only occasional colours are allowed to spring out – the pinks of the Duomo (Cathedral), the bright blues of spring. Milan is best remembered as grey, in black-and-white, and its peripheries can only be imagined in that colourless colour. Finally, Milan is universally recognized as an ugly city – by residents and non-residents alike. The beautiful side of Milan is hidden, locked up, behind closed doors, private.

Danee. Piazza Affari

Milan is a city obsessed by one thing, or rather by two – work and money. The integrative capacities of the city and its cosmopolitan character – the 'small apple' – its American qualities of dynamism, profit and attraction all derive from this ability to produce, invest and circulate money. The Italian stock exchange is in Milan, in Palazzo degli Affari, the main industries have always been in the city, the main banks are here – most around Piazza Cordusio. After the two industrial revolutions of the early part of the century and the boom, Milan was at the centre of Italy's post-industrial revolution where industries such as fashion, advertising and publishing began to dominate the economy of Lombardy and southern Europe.

Fiera Campionaria

From its humble beginnings in April 1920, Milan's annual trade fair soon became the biggest in Italy, and amongst the most important in Europe. The early fairs had their origins in the five international exhibitions held in the city between 1871 and 1906. The opening of the *Fiera* became linked to the visit of the King and posters advertising the exhibition linked images of progress and technical change with Milan itself. By the 1930s, a visit to the Fiera had become a fixed part of the year for over two million visitors from the city and all over Italy. The real boom for the Fiera came after the war. New permanent areas were established and expanded to the north of the city, and the number of visitors had risen to three and a half million by 1948. Technical experiments were centred on the *Fiera Campionaria* including the first television pictures seen in Italy. By the time of the boom, mass consumption had made the annual fair a massive event, too big for any organization to handle: 4.3 million visitors arrived in 1962 and 14,000 exhibitors were involved in the fair. The *Fiera* encapsulated the key regional and European market role of Milan, not just as an industrial city but as a centre of advertising knowhow, of the exchange of information and as a showcase for novelty, progress and technological change. Milan had always been a centre of small and large-scale trade with a powerful and specialized commercial class (Morris 1993; Amatori and Sillano 1996). It had also developed into the 'biggest market in Italy' in parallel with its industrial growth (Dalmasso 1972: 385). After the boom, the massive centralization of the annual Fiera began to be replaced with a series of specialized fairs throughout the year. The annual event dragged on into the 1980s, changing its name to the *Fiera di Milano*, but attention and market forces began to concentrate on events held throughout the year, whilst Milan itself kept a central role (Longoni 1987; *Corriere della Sera*, 13 April 1960).

Bovisa

Bovisa was the classic, stereotypical working-class neighbourhood at the turn of the century. A host to immigrants across the whole century, Bovisa took in new residents first from the countryside, then from the Italian south, and then from Turkey, Morocco and Egypt. Hemmed in by the criss-crossing railway tracks of the commuter system known as the *Ferrovie Nord* (the Northern Railways), in the 1920s Bovisa was clearly separated from the city by the obvious and marked boundary between city and countryside. Huge factories were constructed in open fields, and travellers to the lakes glimpsed the dark, satanic smokestacks as they left Milan. In the 1919 elections, over 70 per cent of the electorate voted for the Socialists, who campaigned with a revolutionary 'maximalist' programme. By the 1960s, there were 40,000 industrial workers employed in the neighbourhood. Immigrants from the south packed rented accommodation in the zone. Yet already, during the 1970s, factories began to close or move out of the city. By 1996, *all* the factories in the zone were empty. Many were demolished. Some were re-used for the new university faculties of architecture and engineering. Others remained as monuments to a bygone era. New immigrants used them as housing. Banks sprouted up in the neighbourhood. Instead of thousands of blue-shirted workers, the mornings in Bovisa were characterized by the arrival of hundreds of students carrying their architectural designs. The famous gasometers, symbol of the zone's productivity, were re-planned as art museums. They had stopped storing gas in 1997.

Centre and Periphery

Milan's periphery began to dominate the city – spatially – in the 1950s. New neighbourhoods sprang up through urban planning or as a series of self-constructed neighbourhoods built by new immigrants. Many of these new neighbourhoods became infamous: Comasina, Quarto Oggiaro, Gratosoglio, Gallaratese. This was the new Milan, the Milan where most residents lived, the Milan of isolation and anomie, but also of housing of good quality for those who had come from shacks and wartime sheds. And this periphery stretched not just to the very edge of the boundaries of the Comune – where the new Comasina neighbourhood was completed in 1954 – but in a huge circle taking in Monza, Sesto San Giovanni, Pavia and later – in the 1980s and 1990s – extending right across to Turin and Venice from west to east. This periphery is made up a mosaic of forms, places, 'non-places', bridges and roads. It is flat, bleak, grey and often foggy, or it is usually represented as such. But this periphery *is* Milan. It is not a non-city, or an anti-city, but part of the huge urban sprawl – the metropolis – which Italian society has created over vast tracts of its territory. Here, by the 1980s, the motor car had become the master, in perfect symmetry with the new, super-mobile forms of work, consumption and study that characterised the transition to the post-industrial.

Populations

Across the complexity of the space occupied by Milan and its endless *periferia*, various, shifting populations have always gravitated towards the city, and away from the city. Milan has always been a city of shifting populations. There have always been commuters from the building workers at the start of the century to the businessmen of recent times. Others used (and use) the city to shop, to demonstrate, to study, to sell, to steal, to barter, to campaign, to build and to knock down, or just to drive through or around. These shifting populations have almost always outnumbered the permanent residents – the Milanese. Yet even the latter have never been particularly attached to a permanent presence in the city itself. The post-industrial city saw the Milanese almost continually on the move, as the new 'industries' which dominated the city demanded flexible hours and above all hyper-mobility. Children were sent to the countryside or the sea on numerous occasions – in wartime and later during the long summer holidays. With the boom and mass tourism (and the mobility of motorization) the city emptied during August and at weekends leaving behind either those too poor to take holidays, or those rich enough to choose their holiday months outside of the classic season.

Box/Parcheggio/Pavement

With mass motorization, the daily problem of space developed into a constant battle over pavements, streets, land rights and legality. The frantic search for parking spots led to the construction of thousands of underground and multi-storey car parks in the 1980s. The price of garages – *boxes* – shot up as Milan became the city with the highest incidence of car theft in Italy. Nonetheless, these plans could not keep up with the huge increases in car ownership (by the end of the 1990s, there were almost a million cars registered in the city) after the boom, and parked vehicles began to invade the space usually reserved for pedestrians, or the courtyards where Milanese children once played in relative safety. This development was institutionalized as architectural devices were modified in order to allow rows of cars to park on pavements. Trees were removed to create yet further space, and the areas once occupied by factories were also re-used in the same way. Still, over half of the 288,000 cars left on the streets every night were parked illegally. The losers were those without cars, or those forced to use pavements on foot –

pensioners, the disabled, mothers with children in push-chairs, immigrants. The daily journey to school, to work and to the shops became a dangerous and tiring zig-zag through and past parked and moving traffic. The city had become a kind of video game where relaxation was impossible and dangers lurked in every corner. Yet, protests were few and ineffectual. *The city was dominated by a culture of individual mobility, and of car ownership.* A cultural revolution would be required to change things, and in the rush-to-spend of the 1980s and 1990s (with the removal of the minor restrictions on traffic in the city centre) the car became the real (and ubiquitous) boss of the city – economically, spatially and in terms of the mass mobility required by the post-modern urban service economy.

Stazione Centrale

The writer and journalist Anna Maria Ortese called it a 'port of work, a bridge of necessity, an estuary of simple blood' (1998: 44). The central station was the main gateway for those arriving in the city (and leaving it) for at least fifty years. It was here that Mussolini met Hitler in 1938. It was from here that Italian Jews were deported to Auschwitz. The three decades from the 1950s to the 1970s saw the arrival of millions of immigrants from Apulia, Sicily, Campania, Calabria, the Veneto. Every summer, many of these immigrants used the Central Station to return to their home towns and villages. The vast central arches hosted a thousand small, daily dramas; immigrants who arrived without even an address or a contact; others weighed down by vast boxes containing their worldly goods. At weekends, the bars and squares of the station became meeting places for immigrants (Moroni 1992: 315–16). Stazione Centrale was a monument to the industrial city, a hulk of stone, marble, glass and iron. Immigrants knew they were entering a *città operosa* (Bigatti 2000), a city with over 200 clocks at many street corners, a city governed by time and deadlines. The station has always been a place of exchange and the settling of accounts, as the title of one of Milanese crime novelist Giorgio Scerbanenco's short stories – *Stazione centrale ammazzare subito* (1993: 93–110) (Central Station Kill Immediately) – makes clear. 250,000 people pass through the station every day, 3,500 crimes are committed there every year and a series of people live, work, beg, sell or buy various legal and illegal items within the station's one-and-a-half million square metres of tunnels, platforms, waiting rooms, offices, roads, shops and markets (Colombo and Navarini 1999; Angeleri and Columba 1985).

Terrorists were to choose the station as a point of protest. The Alto-Adige terrorists planted a bomb in the left-luggage office in 1962, fascists left a bomb in a bank in the station in 1969. Film-makers and photographers have often used the cinematic qualities of the station for key scenes. *Rocco and his Brothers* arrived there in 1960. Alberto Sordi left from the station to return to Sicily in Lattuada's

Il Mafioso (1962). The industrialist in Pasolini's *Teorema* (1968) chooses to undress in the Central Station, ignored by the train-going public. Giuseppe Bertolucci set a whole film in the Central Station (*Oggetti smarritti*, 1980). In Giorgio Leopardi's 1996 film *Hotel Paura*, a businessman becomes a drop-out and lives in the tunnels, abandoned trains and waiting rooms of the station. With the changes in migration patterns in the 1980s, the station began to lose its importance as a place of dramatic human movement, but remained a focal point for business, travel, city users and illegality of all types. Immigrants used the station to move within Italy, and the square outside the station became a meeting place at weekends for domestic workers and others.

Stazione Garibaldi

This station, with its vast modern roof, was not a place of immigration but of commuting for the hundreds of thousands of workers and clerks who rose before dawn to catch the trundling trains of the *Ferrovie Nord*. Novelist Bianciardi went to the Stazione Garibaldi to try to 'find' the Milanese working class on his arrival in the city in the 1960s. He visited the station in the early morning to observe the commuters and the workers, describing the rhythms of the factory in a series of incisive articles (1960; Petrillo 1992b: 57–8). Ermanno Olmi used the station as a key location in his bitter-sweet fable of the city during the boom – *Il Posto* (*The Job*) (1960). In the post-industrial era, the blue-shirted workers began to disappear, but the station was as full as ever. Business users, shoppers, *impiegati* of all kinds packed its long platforms and streamed onto the MM (the Milanese metro), buses and trams.

Water

Milan is a city built on *acqua*, an urban space criss-crossed and ringed by a complicated series of man-made urban canals until the 1930s when most were covered over by town planners. The main canal intersection at Porta Ticinese remained an important working port right up until the 1970s (Moroni 1999: 262). Food, people and, above all, building materials were transported into the heart of the city and unloaded in an urban port, just as the marble to build the city's gothic *Duomo* had travelled into the lake that once stood in the central Piazza Santo Stefano. With time, and thanks to a complicated and controversial series of planning decisions, most of the canals were covered by roads. The port at Porta Ticinese became an area dominated by bars and the fashion industry, and no longer a place of small-time criminality and popular culture. Only nostalgia kept alive the city of water which Stendhal had so admired, although traces of the watery past of Milan remained – dry docks, strange-shaped bars, bridges, floods, street names, the smell. Once again, it was the motor car that triumphed, this time over the boat and the barge. The origins of the water, which had been at the root of Lombardy's first, rural-urban industrial revolution, were forgotten, and the heat of the city in the summer blasted off the hundreds of kilometres of cement that covered the city with the least green space per resident in Europe.

Ringhiere, Balcony, Grattacielo, Car Park

Working-class or popular housing in Milan (and Turin) developed around the form of apartment balconies known as *ringhiere*. Blocks comprised a series of one- or two-room flats, grouped around a common courtyard with collective bathrooms, washing facilities and stairwells. The reason behind this architectural form was economic – the maximum possible number of families within the minimal possible space. *Ringhiere* housing encouraged collective activity and minimized privacy. Every entrance and exit could be observed. Arguments were heard by everyone. Every visit to the toilet was a public event. Residents, literally, washed their dirty linen in public. In *Rocco and his Brothers* the whole block witnesses the triumph and collapse of the Parondi family. But at times of crisis this architectural collectivity could be invaluable, and the balconies and courtyards provided an enclosed and safe play space for children. With the decline of the Milanese working class, the *ringhiere* began to be colonized by richer, childless families. Space was at a premium and numerous strategies were devised to increase it – beds on stilts, the combination of one, two or even three flats, the creation of closed rooms using balcony space. Public space became privatized against strangers, intruders and potential criminals. Doors appeared on balconies and net curtains in windows. Privacy and security took over. Consumer durables, individual heating systems and private bathrooms, replaced the collective services of the past.

New housing dealt with the *ringhiere* tradition in different ways. Often, on the new peripheries, flats were equipped with individual balconies whose view of other flats and balconies was restricted. Other architects tried to recreate the *ringhiere* in concrete, usually with disastrous effects as long walkways became crime blackspots or rubbish dumps. The premium on space in the city remained. Flats and house prices were calculated by the square metre, and builders devised ever more ingenious ways of re-gaining or creating space within the home for the ever-smaller families of Milan.

Milan never gained an 'American' skyline, despite the promises of the planners of the 1950s. The only truly modern skyscraper in the city remains Giò Ponti's sleek and beautiful Pirelli Tower (known as the Big Pirelli – the *Pirellone*), built just before the boom (it was completed in 1958, and opened in 1960) and architectural-political symbol of that period. Over four years of construction, the building site for the tower became an urban 'event'. Pirelli used the site for huge advertising campaigns and signs on the side of the growing skyscraper monitored the progress of the building. A viewpoint was provided with a large notice that presented the building as a 'modern cathedral' (De Giorgi 103–4). A small statue of the Madonna (invisible from below) was placed on the roof of the skyscraper to indicate the fact that this was the tallest building in the city, taller even than the central cathedral with its famous Madonnina, symbol of the city. The Pirelli Tower was perfectly placed to stun new visitors and immigrants arriving in the city as it soared above the Central Station (Cevini 1996), and it was also intended as the centrepiece of a new modern city centre (the *centro direzionale*) to challenge or even replace the old centre around the Cathedral. Communist Party propaganda films depicted immigrants gazing in wonder at the tower (*Il prezzo del miracolo – The Cost of the Miracle*, 1963) whilst the most famous and reproduced photo from the boom years depicts a Sardinian immigrant weighed down by a huge box of his possessions in front of the looming splendour of the Pirellone (Uliano Lucas, 1969 now in Palidda 2000b: 8). The opening credit sequence from Antonioni's *La Notte* shoots Milan in the reflection of the tower from the top down as the camera moves down the skyscraper. During the 'hot autumn' of 1969, the tower was 'besieged' for three days by thousands of protesting workers from Pirelli (Figure 14). In 1975 the company sold the building to the Lombard Regional government, but the Pirelli Tower name remained.

Across the city, close to the *Duomo*, the BBPR group of architects (Lodovico Belgiojoso; Gian Luigi Banfi; Enrico Peressutti; Ernesto Rogers) built the beautiful *Torre Velasca* (1957–60; Brunetti 1996), a mixed-use tower block heavily criticized at the time but now one of the most admired and well-known buildings in Europe. The BBPR humanist tradition dominated the Milanese architectural scene for decades. Their other work ranged from an extraordinary abstract monument to the victims of the Nazi concentration camps (1945–55) – Banfi, one of the 'Bs' of BBPR, had died in Mauthausen in 1945 – to designs for public housing around the city. However, the BBPR legacy was above all linked to the rich cultural and intellectual *milieu* around the Milan-based journal *Casabella* and the Politecnico di Milano.

Palazzo di Giustizia, San Vittore

The huge, imposing marble towers and massive windows of Milan's justice building have been host to some of the key moments in the city's history since 1945 (and before). In 1946 those who had taken part in the famous revolt in the San Vittore prison were condemned there to over twenty years in prison. The bank-robbing 'bandits' who terrorized the city in the 1960s were tried here. In 1970, a trial involving police chief Luigi Calabresi and the revolutionary newspaper *Lotta Continua* transfixed the city and provided the material for Dario Fo's *Accidental*

Death of an Anarchist. The Justice Palace was also important for the trials that did *not* take place there, with the shift of the Piazza Fontana trials to Catanzaro in 1972. After 1992, the 'Clean Hands' corruption inquiry was based in the *Palazzo*, and the dingy courtrooms became the centre of political attention. Stock shots of the *Palazzo* dominated the television news for over five years and demonstrations focused on the area outside the *Palazzo*. In the late 1990s, it sometimes appeared as if the judicial wrangling inside the impenetrable labyrinth of the *Palazzo di Giustizia* were as important as those in parliament or the seat of Milanese local government.

San Vittore prison was built in a modern, Panoptican style in 1879, with six long wings splayed out from a central tower. Throughout the century, San Vittore provided a micro-history of the city, its inhabitants, its dramas and its revolutions. The rioters of 1898 were taken to San Vittore. Mussolini was briefly held here after the war and thousands of militants passed through the prison before and under fascism, from Gramsci to the anarchist Malatesta, often on their way to internal exile in the south. The prison lived through a period of great ferment in the 1940s, with the torture and deportations of Jews and political prisoners under Nazi occupation, the first great revolt of April 1945 and the chaos of the post-war period, when discipline in the prison collapsed, culminating in a four-day riot in 1946 that paralysed the city and left five dead and 150 injured (Foot 1998b). With 1968, the prison (by now very much absorbed within the urban fabric of Milan) became once again a focus for political activity. Riots were common throughout the 1970s and the prison filled with southern immigrants. Special cells were created for terrorist prisoners during the 'years of lead'. For a time, after 1992, the prison was host to a series of politicians and wealthy businessmen, caught up in the dramatic Tangentopoli scandals. San Vittore had always reflected the social make-up of the city and new immigrants became common within the prison of the 1990s. By 1999, nearly half of the inmates were non-Italians. In Milan's juvenile prison, *La Beccaria, all* the prisoners were foreign immigrants (*La Repubblica*, 7 June 1999).

Giorgio Scerbanenco

The Milan of the 1950s and 1960s, with its dark, forbidding peripheries, was the perfect setting for a crime novelist. *Cronaca nera* dominated the popular press as 'the underbelly of Milan', as the radical journalist Paolo Valera had called the lumpenproletarian zones of the city centre in the late 1870s (Valera 1996), shifted to the city's outskirts – to Buccinasco, to Corsico, to Sesto. Scerbanenco captured this moment and these places in a series of unique, violent and unforbidding novels. The titles alone give an idea of the content – *Milano calibro 9* (1969), *I milanesi ammazzano al sabato* (1969), *Traditori di tutti* (1966), *Venere privata* (1966),

I ragazzi del massacro (1968). Scerbanenco's world is one of blurred morals, of extreme violence, of cynicism and evil, of a complete lack of trust. But it is also a Milanese world, with bodies pushed into canals, betrayals in seedy peripheral hotels, teachers murdered ritually by young delinquents, prisons, police stations and foggy streets. Scerbanenco captured perfectly the moment of transition from the non-violent criminality of the urban underworld (the *Ligéra*) to the violent *metropolitan* and *modern* banditry of the late 1960s, where armed and pointless violence was the order of the day.

MM

Metropolitana Milanese. This underground tube system was the real symbol of the miracle for the Milanese. For years, huge building sites dominated the landscape. Debates over stations, design, prices, and routes took up reams of newsprint. The project went way over budget and years past its original deadline. But, finally, on 1 November 1964, just as the boom began to slow down, the first line of the MM was finished. On the opening day the whole city turned out for a free ride on the gleaming new trains. From the Duomo, to the San Siro stadium in the north to the new Gallaratese neighbourhood, the red MM line 1 linked up neighbourhoods, peoples, monuments, stations, commuters and shoppers. At last, the motor car had a real, fast, modern competitor. Later, the city constructed the second, green line, which extended its tentacles way into the Lombard countryside. The third, yellow line, became one of the symbols of *Tangentopoli* in the 1990s. The parties all took a share of the funds and each brick on the MM3 line cost an incredible one million lire (Stajano 1993: 55). By 1994 the company had amassed debts of fourteen billion lire, yet by 1998 the MM was in profit and expanding even further. Plans for an MM4 were announced in 1999 and the other lines continued to grow into the hinterland. Each new station altered the habits of the Milanese and the uses of specific places, as businesses and traffic shifted to accommodate new nodal points and commuter crowds. The map of the MM reflected the city, but the MM itself also mapped and altered the city and its population movements.

San Siro

First built in 1926, the vast San Siro stadium was hailed as architectural wonder right from the start. It has always been the home ground for both of Milan's football teams, AC Milan and Inter Milan. The most fanatical Inter fans use the *curva nord*, for Milan it is the *curva sud*. Research on the reasons behind support for either team have found no specific social, territorial or cultural pattern, although urban myths survive concerning this support (Natale 1988). Unlike London,

Manchester or Liverpool, there are no Inter or Milan zones in the city. San Siro – *La Scala del calcio* – underwent a massive and costly redevelopment in preparation for the 1990 World Cup. The opening game was held in Milan and the huge steel structures built to hold up the new seating took the capacity of the stadium to 80,000. San Siro was now visible from all parts of the city. With the massive success of the Milanese teams since the war – Inter in the 1960s, Milan in the 1960s and then throughout the 1990s – San Siro has become a tourist attraction and an icon of the city for travellers from all parts of the world. The extraordinary atmosphere created for big games, and the closeness of the crowd to the pitch, make San Siro one of the most impressive sites for modern football in the world.

Circonvallazione

The ring road is always busy, at any time of day or night, apart perhaps from Christmas Day or August. Milan's ring-road is hell on earth. Scene of hundreds of daily arguments, crashes, fires, near misses and breakdowns, it is the artery that both keeps the city moving and symbolizes its deep ecological crisis. By day, the road is occupied by workers, by traders, by lorries, by buses, by scooters and motor-bikes, by those taking their children to school or collecting them, by motorists who are delivering, collecting or providing services.

By night, even after rush hour, the ring road is hardly never empty. Thousands of cars criss-cross the city, stopping at the innumerable traffic lights or jumping red lights when the traffic calms down. After a certain time, the traffic lights themselves are turned off (in favour of flashing amber lights) in many areas, to save money, and intersections become even more dangerous than before. Many of these night-time motorists are single men, prospective clients for the thousands of prostitutes who work the ring road from dusk to dawn (and beyond). In the 1980s, this trade was dominated by Italians, but by the end of the 1990s, the Albanians, Nigerians and Brazilian prostitutes had all but driven the Italians off the streets. The absence of any definable red-light district in the city makes the whole urban area available for trade, and certain areas become specialized in certain tastes, until the prostitutes are moved on by the police, and take up again in other areas.

Piazza Fontana and Via Fatebenefratelli

City of massacres, of mysterious deaths, of political intrigue and plots, secrets and revenge – after the Piazza Fontana massacre of 12 December 1969 the city was plunged into a spiral of violence and counter-violence, which lasted well into the 1980s.

Anniversaries, public space and even basic facts became the subject of confrontation and political struggle. The battles for the release of the anarchist Valpreda, accused of having planted the bomb in the bank, or for the truth in the 'Pinelli case', dominated and divided the city. Fascists controlled certain areas, the left others and certain zones were dangerous merely if you 'looked' like a left or right-wing sympathizer. Monuments, plaques and even graves were controversial and provocative. Each side tried to write in stone its own version of the truth, to the dismay of the other side. Each side had its own heroes, villains and martyrs. This history is now written on the walls and in the cemeteries of Milan, but the full facts about that period are only just beginning to emerge. In 1999, thirty years after a bomb was left in a bank crowded with provincial farmers, the first trial to be held in Milan began, amidst general indifference. In interviews, many young people expressed ignorance concerning the events that had dominated public debate in the city in the 1970s. Just as the mass movements of the 1960s and 1970s had fragmented into a thousand tiny groups and cultural-social centres, so the memory of those events and the dark side of the state became lost in the 'years of lead', which were dominated by political terrorism, by mourning and by ritual.

Driss Mousaffir

Most foreign immigrants are both visible and invisible. They are noticeable as different, but synonymous with other immigrants. They are *marocchini, albanesi, inglesi.* They are nameless. Driss Mousaffir's name became (briefly) famous in 1993. This Moroccan immigrant was victim of a bomb intended to cause chaos and disorder, but not intended to kill him. In fact, the bomb just caused death and destruction. Mousaffir was in the wrong place at the wrong time, sleeping in a park opposite an art gallery. The debates over his funeral, his memory and his short, invisible life in the big city can tell us much about the attitudes to immigration in Milan in the 1980s and 1990s.

La Scala

Other places have marked the post-war history of the city in different ways. La Scala symbolized the reconstruction of the city, and the return of democracy with the return to Italy of Toscanini. Milan embraced the greatest *diva* of them all, Maria Callas, in the 1950s. But La Scala was also the symbol of conspicuous consumption, of wealth, of the Milanese bourgeoisie. In De Sica's *Miracolo a Milano*, the ingenuous central character – Tot' – applauds the fur-clad opera-goers as they leave the opera house. In 1968 Mario Capanna and his student followers chose opening night as a moment of protest, covering the opera-goers with eggs and insults. In the 1980s, the protests changed, reflecting the changes in the city.

Workers protesting against factory closures attempted to block the opening night. La Scala's workers struck in solidarity. Meanwhile, the new image of the city was reflected in the kitsch and design of the opening night opera-goers. Craxi was the star of the show and another Socialist wore a red dress with hammers and sickles designed upon it. By 1993, this élite had been swept away by scandal, and the new star of the opening night was a judge – Francesco Saverio Borelli.

Il Corriere della Sera

Milan has always been at the heart of Italy's publishing and newspaper industries - the city of Mondadori, Garzanti, Bompiani, Rizzoli and Feltrinelli. Above all, the city created the most important newspaper in Italian history, *Il Corriere della Sera*. Founded in 1876 by textile magnates the Crespi family, the *Corriere* became a model for all other newspapers and a school of journalism for all the most important writers who worked for the press. For most of the twentieth century, the offices of the paper were in the central Via Solferino and this area created its own milieu of journalists, photographers and press employees. Editor Luigi Albertini's resistance to the dictats of the Fascist regime saw his removal and the paper became a voice of the government throughout the 1920s and 1930s. With the fall of fascism, the *Corriere* quickly regained its place as the only real Italian newspaper, a role only challenged seriously by *La Repubblica*, based in Rome, after 1976. The *Corriere* became a target for student protesters in the late 1960s, but the editorship of Piero Ottone saw the paper swing to the left and employ such maverick writers as Pasolini and Camilla Cederna. Other key newspapers and magazines have also been based in Milan – the innovative *Il Giorno* in the 1950s and 1960s, a paper that transformed the look and style of Italian journalism; or the key publications in a whole series of other cultural realms, sport (*La Gazzetta dello Sport*); economics (*Il Sole-24 Ore*), fashion, design, tourism, architecture, politics and music (F. Colombo 1998; Ortoleva 1996: 189–90).

Dates: 1881, 1898, 1919, 1945, 1954, 1960, 1969, 1992, 1996, 1997

Certain dates stand out in the contemporary history of Milan: This is an eclectic list of some of them. 1881: a huge Expo is organized in the city, launching Milan as Italy's 'Moral Capital'. 1898: food riots are brutally suppressed by the army, leaving hundreds dead. 1919: Milan comes close to revolution a number of times, as riots and strikes sweep across Italy. In March, the first Fascist movement is formed in the city, in a small palazzo in *Piazza San Sepolcro*. April 1945: Mussolini's body is displayed in *Piazzale Loreto* as partisans parade through the city. The bodies of fascists killed in revenge attacks pile up outside the communal cemetery at Musocco. February 1954: the first Italian television programmes are transmitted from Milan. November 1960: Visconti's film *Rocco and his Brothers* opens amidst controversy. 12 December 1969: a bomb explodes in the agricultural bank in Piazza Fontana. 16 are killed and 88 injured. The 'strategy of tension' had begun.

15 January 1996: the last Falck factory in Sesto San Giovanni, the former 'Stalingrad of Italy', closes. First opened in 1906, by the 1950s there were 10,000 workers in the various Falck plants with their exotic names – Vulcano, Unione, Concordia, Vittoria. Emilo Tadini, artist and author of one of the most acute novels on the state of Milan in the 1980s (Tadini 1993), visited the 'hell' of the one-and-a-half million square metres of land that had once housed the various Falck works. He pronounced the 'myth of working-class Milan' dead, there and then, and called the changes to the city a 'catastrophe'. Once, Tadini wrote, 'those who came to Milan . . . knew where they were going. They knew exactly what the identity of Milan was. Work, big factories . . . But now?' Tadini likened the by-now ex-Falck to a war zone, and a cemetery - with the tombs opened and the gravestones smashed apart (Tadini 1996). February 1992: Mario Chiesa, Socialist Party official and head of the biggest municipal old peoples' home, is arrested whilst receiving seven million lire in bribes from a building contractor. His confessions form the basis of the 'Clean Hands' corruption investigation, leading to the nomination of Milan as *Tangentopoli*. 1997: a new Mayor is elected at the head of a centre-right coalition including the post-fascist party, *Alleanza Nazionale*. Albertini attends both the ceremonies for the Resistance as well as that of the collaborationist Republic of Salò.

My place . . . Piazzale Lugano, 22

Two blocks of flats, connected by a central staircase surrounded by four sets of balconies. A small factory stands in the courtyard alongside a pizzeria, another block, constructed in the 1950s, a cellar and a garage. This is Piazzale Lugano, 22. The house where I live and a microcosm of the history of modern Milan. Constructed in the 1890s in open countryside, the house once looked out upon one of the villas of the Visconti family. A canal ran in front of the houses. Soon, the Bovisa zone became one of the nerve centres of Italy's first industrial revolution. Chemical and metalwork factories sprang up – Broggi, Montecatini, Sirio, Ceretti e Tanfani. Workers began to flood into the zone from the surrounding countryside. New housing was constructed around the area of the railways. Visconti's villa was knocked down to create a bridge over the railway tracks. In the 1950s, the first southern immigrants began to arrive in Piazzale Lugano. Many were employed in the huge post office constructed in the opposite side of the Piazzale. Other dialects began to mingle with the Milanese and Italian. The ring road began to be permanently clogged with traffic. The piazzale was no longer a piazza, but a series of roads curving around the city. The canals were cemented over, the fields disappeared, only some tiny rural features remained. Bovisa became an area of high pollution with the lowest level of green space per person in the city. The osteria (bar) in the courtyard became a pizzeria.

With the boom over, factories began to move out of the city. As the 1980s approached, the debates over the zone centred on the re-use of industrial areas and some factories were demolished. A new station was built and important parts of the university, including the architecture faculty, were moved to the zone, housed in an ex-metalwork factory. Seven banks opened in the high street whilst small shops closed and three supermarkets were set up in the area. Piazzale Lugano, 22 also began to change. Foreigners arrived. An Argentinian woman, an English man, a Kurdish family, an Egyptian family, people from Ecuador, Cuba, Israel. The average age in the blocks plummeted as the older generation left, or died. Five children were born to mothers in the flats in the 1997–9 period. Other languages challenged Italian within the courtyard and on the balconies. Scooters filled the parking spaces. The jobs were also different – film researchers, editors, illustrators, journalists, teachers, university researchers, students and pensioners but also motorbike dispatch riders, tram drivers, door-keepers and builders. The rapid changes to 'my place' – Piazzale Lugano, 22 – over the last ten years reflect those in the city. The mosaic is that of Milan, but it is also unique. Every block, every house is different, and has its own history and future to be written, but the history of every house and every block can also tell us something significant about the whole city, its inhabitants and its future.

The Micro and the Macro: Methodologies

This is a work of urban history, which utilises a series of methods to try and understand Milan over the last fifty years. Above all, the book uses micro-historical methods. The particular, the everyday and the ordinary are often used to try and explain the general, the extraordinary and the exceptional. The scale of research is often reduced to housing estates, individual life stories, families, events, scenes from feature films, and places. Milan, as this chapter has tried to show, is a complicated and complex city, as are all cities, with a long and rich past. These micro-histories do not replace the big picture or a wider analysis, but are part of the whole story. This is not an automatic process – a series of micro-histories do not necessarily make a macro-history. Smaller stories need to be interpreted, drawn together and compared. Finally, this work draws its evidence from a whole series of sources, ranging from the traditional (archives, newspapers, published work) to other, less common sources for a work of history (film, interviews, photographs, participant observation and direct experience, housing plans, surveys). Some of this work is descriptive, but no less historical for that. The historian often benefits from playing the role of reporter, or even detective. Clues, small signs and traces can be as important as broad trends and planned monuments. Non-events can mean as much as real ones. The lack of protest can tell us as much as ten years of street demonstrations.

Narration and description have always played a key role in historical explanation and these techniques have recently begun to take on more credibility in conjunction with other methodologies and alternative sources. Yet, 'no description is neutral' and 'the reporting of concrete facts is a way of understanding the real functioning of society . . . which otherwise would end up as simplified or distorted by quantitative calculations or excessive generalisation' (Pes 1998: 50–1). This micro-approach has been inspired by the work of many historians and researchers, in Italy and elsewhere (Portelli 1985, 1991, 1997, 1999; Montaldi 1994; Ginzburg, 1974; 1980; 1998; Passerini 1987; 1988a; Lüdtke 1995; Muir and Ruggiero 1991; Levi 1991; Civile 1987). There is no claim being made here that this book is a comprehensive history of Milan. This is a personal depiction of a city which its author knows intimately, but other portrayals are needed to fully understand the vicissitudes of Italy's 'moral capital' over the last fifty years.

–2–

Mass Cultures and Popular Cultures in Milan: The 'Boom' and After

1. Concepts and Keywords

Describe your ways of life, if you want to know your history. (Montaldi 1994: 313)

'Culture', conceived as a constant process of communication and interaction between and among strata and classes, is resistant to the drawing of simple boundaries. One cannot establish with a single stroke of the pen . . . which *habitus* is popular, which is proletarian and which is bourgeois. (Kaschuba 1995: 177)

Italy's economic miracle transformed the country's cultural landscape. Television became a permanent fixture in Italian homes. Cars replaced the scooters that had replaced bicycles. Migration brought together populations, dialects, lifestyles and customs. Ten million Italians were on the move from one region to another. Rural labourers vanished from large stretches of the countryside. Rice pickers were replaced by machines. Beaches filled with holidaymakers. Traffic jams became a feature of everyday life. Southern villages emptied, northern cities overflowed with new arrivals. All these developments came on the back of one of the most intense and concentrated periods of economic development the world has ever seen, with maximum growth (GNP) rates of over 7.5 per cent between 1958 and 1961 (Sapelli 1989: 21). The 'capital of this miracle' was Milan, and it is on Milan that this study will focus. There are, I believe, three key questions to be asked about popular culture, the working class and the city over this extraordinary period in contemporary Italian history.

First, what was the content of 'classic', traditional, working-class culture in the city *before* the boom? Second, how did this (mythical) working-class culture change during and after the 'miracle'? A critique will be made of assimilation theories which identify in this period the 'death' of working-class or popular culture under the pressure of mass, consumerist cultures. In short, one 'culture' is supposed to have destroyed (or replaced) another. As one interviewee of the oral historian Portelli put it, the end of popular culture 'corresponds with the release of the Fiat 500' (1997: 240). Did this happen, and if so, *how*? Third, and to answer properly question two, how did specific cultural 'forms', and in particular television (supposedly the most powerful *transmitter* of mass consumer culture) contribute to cultural changes among the working class during the boom?

In order to make any headway with these enquiries, we need to sort out the various forms of culture that have been cited thus far, and try and provide some definitions.[1] *'Culture'* in general will be taken as 'a system of lifestyles, of practices, of habits and customs, of social and familial organizations and structures, of beliefs, of attitudes, of the knowledge and conceptions of values that are found in a social aggregation.'[2] This is culture above all in the sense cited by Forgacs and Lumley as an 'extensive range of practices characteristic of a given society, from its mode of material production to its eating habits, dress codes, celebrations and rituals' (1996: 2). *Working class culture* (or *popular culture*, although the latter is often used in Italy with relation to rural classes and in particular the southern peasantry)[3] will be seen, at the risk of tautology, as *the forms of culture specific to the industrial proletariat* (similarly, the dominant culture, or more anachronistically ruling-class culture).[4] Occasionally, the term *subculture* will also be used, with its implication that the proletariat is in some way subordinate, subaltern or subterranean (but also with implications of *resistance)*. Of course, this is not to assume the *existence* of an autonomous working-class culture or cultures. In fact, one of the key areas of this debate concerns the ability or otherwise of the working class to create and maintain its own, specific, cultures or sub-cultures. Almost as important, as we shall see, have been the cultural forms attributed to the proletariat, which have often been 'distributed' as myths.

Mass culture signifies all that brought by the boom – and above all by television and from the US – the 'enemy' for so many intellectuals on the Italian left during and after the 'miracle'. I also include *consumer cultures* (and *commercial cultures*) within this broader banner. The plurals here are obligatory: Portelli has accurately called our attention to the 'many different, shifting, competing, conflicting mass cultures that circulate on our planet' (1997: 47). Finally, I will avoid employing the concept of *folklore*, despite its centrality to many Italian-based debates concerning popular culture, because of its remoteness from the cultural systems used by Milanese workers old and new in the 1950s and 1960s.

1. It is very rare for research on these issues to even make an attempt to define such terms as 'culture' and 'mass culture': Despite the myriad uses to which these terms have been put, their meaning is usually taken as obvious. In the early 1960s, two social scientists identified 163 different uses of the term (cited in Lequin 1983: 234). The most useful discussions I have located are those of De Mauro (1979: 167–76 and 1992: 5–68).

2. Tentori (1977) cited in Morcellini (1986: 99). See also the definitions used by Geertz (1966 cited in Tullio-Altan 1996: 35) and Ginzburg (1980: xiii–xxvi).

3. See De Martino (1949 now in Angelini 1977: 49–72).

4. For the debates concerning popular culture in Italy see Angelini (1977), Forgacs and Lumley (1996: 4–5) and Filippucci (1996: 52–72).

2. Levelling and Consumerism: Pasolini's Critique and his Critics

If the worker and his boss watch the same television programme and visit the same holiday resorts . . . if everyone reads the same newspaper . . . this assimilation does not indicate so much that classes have disappeared, but that the needs and satisfactions which serve to conserve class interests have been made their own by the majority of the population. (Marcuse 1964: 28–9)

Pier Paolo Pasolini's later journalistic writing insisted on one point – almost obsessively. A cultural levelling was taking place in Italy. The lower classes had been culturally *assimilated* or *integrated* into the system.[5] They had lapped up the consumerist myths of neo-capitalism and lost any kind of cultural autonomy they might have possessed. This concept could easily be filed under other labels – *hegemony, consensus, domination*. Pasolini's critique of consumer culture, and his analysis of its pervasiveness, has been extremely influential ever since his articles first appeared, mainly in Italy's most important daily newspaper, the *Corriere della Sera*, in the early 1970s. His ideas are worth examining in more detail in part because they are so often used to explain or describe cultural change during the boom years.[6]

Pasolini attributed great importance to the urbanization of Italian society and to the disappearance of rural traditions. 'The peasant world . . . after about 14,000 years of life, has ended practically overnight' (1993: 31). The values of the village or the *borgata* (values I will come to in the next section) had been replaced by a cultural 'levelling' – 'mass hedonism'. All the deep cultural values of the popular classes had been reduced to one cultural model: 'to decide whether to dream of having a Ferrari or a Porsche . . . with the pretence of being "free"' (1993: 47). This transformation from 'one human epoch to another, thanks to the arrival of consumerism and mass hedonism . . . has constituted, especially in Italy, a real anthropological revolution' (1993: 138). This 'new form of power, the power of consumerism' was far more powerful and effective than previous forms of

---

5. The word used frequently in the 1960s and 1970s was *integration*, taken in the negative sense to mean (passive) acceptance of dominant values. Similar, influential general conclusions had already been reached by Adorno and Horkheimer (1944 now in 1986) and were later confirmed by the seminal research of Goldthorpe, Lockwood, Bechhofer and Platt (1967) (for the UK). In the mid-1970s a more radical and political critique of the working class and its integration, conservatism or consociationism (at a political level) was to emerge in conjunction with the new social movements (such as feminism, environmental movements, gay movements, student movements) (Della Porta (1996). For integration see the incisive comments of De Felice (1995: 841–56 and 878–80).
6. See Pasolini (1993: 23, 31–3, 39–44; 1992; 1976) and the interviews in Pasolini (1995: 174–7 and passim).

domination, more than 'any other previous form of power in history' (1976: 21).[7] Television was the most important medium in this shift of power and cultural assimilation, assisted by urbanization and the planning policies of successive Italian governments. Consumerist ideology had already superseded all other ideologies and sub-cultures by the mid-1970s, including those associated with the Church and the left.[8]

Pasolini's 'theories' have had an enormous influence on contemporary analyses of Italian society, so much so that they are frequently cited as obvious truths, without any need of further justification. Pasolini, it is said, had 'identified' a trend in Italian society (Pasolini is often given prophetic, god-like powers by those on the left). Yet, the reputation of these articles (and the arguments they contain) is, to say the least, exaggerated. Very little of what Pasolini wrote, provocatively, is either obvious or proved. As Gallino has written with regard to American analyses of the assimilating effects of mass culture: 'research up to now has been conducted above all on its *content* . . . rather than the *effects* really produced by exposure to this culture amongst various kinds of individuals and groups' (1993: 200).[9] In reality, Pasolini's arguments are unconvincing and often contradictory.

In the first place, it is unclear just what was the substance of this 'popular culture' that had apparently been destroyed. Pasolini seems to identify popular culture with rurality, with dialects and, very often, with physical traits, with vitality and 'liveliness'. Fortini, one of Pasolini's severest political critics, accused him of identifying 'the people' with 'ignorance and pure vitality' (1993: 11). Certainly we are not even close to any ideals of 'classic working class culture'. Pasolini failed to lay out *what* had been destroyed, and as such it is difficult to find much credence in his story of destruction. The assumption that there had been an autonomous, 'vital', popular culture before the arrival of the devastating power of televisual consumerism is also, as we shall see, extremely difficult to demonstrate. In addition, the whole use of the concept of culture by Pasolini and others who adopt these ideas is mechanistic and simplistic. *Cultures of one kind are not simply destroyed or replaced by other kinds of cultures.* Cultures are adapted,

7. For the importance of the middle classes in the achievement of consensus see Pizzorno's influential article, 1980, first published in 1974.

8. There are also problems of periodization. If levelling took place in the 1960s, then 'working class culture' had apparently survived twenty years of fascism (and attempts at integration via mass cultural techniques) intact and untouched. Here we are encroaching on an (enormous) historical debate over consensus during Mussolini's rule. The main participants in this (disparate) debate have been Renzo De Felice, De Grazia (1981), Passerini (1987), and Gribaudi (1987).

9. Eco was one of the first intellectuals to criticize the 'apocalyptic' critics of mass culture for their simplistic and one-dimensional approach, which also ignored the possibilities of change opened up by the diffusion of mass culture (1993: 29–64). Levelling could also be seen positively, such as in terms of elimination of 'caste differences'.

moulded, shaped across time and place. The concept of the uncomplicated 'arrival' of mass culture and the disappearance of 'traditional, popular culture' fails to capture either the complexity or the richness of the situation. As Forgacs (1996: 281) has argued:

> changes in cultural consumption, such as that brought about by the advent of television, do not work by a simple displacement or eradication of the old by the new but tend to involve a series of adaptations of existing patterns and rituals.

Second, Pasolini's conception of the all-encompassing nature of consumerist culture allows no place for the contradictions of that culture, for the opportunities as well as the restraints. These contradictions have been intelligently drawn out by Portelli, amongst others (1997). One of the central arguments of this book is that consumerism does not necessarily lead to the passive acceptance of a homogeneous (passive) consumer culture, but also opens up new opportunities for resistance, and for variegated uses of time for different cultural purposes. The purchase of a Fiat 500, for example, could easily allow a family or an individual to break away from the suffocating conservatism of a village or a neighbourhood, at least temporarily (Crainz 1996: 136–7; Piccone Stella 1993; Passerini 1988a: 193). In 1950, there were 342,000 private cars circulating in Italy, by 1964 this figure had risen to 4,670,000. Consumption did not mean 'consumerism' was the only ideology that mattered, and horizons could be and were broadened as well as narrowed. As both De Mauro and Forgacs have argued, we can talk about forms of cultural unity without using drastic concepts such as 'cultural levelling' (De Mauro 1979: 171; Forgacs 1996: 281; 1992: 196–8, 236–41).

Third, Pasolini exaggerates the power of this consumerist ideology in terms of its ability to satisfy the needs and desires of 'the people'. Increased dreams lead inevitably to increased frustrations for many, for those who 'run and run but can't keep up'. This was particularly true for those who arrived in the cities during the boom in search of work – for whom *exclusion*, not integration, was often the dominant experience. Pasolini's methods are also problematic. He apparently came to his conclusions through simple intellectual 'observation' of the places, peoples and cultures he knew – the urban periphery of Rome, his own family, the 'damned who watch television every evening'. Pasolini was undoubtedly an acute cultural commentator and polemicist but we need to dig deeper to discover the links between mass culture, the boom and working-class culture during that key period.[10]

To further understand the lack of a *dialectic* in Pasolini's arguments, and the far more complicated and contradictory situation on the ground during and after the boom, we need to get to grips with the myth of the Italian urban industrial working class, and its culture.

10. For the importance of the boom see Crainz (1996) Petrillo (1992b) and Foot (1995 and 1997).

3. Working Class Cultures in Milan: The Boom and Everyday Life

Nobody is so naive as to believe that there is really a proletarian culture. (Fortini 1993: 140)

Paradoxically, one of the clearest ways to understand the content of working class culture in Italy is to construct a stereotype.[11] Obviously, this stereotype is built from a series of real elements which have been studied by historians, anthropologists, sociologists and writers since the first Italian industrial revolution in the 1890s. I have decided to (re)create two stereotypes so as to also capture the different elements which emerge with the mass worker of the 1950s.

3.1. C'era una volta . . . *The Traditional Industrial Working Class*[12]

In the older working-neighbourhoods of Terni, one can still see people sitting on their doorsteps, halfway between the house and the street: the men sometimes reading the paper or chatting with neighbours (or looking inside at the television); the women often sewing, knitting or husking beans – doing house chores in public. (Portelli 1991: 96)

The traditional working class lived, most classically, in the semi-mythical zones of Borgo San Paolo in Turin or Bovisa in Milan (but you could almost repeat the same type of discourse for Bethnal Green in London, or the Paris Red Belt). The husband worked in a big factory – Fiat in Turin, Pirelli or Breda in Milan. The wife also worked, sometimes in a small factory, sometimes as a shop assistant or as a domestic cleaner. Housing was of a *ringhiere* type – based around long balconies, small living space, outside toilets and collective washing facilities (Selvafolta 1990, 200–2; Saraceno 1988a, 212–3; Rosso 1998: 430–2). The man could walk to work, or cycle, or take a tram. The family were either natives of Turin or Milan, or from the immediate countryside around these cities.

The cultural outlook of these (small, nuclear) families was dominated by work, by socialism and later communism, by hostility towards the state and the Church, by a diffuse shared 'package' of values – a proletarian *milieu*: austerity (or thrift), honesty, solidarity, attachment to neighbourhood, a sense of sacrifice and hard work, *operosità*.[13] The image of the neighbourhood was dour, grey and physically

---

11. One of the first historians to challenge these stereotypes in Italy was Passerini, who asked the question (perhaps for the first time from the left) 'which working class?' (1980: 453–99); Passerini (1987) looks at stereotypes (of self-representation).

12. For this section I have used some classic texts, the entries 'Operai' and 'Proletariato' in Gallino (1993: 463–8 and 519–23, as well as part two of Gelder and Thornton (1997), Giddens (1989: 221) and Petrillo (1995).

13. See Gobetti on the Turin working class and its 'morality of work, sense of sacrifice, dignity of class and intransigence', cited in Passerini (1984: 230).

separated from the rich or middle-class areas of the city (Gribaudi 1981: 15–31 and 97–155). A whole series of popular and political festivals constituted the nodal points of the year when the *rione* would unite and occupy the public sphere – 1 May usually being the most important. Classically, the stereotype also contains clichés such as 'doors always being open', and the courtyard as a collective public space. This 'class' was ready to act, collectively – to *mobilize* itself – both at an everyday level (child-care, help for the ill, and so forth) and during moments of industrial and social crisis (strikes, occupations, riots). Traditional working class culture was thus characterized by high degrees of geographical stability, social immobility, sociability, politicization and resistance to the classic sources of dominant culture.[14]

Much of the historical literature about this class came from a left tradition and concentrated almost exclusively on moments of 'heroic' mass mobilization or crisis – the First World War, the post-war crisis, the resistance, 1968–9. Spriano's classic work on Turin stands out within this tradition (1972). It was not until the new schools of oral and micro-historians began to emerge in the 1960s and 1970s that different periods (and arenas – not just the factory, but the home; not just the streets and the trenches, but the bars and the schools) began to be taken seriously. Defeat (even a defeat as complete as fascism) could be as illuminating and important as victory, periods of political or social peace revealed as much as mass strike action. Others challenged these orthodoxies in different ways: through micro-history, through an emphasis on marginal groups outside of this traditional sector, by an analysis of women, work and gender-based structures (Ginzburg, 1974; 1998; Montaldi 1961; Saraceno 1988a, b; Balbo 1976).

3.2. Before the Boom: Milan and the Lost World

It is instructive to note the widespread use of nostalgia in relation to this form of stereotype and the lost world it represents. This is particularly true in ex-industrial cities – big or small – from Milan to Manchester, from Turin to Terni (Portelli 1985; Hudson, 1994). Many historians and others contrast a semi-mythical lost city to that which exists today (or already appeared to exist in the 1970s). For Leonardi, 'the working class were the bosses of the old urban periphery. Thousands of them swarmed around the area between the stations of Bovisa and Greco, wearing their workers' suits . . . to reach their factories'. For Giovenzana, writing about the 1950s, 'it was clear to everyone what the periphery was like, Lambrate, Bovisa, their social composition, their housing, the transport – everything was clear' (Benevolo 1991: 9). For the film director Olmi the neighbourhood of Bovisa

---

14. Sapelli's work on 'class consciousness' has provided the most useful and analytical analysis of this feature of the Italian working class. See his (1980: 430–2).

was 'an urban continuation of the peasant village' where 'the home was a community' and 'rivers of workers' passed by a certain times of the day (1999).

In the 1970s research on the same zone identified

> a common ethnic culture amongst the great part of the population built up over time at a mass level, through working in the same productive areas and thereby experiencing the same productive and social relations. (Crus 1974 cited in Fiorese 1990: 35)

Often, this nostalgia is reduced to the level of neighbourhood. One interviewee for a research project on the Milanese periphery complained about a decline in community spirit: 'once upon a time there was a neighbourhood, there was a group of people who met up all the time' (Bianchi and Perussia 1988) or 'the neighbourhood is no longer what it was' (Scramaglia 1993: 14). This sensation is further reduced to the level of housing blocks, where women and children are afraid to 'talk in the courtyard, on the stairs . . . the attics and cellars are no longer used . . . [they are] a no-mans' land' (Guiducci 1993: 12). 'Today everyone is cold, everyone thinks for themselves.' The city has apparently been transformed from 'a meeting place to a place of conflict . . . of lost culture' (Interviews collected by La Pietra 1990: 81, 88). In many ways (as with Pasolini) the 'lost world' evoked by these kind of images is not that of an industrial society – where large numbers of people work in factories during the day – but a Gemeinschaft/lumpemproletariat-type community. This could include the classic rural village square – where sooner or later everyone meets everyone else. But the lost world seems closer to the teeming, busy streets of a non-industrial city like Naples. The pre-eminence of the street for community life is much more a feature of these kind of urban or semi-rural areas than of industrial cities where time and place are (or were) controlled by the rhythms of the factory siren. *The city is seen as 'good' when it appears as premodern, as a non-city, as the negation of itself.*

In the mid-1970s a Milanese journalist interviewed a series of public figures for a book highly critical of the direction the city was taking. The book was published with the title *Milano No*. Here, the call of the mythical city was even clearer. One interviewee claimed that 'Milan used to be like a village . . . there were door-to-door salesmen who sang in the streets.' For another, 'Milan [the dates are never specified] was different, a large urban village'. The journalist Montanelli missed 'the urban periphery that existed and which no longer exists, a warm periphery . . . there was a real street culture . . . which has been crushed . . . television has ruined everything' (Moncalvo 1977: 142, 280, 341).

There is a certain amount of truth in some descriptions of today's Milan, especially within the more scientific research projects carried out under the auspices of Guiducci, but all of these judgements suffer from a romanticization of the past. Most of the studies in question make *no attempt to demonstrate* that there ever really was a 'street culture' and uncomplicated 'socialization', or that Milan was 'like a village'. These 'facts' are taken as read, as given and immutable. Yet, it is simply very difficult to show that such a situation ever corresponded to reality, as we have seen and will see in the rest of this chapter. If this past was mythical, how could it have been destroyed, or assimilated? In fact, *the myths become stronger and harder to contest* – more entrenched – as mass cultures become more diffuse. There is certainly a situation of non-sociability in today's Milan, but this does not mean that a process of *de*-socialization has taken place. The lack of socialization *now* does not prove that there was a city that was 'socialized' *then*.

3.3. The 'Mass Worker': 1950s–1960s–1970s[15]

The 'mass worker', a term that began to circulate in the early 1960s but took hold around 1968, applied to the sections of the working class most associated with the post-war generation and above all the boom. The 'mass worker' was most typically a (southern) immigrant, working in the same factories as the traditional worker (most classically, Fiat (Turin) or Pirelli (Milan)). The mass worker lived on the urban periphery either in self-constructed groups of houses, known as *Coree* (in Milan, not Turin, see Chapter 3) or new urban developments, or in rundown housing in the city centre (Turin, not Milan). The most stereotypical neighbourhoods associated with the mass worker were Sesto San Giovanni (just outside Milan), Quarto Oggiaro (on the Milanese periphery), Falchera and Nichelino (on the Torinese periphery). But in general the whole belt around Milan was home to the mass worker, who was associated with high levels of exploitation at work, intense alienation from the urban environment and politics, isolation (the family remained in the south, at least at first) and a lack of solidarity at neighbourhood level (if not at the level of regional solidarity transplanted from the south – a kind of *Gemeinschaft* surviving in the city). In some, more optimistic accounts, the mass worker is identified with collective struggle – as an alienated and non-integrated class which was ready to take part in far more radical forms of agitation than those employed by the integrated and moderate traditional proletariat (Negri 1979; Balestrini and Moroni, 1997). Many commentators were opposed to this interpretation of the immigrant worker – and the whole issue is now (as then) an intensely political one. The mass worker was placed by certain theorists in opposition to the traditional productivist culture of the 'old' working class, and therefore as much more (potentially) radical. After the mass struggles of 1968–9 in Milan and Turin, this interpretation became much more fashionable, being accepted by historians and sociologists of all political persuasions.

15. For the literature on the mass worker see the bibliography in Foot (1999d). For images of the mass worker, see also the photography of Lucas and the films of Petri (*La classe operaia va in paradiso*, 1971) and Wertmüller (*Mimì Metallurgico ferito nell'onore*, 1972).

Two questions now emerge, which clash with each other. First, did these stereotypes have any basis in reality? Second, what was it that supposedly destroyed 'traditional working class culture' in Milan (and at the same time created the stereotype)? To begin with the first question, Gribaudi's study has effectively crushed the idea that there was ever a unified, stable working class at Borgo San Paolo in Turin (and if it did not exist there, it did not exist anywhere). In Gribaudi's words, the neighbourhood had become 'the most widely recognised symbol both of the identity of working class culture as well as the latter's capacity for mobilisation' (1987: xi). His detailed work has shown that the traditional working class, in its strongholds, was neither stable, nor socially immobile. Levels of sociability were not particularly important and were mythologized by the inhabitants. Links to the countryside remained strong. Politicization was much weaker than it seemed and based above all around forms of discourse and symbolic rituals.[16] The myth, however, remains strong – despite its lack of historical foundation.

So, there are profound doubts about the very existence of 'a working class culture', at least in the sense in which those, such as Pasolini, who proclaimed it 'dead' in the 1970s ('the culture of the subaltern classes does (nearly) not exist any more' (1976: 176)) used the concept.[17] Pasolini and others were pronouncing the end of a *myth*, a construction based on a distorted and ideological vision of reality (Samuel and Thompson 1990; Passerini 1988a; Barthes 1994). So what really happened? How did mass culture change the daily lives of the Milanese working class? An essential road towards any answer to these questions is to use a more flexible and dialectical approach towards culture and working-class culture; more than both those who have pronounced these cultures as 'dead' as well as those who have identified continuing signs of life. It is crucial to consider these realms as non-monolithic, as packed with contradictions, as containing elements of the rural world, of the past and of the future, as discourse *and* structure. Only by this kind of flexibility can we 'keep reading culture as a terrain of class struggle, without having to imagine a monolithic working class, a guaranteed identity, or a solidified culture' (Portelli 1997: 50). Let us begin this 'reading' with some comments on television and consumption. A more detailed study of the effects of television can be found in Chapter 5 of this book.

16. For the debates in the UK over the so-called 'linguistic turn' in working-class history and the increasing concentration on discourse, see Cerutti (n.d.).

17. For Lequin, part of the explanation for the 'boom' in studies of popular culture in the 1970s lay precisely with the (presumed) imminent 'death' of those cultures (Lequin 1983: 238).

4. Television and Cultural Assimilation

State television in Italy, which began transmitting in 1954, is normally assigned a central role by historians and cultural commentators in the 'death' of traditional cultures – peasant and worker alike. Bosio, for example, argued that 'the capitalist system organises through television the overthrow of popular culture' (1975: 249). Television, it is argued, helped to spread, rapidly and within the home, consumerist values – mass cultures – *which replaced and overpowered all others*. The ideology of television dictated that, according to Pasolini, 'they [the ruling class] are no longer happy with the "person who consumes", they would prefer that there were no other possible ideologies apart from that of consumption' (1993: 23). This 'function' was attributed, in particular, to programmes such as *Carosello* (a peculiar Italian form of advertising, in the form of short films, which ran every evening from 1957 onwards and was particularly popular with children) and *Lascia o raddoppia?* (a game-show, similar to the $64,000 question, which achieved enormous success after 1955). Pasolini's 'solution' was provocative, 'Swiftian' and amusing – ban television (and school) or demonstrate against the transmission of certain popular programmes (1995a: 255; 1976: 165–71).[18] Yet Pasolini was deadly serious.

This 'analysis' has now become an accepted truth in Italy.[19] The role of television has been magnified into an all-powerful precursor of bourgeois (modern) mass consumer culture. Yet, what real evidence is there that this process (if it took place at all) was due to the advent of television? Let us look at the most 'advanced', rich and modern part of Italy in the 1960s, Milan.

4.1. The Spread of Television – 1963 – Five Neighbourhoods in Milan and their Televisions

In 1962 two research institutes in Milan carried out a detailed study of five neighbourhoods in the city. These five neighbourhoods can be grouped into three social 'sectors' – classic, peripheral working-class quarters (Barona, Baggio Vecchio); mixed neighbourhoods (Forlanini and Perrucchetti) and new, out-of-

18. In 1974 Pasolini claimed that, to save itself, the Vatican should have tried to censor *Carosello*, not political programmes (1993: 51). On the importance of *Carosello* for children see Luzzatto-Fegiz (1966: 1391–2) and in general, Gundle (1986: 585–7) and Giusti (1995).

19. Already, in a widely distributed and read work on the Torinese proletariat in the 1960s, Minucci and Vertone wrote about 'the trap' represented by mass culture and 'the worker who . . . seeks the illusion of a relationship with other men in the squalid reflections of the television screen, but in reality he accepts in his loneliness the pale imitation of a social life' (Minucci and Vertone 1960: 193). Such considerations are common in the literature, old and new, see Foot (1995: 327–9) and La Pietra (1990: 81). See also Piccoli (1996: 192) and Lepre (1993: 185).

town mixed developments (Comasina). Over 2,500 people were interviewed over a period of months. One of the key questions concerned the use and spread of television. The results of these surveys revealed that the diffusion of television ownership was extremely high right across the city in 1962, a mere eight years after the first transmissions (for the full figures see Foot 1999e: 146–8). The maximum level (nearly 90 per cent of households) was to be found in the new housing development of Comasina, an extraordinary figure for an area where many residents had recently been re-housed from shacks and shanty-towns.[20] The lowest figure was to be found at Baggio, the poorest quarter overall in terms of income and the neighbourhood closest, superficially at least, to the classic stereotypes of working-class culture identified earlier. Of course, *ownership* of television should not be confused with its *influence*, but two conclusions can be drawn here. First, the diffusion of television within the private sphere was almost complete, in Milan, even in the early 1960s. The so-called 'myth of the television in the shanty town/ shack', a very powerful image during the boom (see below) seems confirmed by these figures. Many people chose to buy a television *first*, before more apparently 'useful' (and often cheaper items) such as washing machines, vacuum cleaners, water heaters and (in some cases) telephones – but after the fridge (just). Second, the figures do not point to television being more or less of a middle-class or working-class possession. Only the most isolated and classical (stable) working class neighbourhood – Baggio – lagged behind. But even there, two thirds of families had purchased a television.

But what about the *use* of television? The survey added two supplementary questions, 'Do you watch television often?' and 'Did you watch television yesterday?' Finally, the men of working age in the sample were asked if 'Have you watched television for more than four hours in the past week?' The answers to these questions indicated that television was already central to the leisure activities of working-class families in Milan. Large majorities of people in all five areas had watched television 'often' and more than half tuned in on a daily basis. Television had replaced, or threatened to replace, almost all other 'classic' free time activities (radio, cinema, bar-life) for most of the inhabitants of new and old neighbourhoods alike.

So, television was important. However, these crude figures tell us very little about the *effects* of this television watching on the watchers and on their cultural activities and outlook. We could conclude that the increased use of television implied an *increasing* home-based use of 'free time'. But this presupposes that

20. Some international comparisons with Comasina are interesting. By 1956, 86 per cent of all American families owned a television; in 1959, 66 per cent of British families had a set, a figure that was to rise to 90 per cent by 1969, whereas in France, in 1963, a mere 30 per cent had purchased a television. Comasina was thus at a par with or above the most modern industrial societies (Cross 1993: 191 and 193).

before television, free time was *less* home-based, and there is little real evidence to show that this was the case. We could also assume that television changed the cultural world-view of the watchers – but again this has to be demonstrated. We would have to show that any apparent changes would not have happened without television, or that there was a link between the use of television and any cultural developments. In fact, these figures alone can help us only with two, tentative conclusions. First, that television was a key part of everyday life for the Milanese working and middle classes in the boom years of the 1960s. Second, that the possession of a television set was a priority – perhaps *the* priority – for even the poorest of families in the city during the same period, taking precedence over almost all other consumer goods.

More evidence can be gleaned from a study of another zone just outside Milan in the late 1950s. In 1958 a sociologist looked in detail at a self-constructed urban village, one of many around Milan – which were known as *Coree* – where *nobody* possessed a television set (although there were other signs of consumerism, such as scooters). Nonetheless, there was an absence of a 'community' in this 'town' – 'the piazza, he wrote, does not exist . . . a maximum level of selfishness ruled . . . the immigrants were unable to come to any kind of agreement to resolve their problems.' Despite the squalor, the poverty and the lack of basic services, however, most immigrants preferred this *Coree* to their southern home towns. According to the priest the migrants had 'discovered a "superamerica"' in Milan. Television, at least in terms of individual ownership, was not essential to the processes supposedly identified in the Milan of the boom (Diena: 1963 14, 100, 153).

4.2. Images and Implications: The Myth of the Television and the Baracca

> In the peripheries of Rome and Milan, on the roofs of the illegal shacks in the *bidonvilles*, many television aerials can be seen, as if a television was a necessity. (Bellotto 1963a).

> The purchase of a television becomes indispensable when the buyer decides to complete that set of consumer durables without which . . . there is no real status for his family. (Bellotto 1963b).

During the boom, most Italian papers sent correspondents to carry out 'inquests' amongst the poorest immigrants in the big cities. Many wrote moving articles, but one image tended to recur repeatedly – that of a television set in even the poorest of hovels. This image, reproduced in photographs and in popular histories of Italy, provided powerful evidence of the importance of television for the poorer immigrants and the lumpenproletariat of the biggest Italian cities. Crainz's book on the boom – the first academic work to attempt a history of the miracle – takes issue with this image, calling it a 'myth'. He cites a contemporary critic who wrote:

'the discourse of the television in the *baracca* . . . is one of those subjects which inspires particularly irritating forms of conversation on trains' (L. Pavolini 1961; Crainz 1996: 132).[21]

However, this image did capture a particular aspect of consumerism during the boom, the imbalance of consumption away from basic goods and towards consumer durables – especially televisions. Many did choose to buy a television set (on credit) – especially at the height of the miracle in 1960–1 (Crainz 1996: 132–4; Sapelli 1989: 24–30). Many probably saved on more 'basic' items, even food, to meet the repayments. This 'myth' is important for two main reasons. First, the continuing use of the myth strengthens the discourse concerning mass culture and television that has been criticized throughout this chapter. Second, however, the 'myth' also captured an important feature of Italian consumption patterns in this period – and underlines the priority of television for migrant and poor families during the miracle. Certainly, these images provide some evidence of cultural levelling, but are clearly not enough to draw Pasolini-type conclusions concerning mass and popular culture. The separation of consumption and pure survival – the idea that money could also be spent on items not actually *needed* by a family – was also an important form of *liberation* and signified a leap in status even for the poorest of families (Crainz 1996: 135). Many sociologists have dubbed this trend a 'distortion' of consumption patterns, but this assumes that there is a 'normal' model (usually located in the UK or France) to which consumption must adhere. Here we are once again in the realm of the 'Italian case' (*il caso italiano*) with its supposed differences from a 'norm'. In addition, there is ample evidence both that 'consumerism' had begun to influence Italian society well before the boom, *and* that later changes, in the 1980s, have been far more dramatic and important than those of the 1960s and 1970s (Forgacs 1996: 275).

5. Consumerism in General

> Striving, as much as acquisition itself, is an essential part of the process. (Stearns 1997: 106).

The consumer culture which is presumed to have destroyed that of the 'traditional working class' went far beyond the possession and use of a television. We are dealing with a whole new way-of-life – a *model* – which supposedly dominated all the actions, hopes and dreams of a whole population. One of the characteristics attributed to this form of cultural immersion is its pervasiveness – the apparent

---

21. See also P. Pavolini (1963), Di Bella (1965: 48–9), *Il Corriere della Sera*, 18 April 1962 (which described a family at Turin with a television and L.137,000 of debts with local food-shops) and Sapelli (1991: 108).

inability of individuals, classes and groups to escape from its influence.[22] Of course, television has effects way beyond those 'induced' by actually watching programmes – on language, on conversation, on attitudes and habits (see Chapter 5 below). 'The tensions of consumerism have an impact on everybody, including those whose mobility is nil' (Portelli 1997: 91). For Stearns a consumerist society 'involves large numbers of people staking a real portion of their personal identity and their quest for meaning – even their emotional satisfaction – on the search for and acquisition of goods. This characteristic is the hardest but the most essential aspect of consumerism to pin down. It means that people begin to appreciate the time spent looking for consumer items as a valuable part of life and not simply as a necessary evil in a struggle for survival' (1997: 105).

Portelli has identified the changes in the working class after the 1960s as a moment when 'consumption became as important as production' (1991: 91). But consumerism could also liberate, creating a space for rebellion in the face of staid and conservative social rules. Hence the stories told by Portelli of 'Raffaele' who waged a two-year battle to 'grow my hair over my ears' or 'Rita' who went to dances alone and wore make up. Whilst local communists condemned local women as 'Americanized' and snobs ('they won't accept a worker anymore') 'by "painting" their faces, women proclaimed that they *had* a face, and impinged on the traditionally male preserve of sexual aggressiveness and choice' (1997: 236–8). Similar analyses can be made for a whole series of central consumer goods of the 1960s. The car and the scooter allowed families and teenagers to become motorized, and mobile (individually) for the first time. The fridge and the vacuum cleaner also opened up numerous possibilities within the household, whilst closing others. Ready-to-wear fashion clothing allowed certain women to choose their own clothes, alone, for the first time. However, consumerism also meant a continual striving after the next 'purchase' and a series of constraints on behaviours and styles. Consensus was achieved not so much through the actual spread of wealth, but through 'the *possibility* of access to it or to its symbols (the car, other consumer durables, television)' (De Felice 1995: 838).

For most Italian intellectuals in the 1960s, however, and historians since, the supposed advent of consumerism was an overwhelmingly negative process which the 'people' lapped up without thinking twice.[23] In 1964 a major international

22. After 1968, attempts at creating a counter culture, in the wider sense of the word, were aimed precisely at allowing individuals to escape (or block out) this influence. Bosio wrote that 'the mass communications represented by television, by newspapers . . . can only be defeated by another truth' (1975: 220).

23. 'Most' but certainly not all. For an influential study of the debates concerning mass culture in Italy see Eco's fundamental study (1993) and the biting comments of Chiaromonte (1992: 152, 161 and passim). For a positive view of television, especially in the area of linguistic unification but also as a kind of general 'educator', see De Mauro (1973: 107–17).

exhibition was organised in Milan around the subject of 'free time'. The opening rooms of the exhibition were designed to 'create doubts' in the visitor's mind about consumerism. In the first room a series of images linked to consumerism were meant to invoke a 'paradise of evasion' which is where the visitor reached a kind of 'euphoria'. But the second, dark and 'squalid' room quickly punctured these 'illusions', representing the reality of 'empty time' – tiredness, lack of money, indifference. Machines in the shape of juke boxes invited viewers to enter their personal data and gave out tickets identifying each person as a certain kind of consumer. However, the tickets were given out randomly. The relationship between the data and the judgement was false 'just as it is false to believe', wrote Eco and Gregotti in the exhibition catalogue, that, 'in our present condition, we can make a free choice about the use of our free time'. Visitors were then sent through various labyrinthine passages to the end of this part of the exhibition, where a slogan on the wall read as follows:

> one of the dangers of industrial civilisation is that free time is organised by the same centres who organise working time. In this case free time is consumed in the same way as working time. *To enjoy yourself implies that you are becoming integrated.*

The curators of the exhibition concluded that 'we hope that visitors can then responsibly complete their visit, after having cleared up some misconceptions' (Triennale di Milano 1964: 14).

6. Conclusions

> The proletariat is not the magical carrier of a young and healthy 'new' culture, which had previously been hidden. (Fortini 1977: 141)

> How is it possible that we all begin as originals and end up as copies? (Geertz cited in Cerutti, 'Il linguistic turn', n.d. : 8)

In 1980 the workers at Fiat in Turin suffered a defeat which has become definitive over the next seventeen years. The period of struggle which began in the early 1960s had come to an end. A year later, many of Italy's 'radical working class historians' gathered for a conference on 'Workers' memory and new class composition'. Many saw the need to question the whole basis of their work (and of 'proletarian history' in general). It was 'necessary . . . to rethink all that in which we have believed, not only the myths but also the theoretical certainties upon which, for example, the history of the workers' movement has been constructed' (Poggi cited by Bermani 1986: xxxii). Differences within the proletariat could be as important as unity, cultural forms more important than organizational methods.

A radical critique of workerism began to take shape, not without resistance, as the fiery debates, reported in full in the volume, show (Bermani 1986).

In 1988 journalist Gad Lerner published a study of the working class in the most industrial city in Italy – and home to the mass worker – Turin. The book – *Workers* – was subtitled 'the life, the houses, the factories of a class which is no more'. The last chapter was entitled 'The Communist Party and the Radiators' – and tells a story whose implications go far beyond one neighbourhood in one town. The neighbourhood was Mirafiori Sud, built in 1967 right next to the most important Fiat factory to house car workers. Here, in the mid-1970s, the Communist Party regularly won around 50 per cent of the vote. By 1987 this vote had fallen to 35 per cent. In the 1994 general elections the constituency was won by a candidate from Berlusconi's right-wing *Forza Italia!* party. Lerner tells the 'story of the radiators' to explain what he sees as a radical change in the neighbourhood in the 1980s. 'The radiators', he writes, 'are synonymous with collapse, with individualism' (1988: 177). What happened was this. In the 1980s, the self-managed collective heating system began to accumulate debts, and could no longer pay for fuel. The response of 96 out of 260 families was to install their own, individual radiator system. 'Friendships were broken, fights nearly broke out . . . it was impossible to hold a meeting of the neighbourhood committee, the police were called out on numerous occasions'. Lerner's conclusion was straightforward: 'what is happening at Mirafiori Sud is the final dissolution of any form of workers' identity . . . the disappearance of a homogeneous culture and language. The workers' neighbourhood no longer exists . . . even if the vast majority of its inhabitants are workers' (1988: 177, 178, 180).

Pasolini described his own vivid vision of the changes in Italian society in May 1975 in the form of a 'letter' to a young Neapolitan:

> If I, when I was your age . . . took a walk in the periphery of a city, that periphery said to me . . . this is where the poor live . . . the poor are workers and the workers are different from the ruling class . . . if you take a walk in a peripheral neighbourhood today, that area will say to you 'here the spirit of the workers has disappeared'. Workers and peasants are 'elsewhere' even if they still live here materially. (Pasolini 1976: 45–6)

Both Lerner and Pasolini invoke a lost world – be it that of the Fiat workers in Turin or the urban peripheries of Bologna or Rome. Both authors take the (previous) existence of this world as given – non-controversial – and concentrate their efforts on the contemporary situation – the mid-1970s for Pasolini, the 1980s for Lerner. Yet, as I have argued throughout this chapter, the discourse of loss, of change, of emptiness depends on a romanticized 'past'. The representation of the death of socialization and the 'neighbourhood' is relative – depending upon representations of an assumed (and not demonstrated) past which touches a nerve in the popular memory of the post-war generation. Much of the historical discourse concerning mass culture is teleological, caught in the headlights of a 'progress' which supposedly moves forward regardless of all obstacles, leaving the past behind *in toto*.

It is more accurate to pose the question about the working class in the 1960s not through the dichotomy of assimilation/rebellion (which, as Pasolini himself argued elsewhere, might not be either/or options at all) but via the concept of *integration*. As Franco De Felice has written, 'it seems to me that the terms of the problem are not either integration or non-integration, but *which* integration, which possible organisation of different social strata' (1995: 879). What seems clear is that neither model – complete rejection of consumerism or complete subjugation to it – can be seen as 'winning' in a complete sense. To cite De Felice again 'the most "realistic" interpretation is that offered by the simultaneous co-existence of all these values within the subordinate classes' (1995: 880).

Those who became 'caught up' in consumer society during the boom were not merely passive receptors of dominant ideology. As Forgacs has argued, 'in acts of cultural consumption the same person can be at one and the same time dominated and an appropriator of meanings' (1996: 274).[24] Many had made choices about how to live their lives and use their 'free time'. Many chose privacy over socialization, television over the bar and the cultural circle, the home over the street. We need to dig deeper into the interplay between mass, popular and traditional cultures to understand the significance of these choices and their importance for the transformations of the following thirty years. The chapters that follow will look at a series of realms of cultural changes and identity-formation within the context of contemporary Milan.

24. The theme of mass culture as simply a form of dominance and power has always found a wide audience in Italy; Packard's seminal work of 1957 was translated into Italian almost immediately (Packard: 1959).

−3−

City of Movement: Milan and Mass Immigration, 1950–2000

1. Introduction: Movement and Immigrations

Modern Lombardy has always been a society of population movement. From the early growth of the silk and textile industries to the creation of the contemporary metropolis, the region has attracted groups of workers, consumers, pilgrims, traders and administrators. Yet the population movements that have marked the region's development have not only been examples of *immigration*, or at least of permanent immigration. People have always *commuted* to the cities to work and consume and trade, from the building workers of the early twentieth century who arrived in Milan every morning, to the worker-peasants of the 1920s who maintained strong links with the countryside, to the classic industrial commuters of the 1950s (Consonni and Tonon 1984). Often, there was a strong seasonal component involved in these movements, and the cities of the region maintained strong links with the countryside economically, socially and politically. Others, throughout history, have used the cities of the region to buy, to sell, and to enjoy themselves, or simply as ways of moving on to other areas, countries or regions – as nodal transport points. The clock has always been central to these patterns of movement – with the evolution of 'rush hours', motorisation and the increasing importance of flexible work.

1.1. Immigrations: The Missing Comparison

Since 1945 the region has been host to two waves of mass immigration, the first concerned Italians, from the countryside, the mountains and the cities of the south, the east and Lombardy, the second concerns non-Italians, from a myriad of countries but above all from North Africa, Egypt and Albania. These two immigrations have corresponded with two different economic phases. The first immigration coincided with the economic miracle, a period of extraordinary growth based around classic industry and public works. The second immigration has taken place against the background of a vastly different economy, centred around services, small industry and post-industrial scenarios.

Notwithstanding the proximity and shock effects of these two immigrations, very few researchers have attempted any kind of comparison between them (exceptions include Petrillo 1998b and Palidda 2000b). In general, when comparisons have been made, the tendency has been to take refuge in simplistic clichés concerning the first migratory movement. In short, the *Italian* migration is generally seen as a difficult but essentially unproblematic phase. This immigration 'from the south' is characterized as integrative and positive, that after the 1980s as *non-integrative* and *negative*. Little reference is made to the enormous body of research carried out at the time with regard to internal immigration. The immigration to Milan in the 1950s and 1960s (as well as those into Turin, Genoa, Rome and Naples) provoked a series of national political and academic debates. The bibliography referring to the period is huge. Massive publicly and privately funded research projects analysed immigration, the immigrants and the host society. By the time of the new immigration of the 1980s and 1990s, it was as if none of this had ever happened. Little (or no) weight has been given to the debates, institutions, contradictions, laws and processes that characterized the population movements of the 'economic miracle'. Often, and especially for Milan (and perhaps this is an indication of the capacity of the city to 'absorb' social and cultural change) it is as if that immigration had never happened. The two immigrations are also seen as self-contained and separate processes, where the experiences of the former have nothing to tell us about the problems linked to the latter.

How can we explain this 'missing comparison'? There are a number of possibilities. First, there is a widespread belief (already proposed, at the time, by Alberoni and Baglioni (1965)) that the internal immigration of the boom years was absorbed with difficulty but, over time, without enormous problems. This belief is far stronger for Milan – where the supposed 'generosity' and 'openness' of the Milanese is often cited – than for Turin. In the latter city the isolated research projects that were carried out in the 1970s and 1980s revealed a city still divided essentially along an immigrant/non-immigrant divide – spatially, socially and culturally.

A second possible reason for the lack of comparison is the common exaggeration of the importance of the Italian/non-Italian question. It is claimed that the immigrants of the 1950s were essentially different from those of the 1980s and 1990s *because they were Italians*. This basic fact, allegedly, signified a far greater level of integration – linguistically, culturally, socially – than has been possible with those coming from outside Italy. To cite Bocca (1998) these were 'people who had language, religion, skin colour and cultural history in common with the Milanese'. In fact, this 'Italianness' alone tells us very little about the integration processes involved and there are far more similarities than differences between the immigration paths and experiences of the two mass movements than the general academic position allows (or even contemplates). In fact, the racialization of the southern immigrants in particular – their *Otherness*, their *Outsiderness* – went very deep. This was also at the level of language, of accent, of appearance, of their marginal location in the urban fabric – often in very similar ways to those of the later period and precisely in terms of the characteristics cited by Bocca. The exaggeration of the importance of being Italian is often tied up with the slippery and simplistic use of the concept of *visibility* with relation to foreign immigrants. In part, this re-invention of the past forms part of current nostalgic accounts of the period of the boom. But these representations also reveal how Italian immigrants in Milan have seen their status change over the years. They have, like Italians in the US over the twentieth century, *become white* (Frye Jacobson 1998: 4). This has been in part as a result of economic change but has also been a component of the re-invention of identity in the face of foreign immigration. One other important area, which is often absent from these observations, was and is that of *citizenship*. The Italian immigrants had the right to vote, today's immigrants (from outside Europe) do not, and this was a powerful incentive for the mass parties of the 1960s (which no longer exist) to recruit and appeal to the immigrants of the boom.

A third possible reason for non-comparison is far more banal. Methodologically, the vast bulk of the research on the immigration of the 1980s and 1990s has been carried out by sociologists and anthropologists – not by historians. Those working on this period and these processes have simply not been used to looking back for explanations and comparisons, and have limited themselves to a perfunctory examination of the bibliography or, in the worst cases, the simple repetition of a few clichés. Much of this research has been funded by local associations anxious to gather information to deal with immediate and pressing problems – the Church, the voluntary sector, local administrations. Most of the researchers employed on these projects have not even contemplated any kind of backwards look towards the 1970s, let alone the 1950s. The practical aspects of this research ('who lives where and what do they need?') is, of course, essential, but it tells us little about what worked and what went wrong before. Separating the two phases so clearly also fails to capture the continuities of other immigrations that do not fit so neatly into these time capsules, from the mass emigration of Italians in the early part of the century, to the Chinese communities in Milan, present since the 1930s, to the Somalian refugees of the early 1970s, to the odyssey of Milan's Jewish community (Farina, Granata, Cologna and Costa 1997; Cologna, Breveglieri, Granata, Novak 1999). The lessons of the past could prove more useful than the bare facts of the present.

For example, if we take one key area of integration in the 1950s – housing – we can start to pick up some crucial signals about the different treatment of the two immigrations. In the 1950s and 1960s whole neighbourhoods were built from scratch to house the waves of immigrants from the countryside and the south. Most of these were on the periphery of the city. Other immigrants built their own houses – in spontaneous agglomerations that became known as *Coree* (so-called in Milan because of their appearance at the time of the Korean war) – in the province and hinterland. A complete urban periphery was constructed for immigrants. Others chose to live well outside the city and travel to work every day. The immigrants of the 1980s and 1990s have had no neighbourhoods built for them, and have had to make do with emergency prefabrictaed 'housing' (see the section on Via Corelli below) or deal with the saturated and expensive Milanese housing market. Cities have stopped growing in traditional ways. On the one hand this has led to the creation of inner-city mixed quarters near the central stations of the big northern cities – Corso Buenos Aires in Milan, San Salvario in Turin – and on the other to a diffuse presence of immigrant residence right across the city. The 1980s and 1990s has not seen the creation of massive immigrant ghettos like Comasina and Quarto Oggiaro (Milan) or La Falchera, Mirafiori Sud and Le Vallette (Turin). Strangely, the inadequate response of the local and national state to the needs of the immigrants has favoured integration within the city by preventing ghetto formation, but it has also helped to create areas with shifting, rootless populations often in conflict with local communities (Tosi 1998). Comparing the two immigrations, therefore, can help us understand each individual period with far more clarity.

A final, general introductory point relates to the relationship between the city, its residents and the new 'outsiders' who have arrived in Milan (and outside Milan). This difficult insider/outsider question is laced with contradictions and complications. When does an outsider become an insider? When does an immigrant become a resident? What is the relationship between urban space, immigration and social conflict in Milan? How do immigrants become linked to certain stereotypes and images – noise, violence, crime, prostitution (for both periods) drugs (for the 1980s and 1990s)? What happens in an urban emergency? These questions will be analysed through a series of micro-events and habitats in the city.

2. Concepts and Keywords

Before any discussion of the specifics of migration at Milan, we need to clarify some of the concepts involved. Integration will be defined as a *coming together of parts into a whole so as to render it a group or semi-group*.[1] The reasons for the use of this minimal definition are twofold. First, such a definition allows us to examine integration in a number of areas without any preconceptions about the negative or positive repercussions of the process involved. This chapter will argue that the integration of the immigrants in Milan, when it did occur, was *an extremely complicated and contradictory process, which did not always lead to positive*

---

1. This definition is a weaker version of that in Marchese and Mancini (1991: 442–3).

outcomes either socially, politically or culturally. For example, I would argue that 'integration' through the mass media and the pull of consumer society did not necessarily have a positive effect on Italian society or its cultural *milieu*. Other possible definitions, such as that of Gallino (1993: 372) or that used by Alberoni are prescriptive and value laden, carrying with them the preconception that integration was necessarily, in some sense, positive and to be encouraged. In fact, one of the problems with Alberoni's (influential) work of the 1960s lay with his extremely biased definition of integration, which seemed to indicate that integration was the *only means* whereby a subject could achieve both individual and collective ends.[2] Our definition makes no such claims, and will allow us to criticize certain aspects of the integration processes at work in the 1950s and 1960s, as well as to draw out the complicated and contradictory dynamics at work. The vast majority of published work on immigration (in both periods) uses the term *integration* as an *unproblematic* and *positive* (and undefined) term. Only in the collection on Milan edited by Barile, Dal Lago, Marchetti and Galeazzo (1994) and in the work of Ambrosini (1999) and Petrillo (1998b) is integration seen as a problematic concept.

Second, our more 'neutral' definition allows a more open analysis of the mechanics of integration. Integration could take on many forms – complete or incomplete, social, cultural, political, economic, 'urban' – and these 'types' of integration were often in conflict, and at times actually incompatible with one another. Hence, an immigrant might be integrated as a worker, but not as a citizen. He or she could be culturally integrated in the 'host' society, but alienated in the workplace. *Some forms of integration excluded others.* A Sicilian, or Chinese, or Moroccan immigrant who 'integrated' in Milan through contact with other Sicilians was excluded from a more *Milanese* integration. Hence integration in certain cases was compatible with *marginality* – in the city, in the factory, politically (Gallino 1993: 405–6). Forms of integration are not incompatible with criminality, prostitution and exploitation of other immigrants. Integration was not, and is not, therefore, necessarily a positive process. In addition, integration can also imply the loss (voluntarily or otherwise) of cultural norms, language and personal histories. This, again, might not be seen as positive. Without a clear understanding of these divergences and contradictions it is impossible to delineate the two-way outcome of the mass migration in Italy in the 1950s and 1960s. Some migrants became firm supporters of the consumer society, some cried 'we want everything, immediately', many were caught up by *both* 'forms of ideology'. No migrant could

2. 'A subject is integrated into a social system when their behavioural models and interior values . . . allow them to pursue personal ends, and at the same time ensures the collective ends of the social sub-systems in which they operate, in a way that is collectively seen as "good"', Alberoni and Baglioni (1965: 100).

ignore the consumerist aspects of the boom years, nor that of the 1980s, but very few were free from some form of alienation – at work, in the city, during their everyday lives – which could easily lead to rebellion and a rejection of the same society.

Finally, the 'host' society, in this case Milan, should not be viewed as a static and passive recipient of mass immigration. The city itself underwent enormous changes during the boom (it was, after all, the 'capital of the miracle') and again in the 1980s. And the Milanese were also caught up in the whirlwind of rapid and unplanned development, and rapid and unplanned deindustrialization. Migration changed the 'host' society as well as the migrants themselves, and rapid adaptation occurred amongst the Milanese – inside and outside of the factory. All too often, the Milanese themselves are 'invisible' in studies of immigration in their city.

It is useful to clarify, briefly, a series of other terms which will be employed. An *immigrant* will be defined as someone who arrives in the city (or its hinterland) from outside – be they Italian or non-Italian. The term *clandestini* signifies those living in the city in an illegal situation – in the 1950s before the new law (L.5, 10 February) of 1961, which abolished the Fascist 'anti-urbanization' law of 1939. In the 1980s and 1990s *clandestini* is used in conjunction with *irregolari* to identify immigrants without legal status or without the correct documents (and in reality this term masks a whole series of different personal situations – from a newly arrived Albanian without papers to long-term immigrants whose documents have run out). The use of the same word here has been forgotten in recent debates and is another argument in favour of a cross-migration comparison. A much more acceptable and correct term is *undocumented* immigrants. *Regolari* (or *documented* immigrants) are those with the correct papers. *Residents* are those who have a further set of legal rights – including an identity card. This group can also include immigrants. Italian residents refers to those in the city for some time. Finally, the loaded term *extra-comunitari*, which technically refers to those from countries outside the EU but in reality is limited to the identification of certain immigrants (and not, for example, to Swiss residents) – usually those from North Africa – will be avoided as far as possible (Balbo and Manconi 1993; Dal Lago 1999; Bolaffi 1998).

This chapter will seek to compare these two immigrations historically. The location of my research is in the city itself – at a micro-level. Immigration is looked at through the examination of specific places, events, and moments over the last fifty years.

3. The First Wave: Migration and the 'Miracle' in Milan

One becomes very quickly Milanese, without forgetting one's own customs, one's own affections. (Bassetti, Comune di Milano 1963: 13)

From 1951 to 1961 300,000 people moved to Milan in search of work (Morpurgo 1975: 20). Industrial employees in Italy rose by 1,379,000 over the same period and more than 20 per cent of these jobs (279,000 posts) were in the province of Milan alone.[3] Most are still there, or have moved to the vast urban hinterland which dominates the contemporary city. During the heady years of the boom (1958–63) internal migration to the 'capital of the miracle' reached huge proportions: 32,619 came in 1955, 36,970 in 1956, 41,416 in 1957, 55,860 in 1958, 59,856 in 1959, 66,930 in 1960, 87,000 in 1961. In 1962, 105,448 immigrants arrived (Guiotto 1986: 29; Petrillo 1992a: 631–61). The city took in nearly 400,000 residents in 15 years.[4] Certain peripheral areas saw their population increase fivefold. At San Donato Milanese just south of Milan the population exploded from 2,667 in 1951 to 15,422 in 1966 (Pellicciari 1970: 36).

This chapter will take a different look at this period of intense population movement in Italy. By taking four different neighbourhoods on the periphery of Milan – the 'capital of the miracle' – we can compare and contrast the experiences of the migrants who arrived in the city during the boom. The first set of 'quarters', Baggio, Barona and Bovisa, were classic working class areas, defined by their factories and their working class. The other neighbourhood, Comasina, was a modern, new, 'self-sufficient' estate. Research on these neighbourhoods has allowed a partial re-evaluation of the migratory process in the north of Italy, especially in an area typically seen as 'uncontroversial': integration. The 'integration' of immigrants will be analysed in two key areas – work and housing. We will start with an examination of a number of accepted truths concerning internal migration in Italy in the 1950s and 1960s.

4. Myths and clichés: Internal Migration

A considerable mythology has built up in Italy about those years, and the migration of potential workers to Milan. This mythology is based around three main clichés. First, that the migration was overwhelmingly from the 'deep' south of Italy to the north (Passigli 1969: 11; Petrillo 1992a: 632). In fact, most immigrants were from Lombardy, whereas those from the south and islands only made up 24 per cent of the total immigrants to Milan in 1958 (Guiotto 1986: 32; Petrillo 1992a: 632–4).[5]

---

3. Guiotto (1986: 45). In Italy the 1960s marked a brief but intense period when the working class employed in 'big' factories became 'central' for the first (and last) time, see Reyneri (1993: 499–507).

4. 1951 – 1,274,245; 1966 – 1,672,771, figures from Pellicciari (1970: 37).

5. See Moretti in Pellicciari (1970: 148). But it should be noted that these figures are under-estimates, because of general statistical inaccuracies and the prevailing fascist laws ('against urbanization') which were a disincentive to register either at the employment offices or with the *Comune*. Pizzorno estimated that there were 19,000 such 'clandestine' workers at Milan in 1961, Guiotto (1986: 35).

Moreover, not all migration was rural-urban. Urban to urban movement was common, as was rural to rural migration (for the Ligurian case see Cavalli 1964).

The second 'myth' is that the vast majority of these migrants were forced to live in self-constructed shanty-towns, the *Coree* on the extreme urban periphery and in the rural hinterland. Whilst many did build *Coree* – the most recent estimate is that 70,000 were living in this type of accommodation in the early 1960s (Meneghetti 1986: 268–70) – the extent of this kind of housing around Milan in the mid to late 1950s was lower than that of the immediate post-war 'reconstruction' period, and of no comparison with the institutionalized *borgate* around Rome. In fact, the over-concentration on the *Coree* is symptomatic of a wider problem in contemporary discussions of the boom – an excess of concern with two or three contemporary accounts of migration in Milan, published in the early 1960s, most notably Montaldi and Alasia's famous 'inquest' *Milano, Corea* (1960).[6] This is not to under-estimate the extent of the *Coree*, or their impact of the popular consciousness of the migrants and the Milanese (*Coree* were identified by the police and many Milanese as centres of criminal activity, and they were often the first areas 'searched' after important robberies or violent crimes, they were also identified with the region of their inhabitants).[7] Nonetheless, at least eight out of ten migrants did not live in the *Coree*, and the *Coree* themselves became integrated into the urban fabric of the city fairly quickly, as Meneghetti's excellent research has shown. In addition, the *Coree* were not flimsy constructions (like those depicted in De Sica's classic 1951 film, *Miracolo a Milano*) but *real houses*, built by the migrants themselves. In fact, most are still standing and are lived in today, within the boundaries of the city and its hinterland. To construct *Coree* houses, immigrants needed some sort of capital, putting them amongst a kind of élite within their community, not amongst the poorest of all. The real problem in the *Coree* areas was the (near-total) lack of public services, not the houses themselves (Vercelloni 1989: 170–1).

Finally, there has been a tendency to concentrate the effects of migration into the five 'peak' years of the 'miracle' (1958–63). Mass migration to Milan had

6. It should be underlined that the 'myth' that links the immigrants to the *Coree* is a Milanese one. At Turin self-constructed housing did not constitute an important part of the migratory experience, real or imaginary, and the major part of the immigrants started out in small hotels rented by the hour, in the town centre or in huge public projects on the edge of the city, see Fofi (1964).

7. Such as the 'Corea del Sud' near Bollate, to the north of Milan, so-called because of the high numbers of southern immigrants living there. Other *Coree* were dominated by immigrants from the Veneto region. See Meneghetti (1986). The growth of the *Coree*, often built in open countryside, also contradicts traditional images concerning the *urban* experience of Milanese immigration in the 1950s. For the identification between crime and the *Coree* see the Milanese local press of the period, for example 'Gli assassini di Bruno Briani si nascondono nelle "coree" periferiche', *Corriere della Sera*, 31 July 1962 where the police 'searched through the building-sites where southern immigrants work'.

been a fact of life from the early 1950s onwards, and the city's demographic decline, accompanied by rapid de-industrialization even in the older peripheral zones, did not begin until the 1980s. In addition, Milan had been a centre for migration in the past, particularly in the 1890s and in the period of the First World War, but also right through the 1930s.

In some ways these 'myths' have served a purpose – to reinforce the depiction of the early southern immigrants both as 'backward' and as 'helpless' on arrival in the big city – as passive victims/recipients of poor conditions and economic and social repression. In fact, there was another side to these migrants and their lives in Milan. Many came to Milan already armed with contacts – family, regional or otherwise. Many already had a house or a job to go to, or both (Petrillo 1992a: 640–1). Many were not politically naive, but had participated in the last great rural struggles (and defeats) in the south (1944, 1950–1), centre and north of the country.[8]

There is also a fourth, unwritten, cliché that pervades the whole area of boom studies. This is the assumption that, somehow, the whole problem of what was called the 'integration' of these immigrants had been solved almost immediately, or even *before* the migrants had arrived. What Alberoni called a 'frenzy of assimilation' had apparently overcome all divisions within the space of a few years. 'Nearly all [the immigrants in Milan], in a word, were already Milanese and wanted to be so' (Alberoni and Baglioni 1965: 11). In the early 1960s, a series of massive, well-financed and important research projects were carried out in Milan, Turin and Genoa concerning internal migration and the integration of, in particular, southern migrants. Milan's *Istituto Lombardo di Scienze Economiche e Sociali* (ILSES) foundation, under the auspices of sociologists of the quality of Pizzorno and Balbo, undertook detailed surveys of the living conditions of the new immigrants, their work situations and their attitudes to the new city. The results were collected in five huge volumes (ILSES 1964a). Since then, they have hardly been referred to again. The *Comune* also commissioned an exhaustive survey of its peripheral zones (where most of the immigrants ended up) right down to counting the number of phone boxes and grocers' stores in each area. Again, these reports were safely filed away.[9]

Since 1964, and Cavalli's invaluable work, *La città divisa*, very little original research has been carried out on the internal migration of the 1950s and 1960s. Why? Had the immigrants really 'pre-integrated', adhering to the 'dominant cultural values' of the industrial society in the north *before* their arrival, as Alberoni and Baglioni had claimed in their studies of 1960 and 1962? Or had they simply 'integrated' quickly into the urban-industrial societies of the north? Or did other issues obscure those of the 'integration' of the migrant workers – above all the

8. Ganapini (1993: 331).
9. Commissione per il coordinamento dei servizi (1962) and Pietro Gennaro *et al.* (1964).

rise of student protest and class struggle? Certainly, researchers are now lucky to have a large body of untouched material to work from. But others are still forced to rely upon contemporary accounts, written twenty or thirty years ago, for some of the most important chapters of post-war Italian history. Both Ginsborg (1989: 217–27 and 250–3) and Lanaro (1992: 235–41), in their monumental histories, make liberal reference to the fine if flawed and polemical work of Montaldi and Alasia (1960) and Fofi (1964), but do not refer to anything written after 1973. The same is true of Meriggi's short history of the north of Italy (1996: 127–31). The rich, complicated story of Italian immigrants during and after the boom was simply left untold.

5. Four Neighbourhoods: Baggio, Barona, Bovisa and Comasina

This chapter will examine two forms of integration. First, that in the workplace – embracing above all cases of *social* integration, and secondly that involving the immigrant's integration into the city – as a citizen of Milan – with a home, a bed and, perhaps, a network of friends and contacts in the urban environment. These issues will be examined with regard to four different neighbourhoods in Milan: Baggio, Barona, Bovisa and Comasina. All are areas on the periphery of Milan. Bovisa is what was once described as an 'old' peripheral neighbourhood. A village until the 1880s, Bovisa's growth was the child of Italy's first industrial revolution. Hemmed in by the main railway network running out of Milan to the north, Bovisa was a natural home for heavy industry. Once the quintessential workers' quarter and 'red' zone, Bovisa was associated with manufacturing industry and with a certain kind of *operosità Milanese* (Milanese work ethic). During the boom, Bovisa's industries experienced rapid growth – especially the chemical and electro-mechanical sectors – and thousands either commuted to the zone or moved there permanently. Bovisa has always had a close relationship between the jobs within the neighbourhood and the zone's population. Despite periods of hectic change and growth (the zone's population reached 44,391 in December 1967), the zone has retained its 'community', its 'isolation' from the city centre, its 'village' feel. Bovisa is also an area with a strong cultural tradition (Foot 1995: 317 n.5).

Many of these features could also be found in the neighbourhoods of Baggio and Barona. At Baggio, another 'classic' working-class neighbourhood (54 per cent of the active population were classified as 'workers' and 10 per cent as 'builders') on the Milanese periphery, the patterns of sociability were those expected of a traditional 'community'. More than half of all residents (and nearly 70 per cent of men) were members of an association – cooperatives, political parties, *Azione Cattolica*, sports clubs and other organizations. Consumerism had not yet 'taken off' at Baggio in the early 1960s (only 16 per cent possessed a car). Similar social patterns characterized Barona (ILSES 1964c, e).

Comasina presents us with a clear contrast to these neighbourhoods. Begun in 1953, Comasina became the biggest public housing project in Italy on final completion in 1958–60, with its eighty-three buildings and 11,000 rooms (Grandi and Pracchi 1980: 260). A modernist, 'futuristic' estate on the city's borders, Comasina was the first 'self-sufficient' neighbourhood built in Italy (Castronovo 1974: 78; Bai 1984). The estate's layout was based around underground walkways, long concrete balconies and a space-age church. Most of the first inhabitants of Comasina were immigrants from the early 1950s and this was one of the first quarters to be studied by ILSES under the auspices of their massive 'Social Integration in Milan' research project of the early 1960s. As a new neighbourhood, Comasina's community was to be created, or so the town planners believed, through the construction of churches, social centres, shops and bars (1964d: 94–107).

By January 1962 there were over 10,000 people on the estate, grouped in 2,200 families. A third of the heads of families were from the south of Italy, but nearly 80 per cent had been in the city for more than ten years. These were not recent immigrants, but those who had arrived before the start of the boom, in the late 1940s and early 1950s. Within the estate there were clear social divisions. Different blocks were used to house various 'types' of residents, including large groups of the *sfrattati* (evicted), *senza-tetto* (homeless) and *ex-baraccati* (ex-shack dwellers). Tensions soon emerged between families from the more 'respectable' parts of the project and those lower down the social scale. Often seemingly petty issues – noise, childcare, rubbish – were the catalysts for (or masks of) broader social and/ or 'ethnic' divisions. Some immigrants constructed complicated caste-type structures to distinguish themselves from those at the poorest end of the scale (Foot 1995). For these reasons, and others, a 'community' spirit was never really a possibility at Comasina, with serious consequences for some of those who came to live there from the late 1960s.

6. The Road to Integration?

6.1. Work and the Migrants[10]

Many researchers have identified the factory as a focal point of integration for immigrants. There are two 'integration' theses that I have identified in this area. The first, which I shall call the 'conservative integration thesis', argues that migrants were integrated into factory life through their acceptance of the cultural values of northern industrial society. These migrants believed they were part of a common project that involved hard work and shared goals of wellbeing and progress. A

---

10. There are, of course, many other possible 'roads' to integration, such as through political parties or the Church. Catholic institutions played an active role in assisting migrants, then as now.

second, 'radical integration' argument adopts a more critical analysis of this period. The 'radical' analysis argues that it was through the shared experience of the factory, of work conditions, of the speedups and technological changes of the 1960s and finally through the trade union struggles of the early 1960s and the 'hot autumn', that immigrants were integrated into northern life. They became, very simply, part of a *class* of *manual workers*, isolated and alienated from their lives in the depressed urban environment.

Of course, this distinction is a schematic one, and obscures many of the contradictory elements of integration. It is certainly true that many young migrants, especially those moving from the rural south, were already well disposed towards an industrial society. Television and migration 'chains' were the key agents of this 'pre-socialization'. However, this process should not be exaggerated, and the evidence supporting these theories was hardly conclusive then and appears inadequate today. In part, this argument rested on certain stereotypes concerning southern migrants: their 'youth' (not all were young by any means, nor 'new' to urban society) and their 'gullibility' in the face of the mass media and consumerism. On arrival, the migrants who did have a positive view of northern city life often saw their dreams shattered, and quickly. But many others saw their aspirations – for a job, a house, a family – fulfilled. The distinction between 'radical' and 'conservative' integration, useful for the arguments employed in this chapter, thus conceals some of the more subtle processes at work at the level of ideology and socialization.

The various integration-at-work theses can be usefully examined at a micro level, in this case that of a single factory. One, important factory in Bovisa was the FACE-Standard plant, one of the biggest and most modern Milanese factories in the mid-1950s (and the 79th biggest company in Italy by 1964). FACE made telephones, exchanges and telephonic equipment and was owned by the American multinational giant ITT. The boom saw FACE take on hundreds of new workers as the demand for telephones increased dramatically.[11] Between 1957 and 1962 the FACE plant at Bovisa took on 749 new workers and 435 new administrative staff, which represented increases of 36 per cent and 45 per cent respectively. In the absence of specific 'ethnic' statistics, it can be assumed that amongst the new workers taken on were significant numbers of *migrants*.[12] Archive information

11. My sources for this section may seem, at first, a trifle eccentric. First, I have used the 'human relations' magazine, produced by the company itself, called *Collaborazione*. This review is a rich source of information about the development and history of FACE. Secondly, there are the Fiom (the metalworkers' trade union) archives and those of the FACE internal commission, held in the *Archivio Fiom* in Milan.

12. Petrillo (1992a and 1992b) and Franzosi (1995) both argue that high numbers of *southern* migrants were *not* taken on as factory workers in large plants until the mid-1960s. Before that, most entered the world of work via the building trade – the classic migrant bridge-head into industrial society.

also reveals that 1,700 out of 4,300 employees in 1960 were young men and women (Archivio Fiom, FACE, f.2, b.29). Clearly, most of these were migrants, and other evidence also points in this direction. In 1963 the company magazine *Collaborazione* wrote, with relation to one section of the factory, that 'amongst the young technicians . . . there are representatives from nearly the whole of Italy: from Istria, from Umbria' (*Collaborazione*, January 1963: 8–9).

Although FACE propaganda made continual reference to its 'faithful' workers, to those who had been with the company for more than thirty years, their own figures revealed a very different company, one overwhelmingly populated by young workers. Eighty per cent of workers had been with the company for less than ten years. Nearly 50 per cent were under thirty (*Collabarazione*, May 1962: 4). What happened to these new employees at FACE? How were they 'integrated' into the factory system, if they were? Of course, FACE was only one factory in one part of one city, but a detailed look at this plant can give us some important insights into the migration processes affecting Milan in general.

The archives of the Fiom, the biggest trade union at FACE, give indirect support to the conservative integration thesis. Very little mention was made, during the boom, of the issue of migration, and the union concentrated on issues dear to workers since the 1940s – the *mensa* (canteen), factory discipline and piecework pay levels. *Collaborazione*, as its title might suggest, viewed the factory as one big happy family. One older woman worker confessed that her 'her family [was] in the work-place, so much so that she feels a bit like the mother of all the young girls in her section' (*Collaborazione*, July–August 1961: 3). Another spoke warmly of 'this great family that is FACE Standard' (*Collaborazione*, June 1962). The first pay envelope of another new worker was described in the following way:

> my work place [is] a second home and this is right because it is there that we spend the great part of our lives . . . I felt something new: faith in myself and in my work. Finally I realised that I could be of use to society. (April 1956: 10)

Another worker's first impression of the factory 'was the clear sensation that I felt an integral and vital part – even if a tiny one – of an immense whole made up of another 4,500 individuals like me, each one rigidly classified at their correct post' (*Collaborazione*, January 1960). This family included all the immigrant workers. In one section of the factory the workers had organized their own festival at which 'given the heterogeneity of the employees, and the places from which they have been . . . imported, we listen to songs singing the praises of Bergamo, Sicily, Naples and, sometimes, even Milan' (*Collaborazione*, February 1958).

Stereotypes about southerners were occasionally used by *Collaborazione*, but in a way that was designed to endear these migrants to their 'fellow' workers. One interview, with a young worker from Apulia, managed this 'conjuring trick' in a quite extraordinary way:

two very dark eyes, black and bushy eyebrows, a face which is not merely tanned, but really dark . . . A Spanish man? An Egyptian? No, simply a southerner and, to be precise, from Bari. Given this discovery, we were afraid that we would meet with the well-known instinctive diffidence, [which is] almost innate, common to all southerners and to be unable to obtain more than a few strained words. (*Collaborazione*, September 1961: 3)

Yet, the bulk of stereotypes were positive, and involved northern employees. Profiles of Milanese workers emphasised their thrift, hard work and dedication to the company. In classic terms, racist stereotypes work best in pairs. The implicit threat was of being cast as the 'negative twin' – the Other – the slothful, stupid and backward southern peasant or ex-peasant.[13] Only very occasionally did this 'implicit threat' slip out from the pages of *Collaborazione*.

For the company, therefore, and undoubtedly for some workers, integration was swift , relatively uncomplicated and positive. Workers, administrative staff and directors were part of a large, harmonious group working for the good of all. But, of course, this was not the whole story. Other evidence calls into question the idea of any swift immigrant 'conservative integration' into Milanese industrial society. The Fiom had published a 'Libro Bianco' on conditions at FACE in the mid-1950s which painted a very different picture – one of short-term contracts, of 'super-exploitation', of *raccomandazioni* (patronage), of political repression and of sexual harassment. The paternalistic nature of the FACE factory regime was epitomized by the fact that all workers had to ring a bell on leaving the plant, a requirement still in place in the early 1960s in one of the most technically advanced factories in Italy (Lega 'Bovisa' di Milano 1955). Piecework made up 20 per cent of wages in 1960, and workers were under constant pressure from 'speed-ups' and refined Taylorist production techniques (Archivio Fiom, FACE, f.2, b.29). The factory's internal commission complained about the 'continual rotation of personnel' (Archivio Fiom, FACE, b.3, f.1, sf.6). Even in the pages of *Collaborazione*, the mask slipped from the idyllic world of the factory family on a number of occasions.

First , there were a number of grudging references in the paper towards migrants. A worker called Giovanni Antico, in the regular column 'Qui parlate voi', affirmed that he was 'Milanese'. He added that 'by now, considering that we are in a small minority, we have become the "terroni"!' (an insult used towards rural immigrants, especially those from the south) (*Collaborazione*, December 1961). Another employee also underlined that he was 'Milanese, and proud of his three generations' and complained significantly that 'we *were* like a family' (my emphasis) at FACE (*Collaborazione*, January 1962). Later the interviewer reminded readers of those who pretended to be Milanese when in fact they had been born in the countryside

13. For these stereotypes see Virciglio (1991), Dickie (1994b and 1999) and Sciolla (1997).

(March 1962). An innocuous debate on the wisdom of Christmas decorations in the city brought accusations of racism onto the pages of *Collaborazione* for the first time (February 1963).

Secondly, these issues were especially strong at FACE because of the opening, in 1962, of a new FACE factory in the south, in Maddaloni near Caserta. Many FACE workers were transferred to the new plant and wrote in *Collaborazione* about their experiences. Others from Maddaloni came to work in Milan. One employee called the new plant at FACE-Sud 'his' factory, and boasted that he had taken his whole family with him to the south (*Collaborazione*, May 1962). Another group of workers also painted a rosy (and stereotypical) picture. They could not hide their 'enthusiasm for this journey which would take them to the land of sun . . . everything down there is so beautiful . . . our factory, the people, the city, the sky' (*Collaborazione*, November 1961). But other accounts were not nearly so complimentary. One correspondent complained of being 'forced' to write about his life at Maddaloni. He described the barrack-like living conditions and what he called a 'nearly colonial atmosphere'. Work at FACE-Sud was compared to military service and the heat was 'oppressive'. The greatest complaints, however, were reserved for the behaviour of southern locals. Whilst the workers from the north went out for drinks every night they were 'always on their own'. And 'how can you live in a town', continued the piece, 'where a young girl has been severely beaten by her short-tempered father because the other evening she returned home "very late": it was 20.30' (*Collaborazione*, September 1963).

The evidence for immigrant integration in the factory, at FACE, is therefore inconclusive. The lack of attention to the problem from the trade unions gives, in one way, indirect support to the 'conservative integration' thesis. However, the tensions that emerged even in a magazine largely devoted to propaganda such as *Collaborazione* seem to indicate that integration – in either an economic or a national sense – was far from positive. The leading role played by FACE workers in the Milanese strikes of 1960–2, which involved the most modern factories in the city, also warns us against the 'conservative integration' thesis. Young immigrants were involved in these crucial struggles, in strikes that dealt 'a first blow to the new myths in Milan, capital of the miracle' (Bertoli 1980: 42). Marginalization and 'super-exploitation' in the factory and outside had led to a kind of integration for some young workers, but not in the way the FACE management had wanted. Violence often broke out during the 1960–1 strikes, as a 'new' working class flexed its muscles across the city. The city saw a series of minor clashes with police, in a long dress rehearsal for 1968 and after, and even Bovisa had its own, tiny, riot in Piazza Bausan in October 1962.[14] The photos of

---

14. The *Corriere della Sera* of 13 October 1962 reported that many of the demonstrators were FACE workers.

that minor event clearly show the central role of young workers (many of whom were from FACE). As Mannheimer has argued, with relation to the struggles of the *late* 1960s, some immigrants were united with fellow manual workers 'in the cause of a common anti-employer struggle' (Mannheimer and Micheli 1974).[15]

However, we should be cautious about the extent of this 'radical integration' in Milan, especially in the period of the economic miracle. As Petrillo has written, 'there was no Piazza Statuto' in Milan (1992a: 654).[16] No large alienated, migrant 'underclass' was to be found in Milan on the scale of that in Turin. Rioting Pirelli workers in 1962 were still dressed in jackets and ties. Their anger had got the better of them but they had not gone looking for confrontation. After 1962 came a short recession and a series of crucial contractual struggles, as well as the emergence of student radicalism in Milan and elsewhere. At Turin the domination of Fiat helped in the isolation of the 'new' working class and of the southern immigrants, pushing them towards radical integration. Turin was a far more closed and hierarchical industrial city when compared with the complexity and modernity of Milan. The type and weight of immigration to Torino was tightly linked to the development and decision-making of *one* firm, Fiat. As such, Milan was (structurally) far more 'open' to outsiders than Turin, and far more conducive to conservative integration pathways.[17] Milan's more complicated industrial system allowed for more integration between an old and a 'new', mainly migrant, working class (Petrillo 1992b: 384–401, 414).

Integration was therefore a complicated and contradictory phenomenon. Many migrants came to Milan with a positive view of both the city and of 'industrial society', ready to accept poor conditions at work in return for a stable job and a stake in the 'miracle'. Others were shocked by the distance between the harsh, grey reality of Milan and the glittering photographic, celluloid and tele-visual images with which they had become accustomed. Many were already politicized via the rural struggles in southern and central Italy, or by previous experiences of emigration, and held to a more realistic view of what awaited them. Some workers were rejected by the 'native' proletariat, others were abandoned by the city itself, and its citizens. Changes in the workplace, Italy's 'late' but rapid industrialization, pushed workers together and favoured 'radical integration', whereas changes in society itself – television, consumerism, the changes in family roles – helped 'conservative integration'. These contradictory processes led to Milan becoming,

15. For the 'integration as class' thesis see Petrillo (1992a: 637–41 and 655–6), who also underlines the role of the Church, and Ganapini (1993: 331–3).

16. Piazza Statuto was the scene of a series of urban riots at Turin in July 1962 involving many young southern immigrants, see Lanzardo (1979).

17. For the hostility of Turin towards the immigrants the work of Fofi (1964) remains fundamental but see also the articles collected in CRIS (1962) and for FIAT and the immigrants see Revelli (1989: 28–31). For Genoa, where the 'rifiuto' of the city was also extremely strong, see Cavalli (1964).

undoubtedly, the 'capital of the miracle', but also the 'capital of 1968' and a stronghold of the workers' movement. Workers were pulled in many different directions, and the final outcome of these 'struggles' did not become clear until the 1980s.

If jobs were relatively easy to come by in the Milan of the 'miracle', 'a roof' was a different matter and the search for decent housing was the main preoccupation of immigrants in the city throughout the boom years.

6.2. Housing

It would be difficult to claim that Milan, as a city, welcomed the migrants of the 1950s and 1960s (Balbo 1962; Albertelli and Ziliani 1970). Most were forced to seek housing either on the extreme urban periphery or in the newly urbanized belt of towns around the *Comune* (Ascoli 1979: 143; Pizzorno 1960). However, this was not a problem that affected immigrants alone. Milan had, historically, 'expelled' its workers *en masse* to its endless urban fringe (Cavallazzi and Falchi 1989: 195; Foot 1991). Visconti claimed that he shot *Rocco and his Brothers* in black and white because that was how Milan would have looked to a family from the south (Servadio 1981: 168). Many of these peripheral residents rose at 4.30 in the morning to travel to work, not reaching home until 8.00 or 9.00 in the evening (Bocca 1980: 84–90). This crucial separation between work and home, between the 'point of production' and the 'point of reproduction', analysed in the American context in Katznelson's *City Trenches*, was a harsh and daily reality for these citizens (1982). Others found poor-quality housing closer to their place of work, in the 'historic' periphery that had developed around Milan's first industrial revolution at the turn of the century.

6.3. The 'Old Neighbourhoods': Bovisa, Baggio and Barona

Bovisa is a zone without any public housing. As such it represented an extreme of the housing equation at the opposite end to new estates like Comasina. Immigrants found rooms or beds at Bovisa through advertisements, private contacts, work contacts, private organizations or house-to-house enquiries. Many found rooms in the older tenement blocks to the north of the zone. Certain streets became known as those where 'the immigrants lived', and maintain that 'reputation' even today. In the 1970s, as space began to dry up, many of these blocks were occupied by protesting immigrants looking for rooms, but in the 1950s accommodation was available. Speculation had not yet pushed the market out of control and immigrants could often find cheap, poor quality and short-term accommodation in peripheral neighbourhoods like Bovisa or in the more central zones around the canals (the *Navigli*) and near the key railway stations (Garibaldi-Isola, Stazione Centrale).

Certain types of 'solidarity networks' helped immigrants find short-term accommodation at Bovisa ('everybody had a spare mattress').[18]

There is no evidence of great tension over housing and migration at Bovisa until the great struggles over rent and the occupations of the early 1970s, when the boom had already run its course. But Bovisa residents, immigrants and Milanese alike, could certainly complain about the lack of services in their zone. According to a 1962 *Comune* publication, the zone needed two chemists, a covered market, two playing fields, 95 school rooms and a civic centre (Commissione 1962: 197). It is interesting to note that the *Comune* believed that just as a zone of 40,000 people needed eight chemists and 243 school rooms, it *required* fifteen party sections and circles (Commissione 1962: xxxii). The *partitocrazia* (partitocracy) system was in full swing. Research on integration at the time also assumed that the road to cohesiveness in society would come through the politicization, in the sense of activity in local party sections, of new immigrants.

Conflicting evidence about integration within 'old' Milan emerges from surveys carried out in the 1960s in two other peripheral neighbourhoods in the city, Baggio and Barona. In Baggio the *local* population was relatively stable – 60 per cent were natives of Milan or its province and 17 per cent had been born in Baggio itself. 41 per cent had been resident there for more than ten years. Relationships amongst these people were 'face-to-face', daily and street-based, conforming to the 'Bethnal Green' model of the proletarian community. Modern consumerism was not yet dominant in Baggio and oppositional subcultures, symbolized by traditions such as civil funerals – with just a red flag – survived. By the mid-1950s, this apparently quiet, settled world was being torn apart by one process – mass immigration.

As one 'old' resident of Baggio put it in 1964: 'from 1953 onwards Baggio began to change, the first big groups of immigrants started to arrive, *chaos broke out*' (my emphasis) (ILSES 1964c: 53).[19] Immigration, especially from the south, created huge problems in this area with its settled, long-term worker population. Four thousand people settled in the quarter between April 1962 and 1964. Immigrants were assigned public flats in the 'new' part of Baggio, or took over ex-farm house-courtyards in the older areas of the neighbourhood. 'Real islands' were formed between different housing blocks, similar to those at Comasina (where divisions were more socially based). The complaints against the immigrants were familiar ones: they were too loud;[20] they argued ('many were dirty, they shouted continually'); they had criminal tendencies ('there were always police sirens');

18. Interview. Luigi Mazzari. Conducted by the author, 1992.

19. All the quotes in this section are from anonymous interviewees cited in this report.

20. 'Noisiness was, in those years, one of the most important aspects which helped to bring together the host society, helping to create discrimination against the southerners', Virciglio (1991: 88).

they had isolated themselves ('they are tempted to close themselves off in clans') and were hostile to Milanese; they left their children unattended; they were 'backward' ('they have a modest love for their cultural and civic backwardness'). They were, in short, different: 'they have another kind of character, they do not easily adapt to our ways and traditions'. Bars were either frequented by southerners or 'locals', very rarely by mixed groups. And in Baggio, this hostility and spatial isolation even ended in violence (ILSES 1964c: 71–2).

Finally, immigrants in Baggio were also accused of political 'crimes'. They were consumerist ('whilst on the one hand they said they had no money . . . on the other they would have needed money to buy their new furniture, their electrical goods and even their cars'). In short, although the charge was not made explicit, the immigrants were also criticized as familists. And these arguments were not without contradictions. On the one hand, the immigrants were seen as 'closed' within an ethnic group, as having reproduced the same social relations from their southern villages, of *collective* hostility towards Milanese people. On the other hand, the immigrants were seen as family oriented, as ignorant of any collective interests outside of their own immediate kin relations. As ILSES put it (in a discussion of an 'immigrant' block in Baggio):

> each family lives in isolation from the others, without communicating either with the
> other inhabitants of the neighbourhood, or with their neighbours . . . their children don't
> play with other children in the neighbourhood and they have *no contact* with the external
> environment. (my emphasis) (ILSES 1964c: 15)

This was about as extreme a level of negative or downward integration as could be imagined. Immigrants at Baggio had certainly integrated into the value system of modern capitalist society, but at the level of housing, of community, of the city, of class, they had closed themselves off (and the closure was also reciprocal, as the hostility to them described in this section has shown) from the Milanese and from Milan as a whole. They had accepted 'Milan' and the 'Miracle', and all it stood for, but rejected Milan at an everyday level. They had integrated as ethnic groups, or families, but not as citizens or workers.[21]

Research on Barona, another Milanese working-class neighbourhood, confirmed the impression from Baggio (ILSES 1964e). Barona was a less settled quarter than Baggio, with only 7 per cent having been born in the neighbourhood and 35

---

21. Many on the periphery found their only route to any sort of common associational life amongst groups of their fellow migrants. At Seggiano near Pioltello, Sicilians from the same village (Pietraperzia) organized the religious processions that had been a feature of their previous lives, Baglivo and Pellicciari (1970: 66). See also the example of immigrants from the small village of Agira in Sicily who settled in Garbagnate outside Milan, Associazione Famiglia Agirina di Milano (1997).

per cent resident at Barona for over ten years. Here, as at Baggio, there were strong spatial divisions between the Milanese and Lombard populations and immigrants in the zone. In fact, Via Biella (and the street numbers were also specified) became known as an 'ethnic island'. The immigrants there, who were 'exclusively southerners', were again seen as criminals, noisy, argumentative, hostile and as uncaring parents. According to ILSES, the inhabitants at Via Biella had reconstituted their previous 'small communities . . . closed in on themselves . . . a real small village within the neighbourhood'. Relations between ethnic groups were, at best, strained. Immigrants had been thrown out of some bars, and kept to 'their' two bars in Via Biella itself. Milanese were insulted in the street. Via Biella was known as *La Casbah* locally (ILSES 1964e: 6–8).

At Barona as well, then, the working class was divided, spatially and along ethnic lines, although there were cases of inter-ethnic integration in other parts of the zone. Via Biella was not even at the lowest end of the social scale. In Via S. Rita towards the extreme periphery of the city, there had been a spate of suicides and residents were accused of allowing their children to 'disturb people' and vandalize public gardens. It was extremely difficult for local associations to attract immigrants, and the latter were accused of taking an instrumental attitude to membership. In all of these zones there was an extremely dynamic situation of instability and of rapid and unplanned change. 'The zone', argued ILSES, 'is in great ferment, the population changes continually, there are houses where in the arc of two or three months the occupiers have changed two or three times.'

What can we conclude about immigration and integration at Baggio and Barona from this survey, based on research from the 1960s? First, that these communities, once so (apparently) united, had been torn apart by immigration – with a 'double refusal' on the part of both immigrants and Baggio-residents, and the creation of well-defined spatial ghettos and boundaries between the various ethnic and social groups. Second, that many immigrant families had serious problems adapting to the Milanese urban environment – hence the talk of suicides, frequent family arguments and crime reported by ILSES. They found strength in two forms of integration, within well-defined ethnic groups or simply as families, united against a hostile outside world. Third, that the class unity of the 1940s and 1950s had been replaced by internecine struggle – a 'war amongst the poor' within the neighbourhood in which the social and environmental problems of the quarter were marginalized. Finally, the classic, proletarian communities of Baggio and Barona had great problems in dealing with 'Others', with outsiders of any kind, and this was part of both its strength and its conservatism. Without the shock impact of the boom, and the mass immigration that accompanied that development, Baggio 'Vecchio', with its Milanese bars, its street life, its male-dominated associations, political parties and co-operatives, would have continued to dominate the neighbourhood. The 'dark side' of the proletarian community was laid bare by the rapid and spontaneous economic forces behind the 'miracle', and the creation of ghettos like Via Biella and 'Baggio Nuovo'.

6.4. The 'New Quarter': Comasina

The ILSES enquiry team of the early 1960s made a thorough investigation into living conditions and social integration at Comasina. They discovered a contradiction. Although the houses themselves were generally judged favourably by the new residents (there were differences between various housing blocks) – the quarter outside of the four walls of the family home was already in decline. Dark underground walkways were filling up with rubbish and were centres for crime even before the estate was finished. Even the internal courtyards in certain blocks, which were designed as arenas of social interaction, were being used as rubbish dumps in the early 1960s, (Commissione 1962: 237; ILSES 1964c: 7). Residents complained about the lack of consumer choice, the dearth of areas to meet people, the absence of shops. The area was described as a 'dead zone, isolated [and] lifeless' (Pietro Gennaro e associati 1964: 35; Commissione 1962: 237). The estate possessed no phone box. 86 per cent of houses had a phone, so the remaining 14 per cent, at least 1,300 people, had no local access to one (Gennaro 1964: 17–22). By 1962 there was only one post box to serve over 10,000 people, and no post office. Nine out of ten residents felt unsafe at times in the quarter and called for a heavier police presence (Gennaro 1964: 11). Communications to the centre of Milan and even to the next neighbourhood were infrequent and slow. Only 30 per cent possessed a car. Shopping was difficult on the estate and judged as expensive and of poor quality by many of the residents. The supposed 'self-sufficiency' of Comasina, it was admitted, had already failed almost as the last brick was built on the estate (Gennaro 1964: 36).[22] Distrust of fellow Comasina residents was extremely high. Nearly half the residents claimed that there were 'many ill-mannered people'. Twenty-three per cent found it difficult to make friends (Gennaro 1964: 11–12; Pellicciari 1964: 28).

This isolation of the urban immigrant, the alienation from the urban environment, is confirmed by other studies, notably that undertaken (by the journal *Classe*) on manual workers at Alfa Romeo. This research found that a third of migrant manual workers (many of whom were immigrants) at Alfa spent their free time 'resting . . . at home', a quarter helped out at home, 20 per cent went to the bar

22. See also IACPM (1958), Alasia and Montaldi (1960: 112–3) and Rigoldi (1978: 50–1). Grandi and Pracchi (1980: 260) have criticized Comasina for its location, its size (too big) and its 'rigid residential monofunctionality'. However, these authors also pointed out that, architecturally, Comasina was better than many of the later estates at Milan (for example Ponte Lambro), which often consisted merely of parallel tower blocks.

and only 6 per cent were visited by friends or family. *Twelve per cent admitted to having no friends at all.* 90 per cent had to travel for more than an hour to arrive at their place of work. Similar patterns were to be found amongst immigrant building workers (Tavolato and Zanuso 1974; Pellicciari 1963). Television was already central to the leisure time of Comasina residents. There was little alternative. Milan's provision of open spaces and parks was the lowest in Europe. Each inhabitant could count on one square metre of green space in 1953, and only 52 square *centimetres* in Bovisa (Morpurgo 1975: 21; Iosa 1971: 104).

Comasina, therefore, became the classic 'ghetto', empty by day except for the old, the very young, the unemployed and non-working women, and full by night, but barren and lacking in informal social structures (the estate was well-served in other ways, having *three* social centres and a church with sports and cultural facilities). The quarter was at the extreme edge of the city, and those re-housed from the *barrache* were located next to the northern boundaries of the neighbourhood. Their chances of integration with the city itself were limited indeed. Some of what had been gained in terms of 'privacy', of 'liberation' from the oppressive aspects of the courtyard or village square, and through the great improvement in the quality of housing for the vast majority of residents, had been lost in the absence of community and in the relationship with the city. *Most inhabitants in Comasina, however, seemed quite happy to pay this 'price'.* Many (but not all) had traded traditional forms of urban integration (the 'community') for other values – privacy, status, a spacious living room. For many, the internal, private life of the family had taken precedence over other forms of social relationships.[23]

7. Which Integration? City, Work and Culture during the Boom in Milan

In Fofi's classic study of immigration to Turin the 'moment' of class-based integration of southerners is symbolized by this incident:

When, at Mirafiori [the biggest FIAT factory], another southerner, little more than a boy, was applauded by the other members of the picket as he insulted a scab, an old Piedmontese, with the terms 'napuli' and 'marocchino'. (1975: 177)[24]

23. The situation at Comasina was much more complicated than this. For example, groups of those re-housed from shacks maintained lively systems of informal social networks. For all these issues see Saraceno (1988a: 185–227) and Foot (1995).

24. See also Guiotto's comments on the generic use of the term 'napoletani' (1986: 31) and Castronovo's reflections (1977: 660).

'Radical integration' in the factory had taken place via the exclusion of other groups, and even the self-exclusion of one worker's own identity. But Primo Levi, Turinese, in an interview in 1986, described this moment in another way:

> At Turin we have experienced the mass immigration of 600,000 southerners. This process was traumatic at first; they were seen as foreigners. But over the course of one generation, only one, this hostility has ended. There have been mixed marriages, children who have been educated in local schools. Nowadays the southerner at Torino is no longer treated like a stranger. (1995: 82)

Integration had clearly taken place, over time, even in 'hostile' Turin, but what kind of integration? In the 1960s, tendencies towards forms of integration were contradictory and flexible. Many migrants found a role as members of a class at work in the factories of Milano. For a long period (1968-1980), this class was a protagonist of struggles on the national stage. Whilst many immigrants found life difficult in the city – and were forced to deal with social isolation and rejection in the urban environment – as a class the new migrants were able to carry forward certain *collective* values. And even the 'isolation' in the city should not be exaggerated. Recent research has revealed that the improvements in living conditions experienced by many migrants outweighed, for them, the negative aspects of the city. Isolation also implied privacy. The decline of neighbourly or community-type relationships was compensated for by the conquest of social space in the home. The contradictions of the integration processes in Milan are perfectly summarized in the testimony of a young schoolteacher from Apulia, who arrived in the city in 1962:

> I remember that first winter. It was terrible looking out of the window: fog everywhere, you could never see the sky . . . we were forced to spend day after day at home . . . we were six children in three rooms. My father had a job at Alfa Romeo found for him by his brother. My mother was scared to go shopping. But it was our first happy year. There were no longer arguments at home . . . we ate well and we had a home which for us was like that of a Lord. (cited in Di Biase 1985: 140)

8. Milan and its Foreign Immigrants: Three Stories from the City

> One of the tasks before the historian is to discover which racial categories are useful to whom at a given moment and why. (Frye-Jackson 1998: 9)

In the sections that follow I will consider three stories of immigration from the Milan of the 1980s and 1990s.[25] The comparison with the migration of the boom

25. The most detailed work on immigration in Milan in the 1980s and 1990s is to be found in Barile *et al.* (1994) especially Dal Lago: 135–240 and Marchetti: 241–366. See also Allievi (1993),

(based around the concept of integration) will focus on the areas of crime, housing, hierarchies and 'foreignness' and urban conflict.

8.1. The Emergency: Via Corelli

The first mass immigrations from outside Italy in the late 1980s caught both the state and local authorities completely unprepared. Milan itself was in the throes of a deep housing crisis, due to excessive rent controls, speculation, the financial problems of the local administration and housing authorities and the transformation of many residential areas into offices or transport links. Many of the first foreign immigrants, especially those living illegally, found shelter in the thousands of disused factories on the Milanese periphery. Even more desperately, many slept in train carriages stored in rail hangars (dubbed 'hotels of fear' by the Italian press). Others formed caravan camps or mini shanty towns in areas of wasteland such as train terminals or abandoned building sites. Numerous evictions (or 'clearances', known as *sgomberi*) took place around the city in the 1990s, and were followed by summary expulsions or the issuing of expulsion orders (Balbo and Manconi 1992: 27–8, 81). These immigrants occupied the slow lane of a two-speed urban environment characterized by industrial decline, the fragmentation of the prol-etariat, and an erosion of communal identity, in a deindustrialized West with creaking welfare states. They have joined a new, shifting underclass which is vulnerable to unscrupulous employers and petty criminals.

Following the first Italian immigration law in 1990 (the so-called 'Martelli law' – law 39) Milan's Council, unlike many other administrations, made an attempt to provide temporary housing for homeless immigrants. Council housing has also been allocated to resident immigrants, mostly Eritrean refugees, since 1982. Ten reception centres, known as *Centri di prima accoglienza* (Cpas) were built or opened, including the large immigrant camp constructed in Via Corelli, opened in the summer of 1990.[26] This 10,000 square metre concrete space consisted of 100 pre-fabricated containers (built to house four people each) surrounded with barbed wire, located on the extreme periphery of the city under a main underpass. Local protests tried to stop the construction of the camp (and similar protests accompanied the opening of nearly all the Cpas). Conditions were hardly luxurious. There was little shade and the containers were unbearably hot in summer and freezing cold in the winter. Elaborate rules (which quickly broke down) were drawn up under which the male occupants were forced to evacuate their 'homes' during the daytime

---

Palidda (2000b) and Cologna (1999). The best general synthesis is Pugliese (1996: 933–84) and see also Signorelli for an anthropological approach (1996).

26. For the history of Via Corelli see Tosi (1993), Granata and Novak (1999: 187–8) and Fazio (1999).

– even at weekends – and smoking, women, friends and card-games were banned. Via Corelli quickly became the symbol of the failure to deal with the immigrant housing problem. By 1991, the centre was seriously overcrowded, the prefabs were not being maintained and there were constant reports of violent incidents. An estimated 700–800 immigrants were sleeping in an area built for 200–300. The law also required that such housing should only be provided for a maximum of six months, so the need to periodically evict all Via Corelli's inhabitants created a situation of fear and police intimidation (in reality the occupants stayed for an average of three years). The site (and the Cpas in general) became a costly embarrassment. In April 1993 the site was described as a 'powder-keg' and 'unmanageable' (*La Repubblica*, 1 April, 6 April 1993). The original decision to contract out the management of the centres to co-operatives had proved disastrous in the Corelli case, as they were unable to keep any kind of control over the inhabitants. Both the regionalist Northern Leagues and the neo-fascist MSI called for their immediate closure. The 1993 election campaign saw these promises dominate the campaign of the winning candidate – Formentini of the Lega.

In May 1994 Formentini maintained his election promise and 'closed' Via Corelli. This was against the wishes of the Assessor for Social Services who, faced with the reality of 800 immigrants to re-house, appealed for time to find an alternative and 'humanitarian' solution. The administration also entered into conflict with the more realistic priorities of the state authorities. In reality, Via Corelli continued to be occupied by over 200 immigrants, despite its official closure. Christmas 1994 saw the electricity company turn off the gas and lighting to the centre, and eleven immigrants were taken to hospital suffering from hypothermia (*Corriere della Sera*, 7 January 1995). In October 1995 the last 107 immigrants were evicted and the remaining prefabs crushed by cranes (*Corriere della Sera*, 15 October 1995). For three years, the area remained empty, but in 1998 the spectre of Via Corelli was raised again. This time the zone was chosen to 'house' a detention centre for those awaiting expulsion under the new immigration law (L. 40/1998) passed by the centre-left government. These centres were to be known as 'Centres for temporary permanence and assistance (sic.)'. After a series of debates and protests, 'Via Corelli' re-opened in January 1999.

The new detention centre was made up of a series of nineteen containers, similar to those that had been there before, but this time the whole area was surrounded by a huge metal fence and barbed wire. The police were in charge of running the centre, along with Red Cross workers. Very quickly, Via Corelli returned to the front pages of the newspapers. Human rights groups complained that those detained had committed no crime, and yet were in a worse situation than 'normal' prisoners. In fact, detainees could make phone calls, but many were not told of their rights to legal protection and appeal. It was very difficult for observers and the press to gain access to the centre. Throughout 1999 Via Corelli was host to a series of riots, attempted suicides, rapes, escapes, demonstrations and protests. The chief of police, it was said, would ring up Via Corelli to see if there was 'space'. If there was, he would order a 'roundup' of immigrants who were then taken to the centre. Men and women were not separated, leading to a number of attacks on young and vulnerable prostitutes. In March 2000, after a series of nationwide demonstrations against detention centres (and a number of deaths in the centres, including three in Trapani and one in Rome) the new interior Minister, Bianco, decided to close Via Corelli. Over fifteen months, 2,724 immigrants had passed through the gates of the centre. The centre was again emptied and the prefabs were again demolished. Plans, however, were soon made for a new 'more human' centre – Corelli 2 – on the same site. In October 2000, yet another 're-opening' took place in Via Corelli, this time of a more prison-like structure with proper buildings and the same high fencing. Soon, Via Corelli 3 was in the news (again), as doubts were raised by a series of judges over the constitutionality of the 'centre' and the imprisonment of immigrants who had committed no crime therein. The story of the new Via Corelli perfectly symbolized the change in the attitude towards immigrants in the 1990s. *From a social question, the immigrants had become a security issue* (especially after the moral panic in Milan following a number of murders in January 1998).[27] It also symbolized the abject failure of the local and national state in its dealings with the immigrants. This securitization of the immigrant issue mirrored processes in other countries and seemed to indicate the growth of a new, right-wing 'authoritarian' consensus around the issues of crime and race (Hall, Crichter, Jefferson, Clarke and Roberts 1978; Huysmans 1995: 53–72; Palidda 2000a, b; Foot 2000b).

To return to the first incarnation of Via Corelli, not only did the Cpas create expensive and ugly ghettos, but they failed completely to deal with the problem of immigrant housing. In the 1990s only 11 per cent of all documented immigrants were housed in these centres, and little or no new cheap housing was built in the city or outside. This approach contrasts strongly with the construction of new, economic neighbourhoods for the immigrants of the boom years, usually on the urban periphery. With the foreign immigrants, therefore, the second, stable home has been almost completely ignored as a problem. There is an assumption that these immigrants are temporary urban dwellers, whereas with those of the 1950s, the supposition was that they were permanent.

Nonetheless, we can also pick out some similarities between the situation at Via Corelli and that involving southern immigrants in the city in the 1960s. First, there is a strong association between crime and immigration – linked to the territorial presence of immigrants from the same region or country and tied up with a widespread fear of these areas. This is as true for Via Corelli as it was for

27. For an alternative view, claiming continuity between the two Via Corellis, see Quagliata (1999).

the *Coree* in the 1960s, or the urban ghettos inhabited by southerners such as those in Baggio. Every proposed new centre for immigrants, or drug addicts, or the homeless provokes protests from local residents in areas where collective action of any other kind is a distant memory. A second comparison is the link made by local residents and the press between immigration and a series of urban anti-social activities – noise, dirt, violence, crime. Via Corelli and the other Cpas, like the *Coree*, also became centres of attraction for police activity, being subject to frequent raids and controls. In the 1960s, after certain crimes, the police would often sweep through the *Coree* picking up a series of 'usual suspects'. Even at a micro-level, certain 'immigrant' streets (or even certain housing blocks) in certain areas became associated with crime and wrongdoing. Often these areas were racialized and given nicknames – such as *Casbah* or *Suk*. Similar terms are often used today.

The whole saga of Via Corelli was important and damaging in the city for a number of reasons. First, it reinforced the stereotype of the immigrant *extra-comunitario* as Moroccan, probably a criminal, male, young, unemployed, violent, desperate, costly. Via Corelli was a highly visible site and 'problem – both in the press and literally, as thousands of Milanese passed over or next to the camp every day in their cars. The realities of *invisible* immigration in the city were not present in Via Corelli – peaceful, not mainly male (45 per cent of immigrants are women), employed and from a whole range of different nationalities (Vitone 1998; Ambrosini 1999). Second, the (costly) emergency model (never adopted for the immigrants of the 1950s, who were able to benefit from a whole series of local government initiatives – from a welcome centre in the Central Station to a guide to the city published by the Council) was never transformed into a model resembling something like normality, with serious consequences for immigrants, administrators and Italians in the late 1990s. Lastly, Via Corelli, although built to house 'regular', legal, documented immigrants soon became a symbol of the problems linked to illegal, undocumented and so-called clandestine immigration. The whole purpose of the centre – to provide short-term housing for those working regularly in Milan – was overturned in reality and even more so in the public mind by a combination of incompetence, lack of planning, criminal activity and a permanent sense of 'emergency'.

8.2. Representation and Memory: The Life and Death of Driss Moussafir

The case of Driss Moussafir's tragic death in 1993 represents an illuminating and complicated example of the treatment and representation of immigration in Milan and elsewhere. On 27 July 1993, at 11.15 pm, the fire brigade and traffic police were called to what was described as a burning car in the central Via Palestro. As three fire-fighters and a traffic policeman moved towards the car a massive bomb exploded, killing all four, injuring seven others and destroying an internationally famous art gallery. A few moments later, in the park bordering Via Palestro, another body was found, that of Moussafir, a forty-four-year-old Moroccan immigrant.

Initial reports named the three fire-fighters and the traffic policeman and referred to 'an *extracomunitario*'. Only later was a name given. Other reports referred to 'an immigrant' (although Judge Borelli optimistically used the term 'citizen').[28] In almost all the reports Moussafir's death was reported last. A series of small hierarchies began to emerge in the treatment of the fifth of five tragedies. Mayor Formentini forgot Moussafir altogether in his initial statement, referring to those who had died 'in the pursuit of their duties'. The next day Michele Serra wrote a bitter piece for *L'Unità*, where he noted the irony of the 'egalitarianism' imposed on Driss by the bomb (1993). Moussafir's friends expressed similar ideas in a message placed on his coffin: 'this blood will help us to escape from our clandestine status'.

Small but important details began to emerge about Moussafir; he had been in Milan for around fifteen years (some reports said seventeen, others eleven) and had got by through a combination of short-term work, street-trading and petty crime. He was well known to the police and within the Moroccan community. He was, apparently, homeless (although his friends later argued that he lived nearby and had not in fact been sleeping on a park bench – but the image of the tramp persisted). He had a permit to stay in the city, which had run out (*L'Unità*, 29 July 1993). Formentini began to mention Mousaffir on the 29 July, referring to a 'poor man forced to live like a tramp'. Yet Mousaffir's coffin was the only one not visited by the Mayor or public officials at Lambrate Cemetery and he was not given the city's Gold Medal unlike the other victims (causing a short-lived debate in the Milanese press). More problems emerged during the funeral, as Mousaffir's body was displayed with the others (entering last) in Piazza del Duomo and then taken for a small Islamic service at Segrate, attended by two left wing councillors (*L'Unità*, 30 July 1993). No transport was provided for the mourners to reach the Mosque and, with all public transport closed for the day, the small group was forced to remain behind. Nonetheless, many citizens showed their respect with poems and cards. Some of these were collected in an official book (Comune di Milano 1993). Moussafir's body was flown to Morocco for burial.

The Morrocan's name was commemorated in the dedication of a school in the Stadera neighbourhood, one of the most important zones for immigration in the city and the scene of violent clashes in 1998 (see below). Even here, memory played some tricks on the dead immigrant. The initial naming of the school was taken by Italians from an official banner hung in Via Palestro, where the spelling was wrong. The name *Wousaffir* was used. None of the immigrants attending the school understood who this person was – the name Wousaffir having no meaning

28. See *L'Unità*, 28 July 1993.

in Moroccan (whilst Moussafir means 'traveller'). Only after some months was the mistake put right and the meaning of the school's name became clearer for those immigrants who learned their Italian there. In 1994, a year after the explosion, an official plaque was unveiled in Via Palestro. Moussafir's name was correctly spelled this time, and he is described as a 'Moroccan citizen', but his name remains last in the list, below the four Italians listed in alphabetical order. In addition, the reference to 'the sacrifice of young lives' does not appear to refer to Moussafir, forty-four at the time of his death (Lisbona and Brunasti 1998: 74).

Moussafir's insignificant life and significant death raise a number of questions concerning the place of foreign immigrants in Milanese society. First, there is the issue of *visibility*. It is often assumed that foreign immigrants are particularly visible in a city like Milan, unused to significant numbers of non-Italians amongst its residents.[29] *Driss was both visible and invisible.* He was 'well-known' to the police, and to local shopkeepers, and to those who regularly purchase contraband cigarettes from his improvised stall. He lived his life on the street, not behind closed doors. He was a *public* figure. Yet, he was invisible to many others – a man without a name, without a family, without a home. He could be reduced, easily, to an *extracomunitario*, to a category. The concept of visibility, used so often and so sloppily by many writers on immigration, is both contradictory and extremely problematic. The question that needs to be asked is not 'visible or not?' but 'visible or invisible as what and for whom?' Southern immigrants were also assumed to be particularly 'visible' during the boom. Over time, their 'Otherness', like that of Italians in the US, has been assimilated into a general 'whiteness', which has been constructed in part against the new immigrants. New inclusive identities have been created that exclude many non-Italians. As Frye Jackson (1998: 4) puts it in his brilliant study of the creation and perceptions of race in the US, 'Caucasians are made and not born'. The cliché of visibility also simply reproduces the stereotype of immigrant as street-trader, prostitute, criminal, beggar.[30] It ignores the vast majority of invisible immigrant jobs in kitchens, sweatshops, building sites, nurseries, old-peoples' homes, hospitals and small factories.

Second, Milan is a society where foreign *extracomunitari* naturally fit into hierarchies that penalize them imperceptibly at a whole series of levels. Moussafir's coffin was 'naturally' last into the Piazza and first to leave, his name was 'naturally' last (or missing) in almost all the official communications and in the reporting in the press and on television, his name was 'naturally' the only one misspelled on

29. It is worth noting that non-Italian immigrants were already 'visible' in the 1970s, see the work of photographer Lucas (1977). The historic Chinese community is often forgotten, Farina *et al.* (1997).

30. This link between street-trading and immigration was also made for the southern immigrants in the 1950s (with a particularly strong image of lemon-selling at street markets, a trade now adopted by foreign immigrants) and the first Chinese immigrants in the 1930s.

the official memorial. The fact that one of the traffic policemen who died was a Neapolitan immigrant, who had been in the city for far less time than Moussafir, was hardly mentioned and not seen as important. Finally, the city itself (any city) does not discriminate with its 'egalitarian' dangers. A bomb can kill anyone who happens to be passing. Car crashes do not choose their victims and pollution affects almost everyone. The city unites and divides in complicated mosaics of fear, real hazards and anxieties. The arguments in Milan over the construction of fences around the major public parks, and the rise in urban crime tell us much about the power of barriers and locks and the gap between real danger and insecurity.

8.3. Violence and urban conflict. Via Meda 1998

These fears and conflicts, linked as they are to the use and abuse of urban space, exploded briefly in Milan during the summer of 1998. The Stadera area, at the extreme south of the city's boundaries but only ten minutes by tram from the city centre, is characterized by ageing and badly maintained public housing estates. The Porta Venezia area near the Central Station (with its plethora of rented accommodation) performs the function of a first port of call for many immigrants in the city – similar to that of San Salvario and Porta Palazzo in Turin, or the historic centre of Genoa, or Stoke Newington in London – but Stadera is the area where many immigrants go to find a more permanent home.[31] Most of these immigrants are unable to procure public housing through legal means (the waiting lists are extremely long) and have decided to occupy empty flats on these estates. By 1997, over 200 flats on the estate were occupied illegally by Italians and non-Italian immigrants. The authorities more or less tolerated this situation, given the lack of alternative housing available and the closure of the Cpas in the 1990s. Every so often, for political reasons, the police would raid specific flats and evict the occupants. In many cases, the flats were reoccupied almost immediately.

In this zone, given the relatively high numbers of non-Italian immigrants and the fact that many had regular jobs, a number of businesses began to open linked to the immigrant presence. One of these was a bar catering for immigrants called Bar Skirrat in Via Spaventa near Via Meda. In the late 1990s, this bar began to become the focus of conflict over social space, urban space and immigration. Local residents (mainly Italians but also foreign immigrants – the dividing lines were not always immigrant/non-immigrant) complained to the council and the police on numerous occasions of excessive noise, violence and drunkenness. The authorities often ignored the protests of these so-called 'locals'. On a hot night in June 1998 this situation reached the point of violence. After two days of street

31. For the city-immigrant relationship in general see Tosi (1998), for Milan see A. Colombo (1998) and Cologna *et al.* (1999). For Milan's Central Station see Colombo and Navarini (1999).

protests, where demonstrators sat on trams lines and distributed leaflets, around 300 people gathered in the street and began to surround the bar (and the fifty immigrants inside). The police arrived. Stones were thrown towards the bar and a number of immigrants were beaten up (some by the police) and seven were injured. There was only one arrest. These incidents went on for a number of hours and were reported in the national press and on television.[32]

The reaction of the authorities to these events was informative. First, the police sent hundreds of officers to the zone where they remained night and day for over three weeks. This highly visible presence secured the attention of the mass media for at least a week. Second, the political authorities took immediate action. The bar was closed – officially because of an administrative error in its licence – but obviously as a result of the protests. This decision heartened those who had demonstrated against the immigrants, who called for the permanent closure of Bar Skirrat. In addition, the public statements of the Mayor, Deputy-Mayor and Social Services Assessor more or less backed the actions of the 'locals' and blamed the violence on the immigrants. Deputy-Mayor De Corato spoke of a 'widespread problem. The immigrants meet in some bars and transform them into fortresses under siege'. Colli, responsible for social services, argued that 'this is no longer immigration, it is an invasion', Mayor Albertini claimed that 'the people cannot take any more' (*Corriere della Sera*, 6 June 1998). The only representative of the state who criticized the violence with any clarity was the Prefect, Sorge, who had often in the past attacked the administration's purely repressive attitude to immigration. Two clear and contrasting versions of the 'facts' emerged. The first, sustained by the political Right but also by many on the Left, and backed by the mass media, argued that, as in other areas of Italy (above all San Salvario in Turin) the 'citizens' (i.e. Italians) were tired of the antisocial and criminal behaviour (such as drug dealing and prostitution) of foreign immigrants, above all Moroccans. To cite the journalist Cervi, these residents wanted to live 'in a decent environment, not in an illegal *casbah*' without 'the incessant night patrols of the North Africans'.[33] For these commentators, a 'pressure-cooker situation' had exploded spontaneously in Via Meda and the 'locals', who merely wanted a quiet life, had understandably taken the law into their own hands. The second version, that of the Prefect and of some of the immigrants, describes a planned attack on the bar controlled by local criminals (linked in the press to Italian southern immigrants) and far right elements using the cover of 'local' anger over noise and violence. The victims in the first version are (Italian) 'locals', in the second foreign immigrants.

32. See Bocca (1998).

33. *Il Giornale,* 6 June 1998. See also R. Sorge 'Colpa di pochi teppisti la protesta anti-immigrati', *Il Giornale* 6 June 1998, and Cervi's reply. For the reporting relating to immigrants and the discrimination in the press and the legal system, see Dal Lago (1999). For the very low figures of murders actually committed by immigrants in Milan, see Calvarese and Breda (1998: 517–28).

The actions of the local authorities over the next few days were all in favour of the demonstrators. Bar Skirrat remained closed. Evictions (with the presence of the press and local television stations) targeted immigrants despite the widespread *Italian* illegal occupation of houses in the zone.[34] Public pronouncements spoke of a war on *clandestini*. The message was clear. Violence pays. The real problems of Stadera (housing maintenance, social services, transport) managed to filter through to the institutions for the first time in years. Cosmetically, the state attempted to provide at least the appearance of non-discrimination. A series of controls were made on all the bars in the area (but no others were closed), and, two weeks later, Bar Skirrat reopened (despite protests) with vastly reduced opening hours. The situation remained tense, but there was no repetition of the violence of June.

Via Meda is an instructive case of urban conflict over a series of contentious issues. First, the right to silence (and the right to be noisy). Throughout the history of post-war Milan, immigration has been linked to a series of 'anti-social' attributes that threaten the 'tranquil' life of locals – noise, drunkenness, violence, threats to women, dirt. The connection of these features with immigrants is a crucial part of the construction of negative stereotypes (Ambrosini 1993: 347–64). The positive 'twin' of this stereotype is the 'non-racist' Milanese tired of being disturbed and hassled during his or her daily activities.[35] In the Stadera zone, these negative stereotypes are linked above all to young Moroccan men, whilst the vast majority of immigrants in the zone are Egyptians (many of whom live with their families). Noise transcends urban space and creates conflict between the noisemakers and those who wish to work, sleep or simply live in silence (or relative silence). It is also worth noting the role of the street and the market in Moroccan and Senegalese culture – the importance of public space, and the lack of private space for these immigrants to use in their free time (Dal Lago 1994; Marchetti 1994; Ottieri 1998: 36–7; Palidda 2000b). The local residents are defending (collectively and in public) their right to silence within their own, bounded private space. Finally, the link between crime and immigration is an extremely controversial one and has begun to provoke a bitter scholarly debate (and political debate) in Italy (Lagazzi 1996; Coluccia and Ferretti 1996; Palidda 1994, 1997 and 2000a, b; Melossi 2000; Dal Lago, 1999; Barbagli 1998; Melotti 1996: 448-88). This link was made explicit in Via Meda by the protesters and found agreement amongst the city's administrators.

Similar problems of co-habitation in the city had emerged with the mass internal immigrations of the 1950s and 1960s. Southerners were accused of various 'crimes'

34. *Corriere della Sera*, 19 June 1998. The first three evictions (the only ones carried out that day) all involved Moroccans with regular residence permits.

35. See former Mayor Tognoli (1983: 9–10). Part of this stereotype is also linked to a mythical re-working of the immigration of the 1950s and 1960s when the Milanese supposedly accepted southern immigrants with open arms.

that were linked to classic stereotypes – jealousy, excessive noise, violence, lack of respect for the others. On public housing estates such as Comasina in Milan the divisions were often along immigrant/non-immigrant lines, which often coincided with social fissures. Often, bars and public spaces (like playgrounds) became known and frequented by southerners or northerners. The Bar Skirrats of today were the Bar Sports of the boom (Foot 1995). Yet, the differences with today are important – the housing market allowed immigrants during the boom a house and their own space, this is far more difficult today. The possibility of factory work, and the integration provoked by such activity, no longer exists in Milan (aside from small industry). Most immigrants find work today in the service sector where integration is far more difficult and unionization virtually non-existent. During the boom the vast majority ended up in industry after a period in the building trade. Finally, the legal position of the 1950s immigrants became stabilized with the changes to the laws in 1961. Up to that point, despite being Italians, immigrants were often denied basic social and political rights in the city, and were also known as *clandestini*. They could be 'expelled' from Milan (if not from Italy) in similar ways to today. After 1961, these immigrants were put on the same legal level as non-immigrants, and were able to vote and claim social services in Milan. Foreign immigrants have to go through a far more difficult and dangerous process to gain basic residence permits, and all non-EU immigrants have no political rights. Political parties that organized the immigrants of the miracle years had much to gain – votes, members, militants. The new immigrants have much less to offer, and in any case the biggest parties in Milan are unlikely to attract immigrants.

Via Meda is at the frontier of integration and conflict over the use of the city, the management of space and the focus of social problems. Neighbourhoods like Via Meda can either move towards the ghetto-type model that has evolved, for example, in the US or around Paris, or towards a more successful if fragile mosaic model found in parts of a city like London. Which of these 'two roads' Milan takes in part depends on the attitudes and responsibility of the city's politicians. The rise of political racism in Milan and Italy in the 1990s provides cause for some pessimism in this area.

9. Conclusions: Needed but not Welcome – Lessons from the Past and for the Future

By the end of the 1990s Milan had a 10 per cent foreign immigrant population, the vast majority of whom worked in the low-level service sector (restaurant workers, cleaners, maids) or in factories. Even in the regionalist North-East (especially around Brescia) many of the workers in the steel furnaces were (cheap and often non-unionized) African immigrants. This integration at an economic level is necessary to keep the Milanese economy alive, as the 'Italian' city ages at an alarming rate. Nonetheless, it is clear that these immigrants are, to cite Zolberg, 'needed but not welcome . . . there is a contradiction between their presence as economic actors and the undesirability of their social presence' (cited in Ambrosini 1997: 49). The increasing urban fear and tension linked to deindustrialization, rises in criminality and the spatial segregation of the city have created tensions that Milan appears to be unready and unwilling to confront. Yet the immigrants of the 1950s and 1960s were also 'wanted but not welcome' – in different ways. This phrase is not enough to encapsulate the differences and the similarities between the two mass immigrations experienced by Milan over the last fifty years. We are also dealing with two very different cities. An industrial and financial centre going through a period of extraordinary development as opposed to a service-financial conurbation whose economy is based on mobility and flexibility. It is impossible to deal with the complications of these two immigrations without grappling with the changes that have transformed Milan itself.

The immigrants of the 1950s nearly all arrived in the same way and in the same *place* (the Central Station). Their experiences were focused and in many ways linked with those millions of Italians who had once emigrated abroad. This link is not there today, and the *memory* of the experiences linked to these movements appears to have evaporated. The immigrants arrive in hundreds of different ways and through hundreds of different entry points to the city. Their subjective experiences, despite the rhetoric of some writers and filmmakers, have little in common either with internal Italian immigration or emigration. They are 'needed but not welcome' and often made to feel decisively unwelcome. The economic space, at the dirty end of the economy and in the dirty corners of the city, is there, but the political, social, cultural and urban spaces are all extremely limited. The city is not ready to absorb these new immigrants, and their presence is and will continue to be marked by a series of conflicts that range from the micro and everyday to the global.

−4−

Divided City: Milan and Cinema, 1945–2000

Every city offers to the cinema a ready-made set, which, however, has to be explored, re-edited, divided and reconstructed. The film camera and editing of the images 'make' the city. (Raffaele De Berti)

1. Milan and Cinema: A Non-Cinematic City[1]

Milan is a flat city without a river. The light is often bad. It has few monuments of note. These physical and aesthetic qualities alone go some way to explaining the very few films made in Milan since the war. Milan is not, and never will be, 'cinematic' in the traditional sense of the word – its 'cinematic' qualities have always been much more modern, ephemeral and hidden. Rome was, for many cinema-makers and cinema-goers, the epitome of Italy. Milan never has been a typically Italian city. Whole categories of 'city films' (as identified by Bass 1997: 84–99) are almost impossible in Milan – the postcard film, the Hollywood blockbuster, the historical epic. Totò, the most successful comic actor of the post-war period, made very few films in Milan. Visconti, possibly the most Milanese of all modern film directors, made only one full-length feature film in the city – *Rocco and his Brothers* (1960). Fellini never made a film in Milan. Antonioni made *La Notte* (1961) and *Cronaca di un amore* (1950). Pasolini only shot (some of) *Teorema* (1968) and *Edipo Re* (1967) in Milan, and wrote the script for *Milano nera* (1964). De Sica made *Miracolo a Milano* (1951). Rossellini made no films in the 'moral capital', neither has Rosi, the same can be said of Germi, Bernardo Bertolucci, the Taviani brothers and so on. The lure of Rome, and the south, has been overwhelming – for aesthetic reasons, certainly, but also for economic, political and institutional ones. The school of cinema is in Rome, most actors have always been based in Rome and, of course, *Cinecittà* was built in Rome. The state is in Rome. Milan threatened to have its own film industry at the start of the century, when a number of studios were opened on the periphery of the city – such as *Milano Films* (Pasculli 1998; De Berti 1996). A few important silents

---

1. For Milan and cinema see also Pasculli (1998), Zenoni (1994), Escobar (1993) and Comune di Milano (1999). For cinema and the city more generally, see *Segnocinema,* 33, 1988, Galbiati 1989, *Segnocinema*, 78 and 79, 1996 and Sorlin 1991.

were made in the first decade of the century, but these studios all failed and all that remains today are some battered signs and a couple of obscure works of history.

Since 1945, the relationship between Milan and cinema has gone through four broad phases: first, a barren neo-realist phase, linked only to the last and most un-neo-realist film of all – De Sica's *Miracolo a Milano*. With the boom, Milan briefly but excitingly attracted young and old film directors. *Rocco* and *La Notte* were released within months in 1960–1. A group of young film directors, many of whom had come from documentary film-making, all made films set in Milan in this period – Ermanno Olmi with *Il Posto* (1961), Visconti's nephew Eriprando with *Una storia milanese* (1962), Damiano Damiani with *La Rimpatriata* (1963). The short but rich experience of the *22 Dicembre* company ended in the early 1960s and most of these directors moved elsewhere or stopped making films altogether. The movements linked to 1968 were also centred on Milan and provoked a new flurry of political film-making, from Elio Petri's stunning *La classe operaia va in paradiso* (1971) to Bellocchio's *Sbatti il mostro in prima pagina* (1972) to Cavani's *I Cannibali* (1970) to Pasolini's *Teorema* (1968). The 1970s saw Milan become a centre for popular gangster movies, beginning with Lizzani's hyper-realistic *Banditi a Milano* (1968). Milan, its under- and over-passes, its bleak peripheries, proved to be the perfect location for this kind of film – with car chases, shootouts, blood on the streets. This was Milan as Chicago.

In the 1980s, perhaps for the first time, Milan began to challenge Rome as a cinematic centre and a cinematic city (whilst becoming the national centre of private television and advertising). Amelio's *Colpire al cuore* (1982) is probably the most interesting 1980s film using modern Milanese locations (and the best film Italy has produced about terrorism). Other directors, especially Nichetti and Salvatores, based most of their work in Milan. Salvatores's group of Milan-based actors, whom he had cultivated in theatre productions, provided a new Milanese base for film-making – Cederna, Abbantuono, Bentivoglio, Orlando. A new generation, led by Silvio Soldini, also embraced the non-cinematic qualities of the city.[2] The 1980s also saw a new genre of yuppy-films set in the city, from *Sotti il vestito niente* (1985) to *Via Montanapoleone* (1987) – the perfect reflection of that *Milano da bere* invented by an advertiser for an after-dinner drink. Many of these films appeared as extensions of advertising, and a series of directors and writers passed from advertising to film-making and back again. In *Strane storie* (1994) Sandro Boldoni made a film which parodied the world of advertising from which he had come. In the opening sequence a man attempts to pay his oxygen bill which is overdue, amidst general indifference and bureaucracy.

---

2. Milan has become Italy's centre for experimental film-making, with important initiatives such as the Filmmaker festivals and the student laboratories at the Politecnico.

Whilst Milan has almost always been at the centre of Italian history – usually pre-empting changes for good and bad – film makers have often ignored some of these major themes or moments. No film (apart from propagandist documentaries) was made about the Piazza Fontana massacre of 1969, or the dramatic events of the 1970s in the city (De Berti, 1996: 442). No film has been produced about the intensely cinematic scandals that became known as *Tangentopoli*. Luchetti's prescient *Il Portaborse* (1991) was set in Mantua. Milan-based films have tended to confront the city through a series of overlapping themes.

2. Outsiders: Arrivals, Integration, Alienation

The outsider/insider dynamic is central to an understanding of certain key Milan movies. Often, the city is seen through an outsider's eyes – or through that of a voyeur. The key location of the Central Station is important to this fixing of Otherness – the arrival or (much more rarely) the departure of characters in the anonymous cathedral of work and movement underlining the non-Milanese or transient nature of the characters and the hostility of the city.

Outsiders in Milanese films are immigrants, or militants, or new workers, or non-militants. Visconti – an insider in cinematic and regional terms – chose to make a film about outsiders in the city – southern immigrants. The southern family in *Rocco and his Brothers* is marginalized spatially, socially, sexually and ethnically.[3] In Pasolini's *Teorema* a saint-like figure arrives and tears a Milanese family apart, and then leaves. Petri's larger-than-life creation, Lulù Massa, played by Gian Maria Volonté in *La classe operaia va in paradiso* (1971) is twice the outsider – first as a stakhanovite worker who ignores his colleagues, and then as a militant who refuses to work. In Olmi's *Il Posto* (1961) the young worker at Pirelli is an outsider both because of his origins (he is from the countryside) and because of his newness in the office. In the city he finds it difficult to cross the road and even ordering and drinking a coffee is a major achievement. The rich professor played by Trintignant in *Colpire al cuore* is an outsider in the squalid periphery where his student lover lives. He carries a map. Jeanne Moreau is lost (and excited by) the wild periphery of Sesto San Giovanni in *La Notte* (1961) even though she is revisiting certain well-known locations. De Fillipo's immigrant protesters in *Napoletani a Milano* (1953) are obvious outsiders in the big city of the north, even after finding factory work. Kusturica's Milan-based gypsies (1989) live in a twilight world of criminality where the city is a mosaic of bright lights, dust, money and violence. Their world is a 'non-place', recognizable as nowhere (apart from the advertising hoardings) – a ubiquitous 'periphery'.[4]

---

3. For a detailed study of this film, and its relationship with Milan, see Foot (1999a).
4. For the periphery and cinema see De Berti (1997: 34–45) and Ferzetti (1988: 21–44).

How is this otherness represented, or hinted at, in these films? Firstly by set-piece moments illustrating the arrival of the outsiders in Milan. The arrival is a key moment in these films, often using one of the most cinematic arenas in the city – the Stazione Centrale. As De Berti has written, 'the central station with its imposing architectural structure became one of the dominant and fixed reference points of the Milanese map' (1996: 436). Hence, the Parondi family are left alone on the station platform, not knowing the way even to the tram stop.[5] They are astounded by the lights and skyscrapers of the city – they speak vaguely the same language as the locals but there is no communication. In *Rocco*, even the same words used by immigrants and locals lead to complete incomprehension.[6] The Parondis' first house is a cellar, and they slowly move up towards the light as they become more wealthy. Kusturica's gypsies arrive in caravans and park on the dusty edge of the city. Milan's wealth and power is represented by enormous advertising hoardings and bright lights. In Wertmüller's *Tutto a posto, niente in ordine* (1974) the immigrants get lost immediately and have their bags stolen (the director of photography is the same as *Rocco* – Giuseppe Rotunno). In *Miracle in Milan*, the young protagonist understands nothing of the big city and is also robbed. He gives himself away as an outsider and arouses suspicion by saying 'hello' to a series of strangers he passes. The hostility of the replies he receives becomes the *leit-motiv* of the film ('what do you mean by "hello"'). He also applauds the rich opera-goers at La Scala, amazed at their ostentatious jewels and furs.

Outsiders are 'lost' physically and culturally. They are unable to move within the city without arousing comment, suspicion, criminals who want to rob them, strange looks, racism. They stand out; they are laughed at; they are ignored: they get lost. Simple tasks are beyond them. In *Teorema* the factory owner chooses to undress in the Central Station, virtually ignored by the passers by. Domenico Trieste in *Il Posto* spends his lunch break window shopping.

The central station is a place for some, a 'non-place' for others.[7] Like all stations, it is a place where most people remain for a short time, but many others (tramps, pick-pockets, railway workers) stay for longer periods – becoming part of the station scene itself. Similar feelings surround public transport, where anonymity reigns supreme. Most Milanese films use trams at some point – *Rocco*, *Il Posto*, *Napoletani a Milano*. Olmi in *Il Posto* (1961) highlights the commuter trains of

5. Amelio pays homage to this scene in his latest film, based in Turin during the boom, *Così ridevano* (1998). During the immigrant's arrival at Turin station, Amelio cites the music from *Rocco*.

6. As in this conversation: 'Ticket collector: Capolinea . . .; Rosaria: Capolinea?; Ticket Collector: Lambrate . . .; Rosaria: Lambrate?; Rosaria: Mio figlio; Ticket Collector: Suo figlio?' As Brunetta has written, 'the repetition of the words is a sign of an absolute estrangement between the two worlds, of the nearly-galactic distance between them . . . to communicate they are reduced to single words, gestures, photographs' (1993: 89). See also the comments of Tonetti (1983: 83).

7. The Station is an intensely cinematic setting, with its cathedral-like dome, pillars and lights. See also *Kamikazen*, *Hotel Paura* and *Oggetti smarritti*, G. Bertolucci (1981).

the *Ferrovie Nord* which still flood into the city from the provinces every day. Soldini is particularly fond of the MM – the *Metropolitana Milanese*. It is on the metro where strangers and half-friends meet, exchange glances, recognize or fail to recognize each other. In *L'aria serena dell'ovest*, Bentivoglio finally re-encounters the nurse whom he has been looking for throughout the film on the metro, but by that point he has almost forgotten her, and fails to recognize her. In *Un'anima divisa in due*, the same actor loses touch with reality on the MM – which becomes the centre of his life-crisis. One of the difficulties in examining this insider/outsider relationship involves the role of the directors and writers. Visconti was an insider in Milan – 'I am the king of Milan', he used to joke. Yet, in *Rocco*, he claimed to be viewing the city through the eyes of a group of outsiders. This contradiction is never fully resolved in the film, which flirts with stereotypical views of southern behaviour in the big city (Foot 1999a).

Some of these outsiders are also voyeurs. Amelio's boy protagonist follows a young and beautiful terrorist to a peripheral estate, and takes secret photos of his father with her in the city centre. The young clerk in Olmi's *Il Posto* spends most of the film watching the others. One character, Dr Tobia, in Soldini's *L'aria serena dell'ovest*, buys a pair of binoculars and watches normal, everyday behaviour in a park with fascination. Jeanne Moreau in *La Notte* comes across a brutal and theatrical fight and then intervenes to stop the beating.

Perhaps the most famous cinematic arrival is that of the comedians Totò and Peppino, dressed in their furs in August. Olmi's worker arrives every morning from the provinces. Amelio's professor travels secretly to the periphery. De Sica's tramps are insiders in many of these realms – such as language (they speak Milanese dialect) – but outsiders in so many others – above all economically and spatially. There are also ethnic outsiders (immigrants or gypsies, as in Soldini's *Un'anima divisa in due*), there are urban outsiders, who are lost in a whole series of ways in the city, and there are insider-outsiders. Many *Milanese* are alienated from the city in which they live – they fail to fit in *and* fail to break away – as in *L'aria serena dell'ovest*.

This outsiderness is also represented by appearance, by movement, by wonder at the bright lights of the city, by clumsiness, by language differences, by naiveté, by strangeness (as in *Teorema*). A final category of outsiderness in Milan is contempt for one's own city. The whole of Salvatores's set of films concentrate on a strong desire to escape from Milan – to run away. De Sica's tramps fly out of Milan. Three of *Rocco e i suoi fratelli* express their desire to return to their home town in the south. Mastroianni in *La Notte* makes no attempt to disguise his contempt for the world of culture of which he is part. Soldini's characters achieve nothing, despite the pretence of rebellion.

Some, however, do make it – perhaps against their own will. They integrate and they become insiders. Ciro, one of Rocco's brothers, gets a job at Alfa Romeo.

Kusturica's gypsy hero finds the American dream (through crime) in Milan, in a fantastic parody of *Mean Streets*. Tognazzi in *La vita agra* lights up the skyscraper he was once intending to bomb with fireworks. In *Napoletani a Milano* the young heroine becomes a successful shop assistant. The writer played by Mastroianni in *La Notte* is tempted by the offer of big wages to become a public relations man for a typical Milanese company. The clerk in *Il Posto* gets his job, his desk and his paperwork. The lure of the city, and its wages, is strong indeed. But the city is a harsh place, and there is a fine line between the insider and the outsider. It is easy to fall through the net into the dark underworld of poverty and despair of the underclass (*Hotel Paura*, Renato de Maria 1996).

3. Divided City

Cinematic portrayals of Milan depict a city divided socially, culturally and above all spatially. The key division here is between centre and peripheries, and (and this is not the same distinction) between something obviously recognizable as 'Milan' (the classic trademarks of a Milan film – the *Duomo*, the station, the canals) and the anonymous wastelands of the periphery. This is not simply a reflection of classic city/country divisions, but a more ephemeral and complicated representation of boundaries. Here I will compare the divisions in *Rocco e i suoi fratelli*, *La Notte*, *Miracolo a Milano*, *Il tempo dei gitani* and *Colpire al cuore* with those in Soldini's *L'aria serena dell'ovest* – which consciously avoids landmarks.[8]

To make a film look *Milanese* – to *site* a film in Milan – many directors have trademarked certain classic, recognizable features of the city. The most classic is the Cathedral and its massive square, used by Visconti (from above), Kusturica (where the main character sends home a postcard of the Duomo to his mother, who constructs a model of the Cathedral, which later burns down). In *Il tempo dei gitani* the Piazza del Duomo is a place of both social division and opportunity. A site for begging but also of opulence, where the transition of the main character from mendicant to the control of an elegant bar, where he is served a coffee, is a key moment of integration. Totò's famous conversation with a traffic policeman takes place in the Piazza del Duomo, and De Sica tramps fly up and over the Cathedral in *Miracle in Milan*. Visconti lovingly includes a whole series of more minor Milanese locations in *Rocco* – from the canals to the Sempione park. Amelio uses the Brera courtyard in *Colpire al cuore*. *La Notte* presents us with the whole city in the stunning opening shot, but very little of the rest lets us know we are in the classic Milan, physically. Many trademarks are more modern – the Central Station, the Pirelli Tower (symbol of the Milan of the boom), the motorways, the

---

8. A 'new visible urban space, anonymous but at the same time recognisable in terms of its colours, its atmosphere and its buildings' (De Berti 1996: 445). See also Gieri (1999: 46).

Torre Valasca, certain factories. Soldini's Milan is one of studied interiors, anonymous housing blocks, parks, hospitals, nightclubs, clocks and airports. Soldini uses imaginative and unknown 'everyday' locations – such as 'normal' bars – not immediately recognizable, even to people who know Milan. This is the real, average, everyday Milan – without fog (and stunningly photographed by Luca Bigazzi). Olmi recreates the tragic life of a lonely clerk from the early 1960s through a brief series of stills summed up in three or four objects, such as a coat hanger and a desk lamp.

Cinematic Milan is not only about exteriors. Amelio uses both the inside and outside of the sad popular housing of the periphery. Visconti recreated the luxurious apartments of the Milanese bourgeoisie in *Il Lavoro* or that of the petty bourgeoisie in *Rocco* (as well as those of the immigrants). Antonioni's interiors reflect those of the Milanese intelligentsia, particularly in the party scene in *La Notte*. Petri's 'affluent worker' flat in *La classe operaia* is lit only by the blue light of his television and is cluttered with useless consumer knick-knacks. The worker is banned by his wife from entering his own sitting room in case he makes a mess. Tognazzi's worker in Monicelli's *Romanzo popolare* lives in a high-rise flat overcrowded with ornaments and domestic goods. Outside, the lifts are perennially broken and the roads are unfinished. Pasolini's unfilmed (a film was made called *Milano nera,* which bore little relationship to the original idea) script for *La nebbiosa* made the image of a city in movement the *leit-motiv* of his whole story, with continual connecting shots from cars or motorbikes of a confused and confusing city; a city that never sleeps (Pasolini 1995b). The theme of barriers is central to some cinematic visions of Milan. These barriers are often real – they can be touched. Antonioni shoots the city in the reflection from the light of the Pirelli tower, symbol of the boom, the Parondi family peer through bars, Amelio's boy protagonist betrays his father to the police from behind a wall of broken glass. Other barriers are far more subtle and far more powerful, from the social divisions in *Miracle in Milan* to the racism in *Un'anima divisa in due*, to the ethnic futuristic cities of *Nirvana*.

Milan, like all cities, is a *divided* city, and is dominated spatially by its huge, flat, endless peripheries. These peripheries are central to the cinematic qualities of the most important Milanese films. De Sica set his tramps and their shanty town in the old periphery, in a field behind the university to the east of the city. Here the tramps and shack dwellers re-build a city with squares, street names, social hierarchies and even a statue. The stark social and spatial divisions in the city are revealed by the visit of the top-hatted rich land speculators, the famous train scene where rich passengers glimpse a nether-world of marginalization, and the visit of the tramps themselves to the businessman's super-opulent offices. In *Rocco*, Visconti filmed the new periphery for the first time, carrying out meticulous research on new locations – which had never been seen before on cinema screens.

The monotonous, often hideous houses built for the immigrants of the boom become almost beautiful and symmetrical under Rotunno's stark black and white photography. This was the unknown periphery, never previously shown on film, 'the map of the city is completely redesigned by Visconti' (De Berti 1996: 438).[9]

Visconti was fascinated by the Milanese periphery in the late 1950s and early 1960s. *L'Arialda*, the Testori play he produced soon after *Rocco*, was set entirely in a working-class housing estate on the Milanese periphery with an amazing set designed by Visconti himself. But what kind of periphery is portrayed in *Rocco*? It is the periphery of the black and white photos taken by Visconti on his documentation trips to the city – dark, foggy, empty, flat, smoky. We rarely see crowds of people or even those going about their daily business. Often the scenes are totally empty – emphasizing the alienation of the urban periphery. This is true, for example, of the long fight scene involving two of the brothers. The only time we see the periphery 'populated' (sparsely) it is by workers – in their lunch break from Alfa Romeo. How realistic was this portrayal? If we compare some photos taken of workers – on strike – at the nearby FACE factory in 1955 with the final scene of the film, the similarity is striking. Visconti had not stripped the periphery of people – in these new neighbourhoods, at night, *that was how it was*. By day, the story was different, as children played in the streets and women shopped. But by night, and we mainly see the periphery at night, this was how it was; bleak, empty, flat, lifeless.

A brief comparison with one of the few films to feature the Milanese periphery before Visconti is also instructive. De Sica's *Miracle in Milan*, released in 1951, also shows an empty city – as in the opening funeral scene. However, De Sica's periphery is, in general, very different to that of Visconti. It is a shanty-town periphery – only populated by the very poor and destitute and homeless – a kind of countryside filled with cardboard boxes. But it is populated and lively – a real semi-community exists there. When De Sica shows the centre of Milan it is only to contrast it with this periphery, as in the scene where Totò comes across La Scala by chance. When Visconti shows the centre of town, it is for aesthetic reasons (the Duomo scene) and never as a specific contrast with the periphery, except perhaps in the opening scene. De Sica's Milanese periphery is pre-boom and pre-mass immigration – its inhabitants are mainly Milanese tramps. Visconti's periphery is that of the boom and immigration – its inhabitants are mainly southerners.

Many critics praised Visconti for having shown an 'unknown' Milan, a hidden city, the dark side of the 'capital of the miracle'. *Avanti!* called *Rocco* a film 'which destroys the myth of the big city of general progress and well-being' (*Avanti!*, 14 October 1960). *L'Unità* claimed that Rocco had revealed the 'dark zones of our

---

9. In fact, the research for locations for *Rocco* was long, meticulous and detailed, see Foot (1999a) for the details.

social and civil life' and had 'uncovered what was rotten'. Undoubtedly, the peripheral Milan of *Rocco* had never made it onto the big screen before, and Visconti himself had been shocked by what he had seen in these neighbourhoods. In this sense, at least, the Milan of *Rocco and his Brothers* was 'unknown'. Later, during the 1980s, similar debates surrounded a controversial documentary directed by Olmi, *Milano '83*.

Antonioni's empty (and dangerous) periphery is shown through a journey – as Jeanne Moreau wanders around Sesto San Giovanni. A series of shooting rockets add a surreal touch. Olmi's periphery in *Il Posto* is further away – the real (almost completely non-urban) countryside of the provinces which he was to explore further and re-create in the *Tree of the Wooden Clogs* (1978). Kustarica's wasteland periphery is that of the gypsies – it could be anywhere – bare, barren, dirty and stark. Amelio's periphery is even newer, the estates of the 1970s and 1980s – inspired by Aldo Bonasia's stunning political photographs from the 'years of lead' (1978). Amelio plays with the architectural quirks of the estate to provide both an orderly and a shocking view of the outskirts, the hidden edge of the city. Petri's working class periphery in *La classe operaia* is similarly generic, centred around fog-bound and snow-covered factory gates and disused warehouses. It looks like Milan, but it is in fact a snow-covered Novara. Monicelli, in his short film *Renzo e Luciana* (*Boccaccio '70*, 1962) contrasts the teeming factories of the boom with the emptiness of the periphery, where the couple in the film get married in a makeshift church during their lunch break. Instead of a church organ, the wedding march is played on a juke box. The couple then return to work. Later, they work separate shifts, sleeping in the same bed (at different times) and even using the same coffee cup. Pasolini's factories, on the other hand, are documentary-like, disturbing, empty and seen from a moving camera. Lattuada's factory, where the Sicilian Alberto Sordi works (*Mafioso*, 1962) is a noisy, frightening but efficient centre of production, technology and power – in contrast with the backward and rural Sicily of the rest of the film.

Social divisions obviously play a key part in *Rocco and his Brothers*, overlaid and underlined by more 'ethnic' divisions involving southern culture, as they do in *Miracle in Milan* and *La classe operaia*. In *Miracle in Milan* 'the poor are absolutely poor and the rich are absolutely rich' (Garcia Marquez 1999). A building speculator called Mobbi arrives in the periphery dressed in a top hat and furs. He invites the tramps to his offices where the furniture and decorations all seem incredibly opulent and large. Visconti films the shifting arenas of lumpenproletarian life in *Rocco and his Brothers* – the smoky bars, the gyms, the boxing rings, the peripheral bars. The rich Milanese are invariably presented as caricatures, either through the horror of their cultural void (and internal architecture) as in *La Notte*, or their brutality and conspicuous consumption (*Miracle in Milan*) – or their moral emptiness (*Il Lavoro*), or their corruption (*Rocco*).

4. Foggy City: Milan and *La Nebbia*

The relationship between fog (*La nebbia*), Milan and the Milanese is a fascinating one. In his novel *La vita agra*, Bianciardi tried to dissect this association:

> they call it fog, they treasure it, they show it to you, they glory in it as a local product. And it is a local product. But it is not fog . . . it is if anything an angry fumigation, a flatulence of men, of motors, of chimneys, of sweat, of smelly feet, of dust shaken up by the secretaries, the whores, the representatives, the graphical designers . . . (1995: 167)

One constant between De Sica and Visconti is the use of fog as a kind of trademark of the city. In De Sica's film the inhabitants of the shanty town huddle together under the rare beams of sunlight that penetrate the fog. In Visconti the fog envelops the periphery and the park where the brothers meet. In both, the fog takes on an unreal quality. De Sica does this deliberately, as the whole film is characterized by a magical-realist style. In *Rocco*, the fog *was* unreal – Visconti had to create artificial *nebbia* because none was 'naturally' available. And despite fog only appearing in one scene, reviewers of *Rocco* made constant reference to the foggy periphery. In one of the earlier scripts, Ginetta asks Rosaria, the mother of the five boys, 'what do you think of Milan and the fog?' A description of Rosaria's unease in the city talks about 'that sea of thick and famous fog which limits her view to a few metres from the house'. Other passages describe 'streets immersed in fog' and of the countryside around Milan being 'a single compact block of fog'.[10] It would be interesting to delve deeper into the psyche of a city whose identity seems to be defined, physically, *by not being able to see it* – by its very meteorological invisibility.

Later directors rejected the fogbound stereotype. The daytime light in Soldini's *L'aria serena dell'ovest* is always bright, the sky always blue – in contrast with the dark and inconsequential lives of the characters he portrays. In a certain sense this came about by chance (the time of filming coincided with weather of this type)[11] – but this new, bright, blue Milan makes a conscious break with the foggy cliché of so many films and books. Weather is also important for Salvatores's *Kamikazen*, set in a sweltering 24 hours in July 1987. Every so often in the film, a caption gives the time and the temperature. Lulù Massa, the worker in Petri's *La classe operaia va in paradiso,* walks into the factory on a path cut through piles of snow – which remains there for the whole film. At one point there is a snowball fight and the cold is also represented by the smoky breath of the workers on the

---

10. 'Trattamento', *Archivio Visconti,* C26: 004868: 12.
11. Talk by Soldini, Politecnico di Milano, 1995.

picket line. *Rocco and his Brothers* also breathe visible air on their station platform. Totò and Peppino arrive in Milan in August dressed in furs. Peppino notes the absence of fog and Totò replies 'when the fog is there, you cannot see it'. Finally, in Salvatores's futuristic Milan (*Nirvana*, 1997), it is always snowing. Film critic Brunetta has also noted the north-weather connection in cinematic terms:

> within the macro-divisions of territories, the north remains an indistinct land for fifteen years, marked in a climatic and anthropological sense in negative terms: fog, cold, snow symbolise the lack of human warmth, loneliness, hypocrisy, the social violence covered up by economic well-being and respectability. (Brunetta 1997: 813–4)

5. Images of the City: Anti-Milan – Portraits of an Empty City

Whilst businessmen and economists continued to sing the virtues of the boom, and the wealth it was creating for all, film-makers presented a different image of the capital of the miracle. De Sica concentrated on the tramps of the periphery, Visconti on the marginalized immigrants, Olmi (in perhaps the most powerful critique of all) on the moral emptiness of the regimented office worker, and the anonymous workings of the Big Company. Antonioni presented an intelligentsia who had sold out completely to the lure of industry and its money, or were on the verge of doing so. Culture was a commodity like any other, and the inner emptiness of the citizens of the city was covered by the trappings of consumerism and wealth. During the famous party scene in *La Notte*, the writer played by Marcello Mastroianni is seduced more by the blatant offer of large sums of money than by the enigmatic beauty of Monica Vitti.

The new Milanese cinema presented an image of the city in stark contrast to that of *Milano da bere* – a rampant and rich yuppy city at the forefront of Italy's second economic miracle. The Socialist administration of Milan was at the centre of this world, with its social events, its congresses, its links to the world of fashion, television and advertising. Milan was widely seen as the city of Berlusconi, of Ferré and Valentino, of yuppies, extravagance, of booming share prices, big cars and good times. Soldini presented an alternative (and quietly ferocious) image of another city – of unhappiness, of squalor, of ignorance concerning the events in the world, of banality. Even worse, there was no desire to rebel against this world and the all-powerful lure of money. Two characters in *L'aria* make half-hearted attempts to change course, and then give in. Only the extraordinary and tragic figure of the nurse – the only character without money in the film – attempts a different kind of life, and is punished for it by the coldness and violence of the city. Salvatores presents us with a series of failures desperate for one big chance on television (*Kamikazen*), or ex-rebels trying to relive the past (*Marrakech express*). Olmi's documentary about the city, *Milano '83*, was rejected by those who had financed it as presenting a false impression of Milan. Where was the stock exchange, the money, the wealth of the city? Olmi instead looked at the invisible people who made everything else possible – the street cleaners, the commuters, the workers behind the La Scala opera house. The battle over images, for once, hit the front pages of the press, as the authorities tried to suppress Olmi's documentary as presenting a 'negative' image of Milan.

6. Crisis City: Milan in the 1990s

The Milan of the 1990s was a city in crisis. This crisis was not an economic one, but social, cultural and ecological. Above all, Milan was passing through a crisis of identity. From a city with a clear industrial mission, it had become a phenomenally successful post-industrial metropolis, but this rapid transition had left many of the city's residents and other populations disorientated and even traumatized. Film-makers from the 1990s tried to deal with these shifts in a series of ways. This section will look at two key Milanese films from the 1990s: Piccioni's *Fuori dal mondo* (1998) and Salvatores's *Nirvana* (1997).

Piccioni's film brings together individuals in crisis, in this case through the discovery by a nun of an abandoned baby in a Milanese park. The photography of Bigazzi is central to the view of Milan in this film, as it is in Soldini's *L'aria serena* and *Un'anima divisa in due*. In modern Milan, it is almost as if people cannot come into contact by 'normal' social, political or cultural means, and it takes a crisis or an exceptional chance event (the lost diary for Soldini in *L'Aria*, the arrest of a shoplifter in *Un'anima*, the abandoned baby for Piccioni) to bring them together, if only momentarily. These crises lead to attempts to escape from Milan and previous lives. Sometimes this takes the form of physical escape from the city, as with the shop assistant and the gypsy in *Un'anima divisa in due*, sometimes it appears as the temptation to change direction completely, as when the nun in *Fuori dal mondo* changes into 'normal' clothes and questions the choices that have dominated her life thus far.

After the discovery of the baby, the nun becomes attached to the baby and begins to question her whole decision to join the sisterhood. This prompts her to look for the parents of the child. An item of clothing leads her to a launderette and its manager, an unhappy and lonely man obsessed with work. Together, this strange couple begin to search the city for the baby's mother. Their search will lead to a crisis in both their lives and move them both emotionally. All this is set against a Milan in movement, a city full of traps and pitfalls, of unrecognizable interiors and traffic jams. There is a conscious attempt (which is perhaps not entirely successful) to talk about 'ordinary people' – cleaners; ice-cream waitresses; nuns; carabinieri; immigrants – who are all seen as *Fuori dal mondo* – outside of the system – but essential to the smooth running of the city. In Milan people are judged by their wealth and by their appearance. Margherita Buy's fragile nun stands out amongst the thousands of commuters at the Stazione Garibaldi because she is dressed differently but also because she is not wealthy and has chosen not to be so.

Finally, in *Nirvana*, Salvatores creates a futuristic Milan, but with strong elements linked to the past. The 'future' of *Nirvana* is a close one, we are only in 2007, in an *agglomerato dal nord*, a northern agglomerate that looks very like Milan from above, and the set chosen for the film was a significant one, the ex-Alfa Romeo factory *Il Portello*, closed in the late 1970s. This factory symbolized the industrial revolution of the boom years (and that of the first industrial revolution of the 1890s) and represented a fascinating mix of the old and the new, thanks to the innovative designs of Giancarlo Basili and Salvatores's vision. In *Nirvana*, the city is strongly divided on ethnic lines, and every place, apart from the rich centre, is a dangerous place. These places are reached in various ways, and in the case of Bombay City, by lift. Bombay City is the only hot place in the city, thanks to its proximity to the heating systems of the metropolis. This scenario, then, is both familiar and disconcerting; a futuristic city which often looks like a teeming market, and where the relationships between people are even more tenuous than before. The only really human character in the film is an invention, a character in a video-game – called *Nirvana* – who can only find peace by being 'cancelled'. The story of the film, if it has one, is of the search to cancel this character (Canova 1996).

7. Conclusion: From Stereotypes to Non-City

Milan has traditionally been viewed, cinematically, as a city of work, of factories, of bustle and of wealth. These images were often seen as enough to understand Milan, and often appear in credit sequences. The credits of Lattuada's *Mafioso*, for example, crash home the image of Milan-as-factory through the use of a tracking shot through a noisy, smoking, impressive metalwork plant. Lattuada has shown us the Milan of the boom, which he then goes on to contrast with the backwardness of rural Sicily. Similarly, if more beautifully, the opening credit sequence of *La Notte* also uses industrial sounds as the camera shoots the city through the reflection of the ultra-modern symbol of the miracle – the Pirelli Tower (Bass 1995–6). With the rapid and traumatic de-industrialization of the city, this image is no longer appropriate. Soldini's credit sequence for his *L'aria serena dell'ovest* is a kind of manifesto for this transformation. A series of 'non-places' are shown through a blue half-light. The city is empty, quiet, animated only by the clanking of empty trams. The places are neither instantly recognizable nor obviously 'Milanese'. Even *La Galleria* is shot from the side and in such a way that it loses its 'postcard' feel. This city is both more difficult to pin down and more interesting than the clarity and noise of Milan-as-factory. Throughout the film, sound and image fail to connect, and we often hear the taped interviews of one of the protagonists whilst the action itself is elsewhere. Salvatores also flagged the new city with his science-fiction hit, shot in the wastelands of ex-industrial Milan – *Nirvana*. The image of a futuristic Milan, shot in the abandoned Alfa Romeo factories that had symbolized the productive nature of the boom, was far closer to contemporary Milan than it seemed, at first glance. The new city had attracted a new type of cinema no longer imprisoned by the urban clichés. These films were about the city itself, and no longer felt the need to locate or identify what Milan is or was in the first five minutes of the movie – or before their films had even begun. In fact, perhaps these directors did not even have a precise idea of 'Milan'. Nonetheless, these varied visions were never merely reflections of Milanese 'reality', but also contributed to the complex and competing series of images that have characterized descriptions of Milan since the war. Milan's relationship with cinema (and other art-forms) helped to define the city itself, and this 'non-cinematic' urban space played an increasingly central role in post-war Italian film-making. The non-cinematic nature of Milan fitted perfectly with the crisis-ridden and image-obsessed Italy of the 1980s and 1990s. Italian modernity, for good and for ill, has always started to appear and take root in Milan, and modern Italian directors found fertile ground for a new kind of film-making in the bleak peripheries and flat landscapes of this post-industrial city.

–5–

Television and the City: The History and Impact of Television in Milan, 1954–2000

1. Introduction

Lascia o raddoppia? succeeded where *The Divine Comedy* failed . . . it gave Italy a national language. (Grasso 2000: 59)

We need to think about television as a psychological, social and cultural form, as well as an economic and political one. We need to think about the medium as more than just a source of influence, neither simply benign nor malignant. We need to think about television as embedded in the multiple discourses of everyday life. (Silverstone 1994: ix)

The impact of television has tended to be viewed in apocalyptic terms by historians and cultural commentators. This is particularly true in the Italian case, where the introduction and diffusion of broadcasting coincided with the period of intense development and consumerism known as the economic miracle. Put simply, television is (and was) seen as an essentially *negative* phenomenon with some positive side effects in the backward south – especially the 'linguistic unification' of Italy (De Mauro 1973; Grasso 2000: 59).[1] Television contributed to a series of supposedly unsatisfactory characteristics of contemporary society – atomization, the disappearance of community, cultural uniformity and home-based familism. Quite apart from the series of theoretical and political problems involved in the equation home-life-bad – bar/community/street-life-good, there is simply very little evidence available from which such conclusions can be drawn. Most of the local studies of the early period of television were based in the countryside, and often in the deep south, as in the case of two of the most interesting early research projects, De Rita's work on Basilicata (1964) and Eiserman's and Acquaviva's study of the Gargano region in Apulia (1971). To date, no historical study has

---

1. This unification tends to be somewhat exaggerated in recent accounts, see for example, Grasso (2000). There is a nostalgic trend emerging in more recent accounts, which tend to contrast the 'innocent' years of early television with the commercial years of the 1980s and 1990s.

been made of the impact of television in the capitals of the miracle – Milan and Turin, although some work has been done on the history of television in Milan (Grasso 1996a; Ferrari and Giusto 2000). These cities were at the heart of the boom, the meccas for millions of immigrants in search of work, the core of Italy's late and brief second industrial revolution.

This chapter aims to address this balance for one city, Milan, picking up on the themes and debates outlined in Chapter 2. The first part of the chapter will analyse the birth and early years of television, in the period 1954–60. The second part will look at the era of private television, developed in Milan, above all thanks to the entrepreneur Silvio Berlusconi. But before we enter into the heart of the first period, it is essential to examine what we mean by the *effects* of television. This analysis takes an extremely flexible view of such effects. That is, we will be looking at the cultural influence of television, and the impact of the particular form of mass culture introduced by television in Milan, but also at a whole series of other effects. For example, changes to the form of households, changes to leisure patterns, the impact upon other cultural forms – especially cinema – as well as more subtle changes to the whole way of experiencing home life and bar life after television. The effects of television were often far more 'micro' and complicated than the grand ideological discourses allow – the shifting of furniture, the re-arranging of interiors, the subtle changes to language or to newspaper reports, the impact in schools. Too little attention has been paid to the gender effects of early television – which allowed women into bars and public places on a par with men for the first time (if only at certain designated times) and began to break down some of the rigid gender barriers that had characterized leisure activities. Previous generational barriers also became more blurred, as children were also seen in specific public and private places with their parents at certain times. Research on early television has rightly identified a 'collective' phase marked by low numbers of sets and high numbers of spectators in bars or in those few houses with televisions (Anania 1997: 24–30). This piece will also try and draw out some of the details of that phase for one key city – Milan. Finally, this analysis of effects does not view these effects as isolated from other cultural, political, social and economic processes at work within society, the home and the family. Media effects can only be seen within the broad context of other changes and neither shape nor necessarily are inferior to other influences from other sphere of life (Wolf 1992; Bechelloni 1984).

Television will be seen as a system of social, cultural and economic phenomena, of signs and symbols of various kinds. Within this system the various aspects of television (the content of the programmes; the audience; the historical role of the medium; the regulation of the media; advertising) will not be looked at in isolation. Television, as Grasso has written, is 'not only a mirror on reality, but something more, which does not only reproduce external facts, but can also provoke them, or even determine them' (2000: 60).

Historical studies of this type are inevitably hindered by the sources available. For Milan, the presence of a series of detailed and wide-ranging surveys of suburban neighbourhoods carried out in the early 1960s (and hardly used by researchers) provides a background for this study. In addition, the local press followed the tentative and then triumphant first steps of Italian television in some detail, and provides invaluable insights into the cultural and urban effects of television. The effect of television *on* the form and content of the press is also an important area for historical research. The time period chosen for this first section is limited to the early years of Italian television, from its introduction in 1954 to 1960, at the height of the boom. This short period will allow for a more detailed analysis and also covers the period of the most important and legendary programme to emerge from early Italian television – *Lascia o raddoppia?* – a quiz show that thrust television onto the front pages of all the daily papers and 'invented' the medium as a mass phenomenon.

By 1960 the collective period of television was coming to an end, and individual sets were taking over. As for Milan, certain neighbourhoods will be examined at the expense of others. This is in part a response to the material available, but also a methodological choice. The micro-changes introduced by television have often been overlooked in the broad sweep of historical narrative. This chapter aims, in its own small way, to re-establish the importance of these tiny, but significant changes and continuities in the late 1950s, and then again for the 1970s and 1980s. Television had contradictory effects in all sectors of cultural and economic life; it encouraged atomization as a family unit, but also promoted collective consumption in places designed for other activities. It educated and opened horizons, but also tended towards a levelling (up *and* down) of cultural and everyday outlooks. It both liberated *and* imprisoned the mind. It encouraged consumerism, as well as criticisms of that consumerism. Some effects were short term, some are still being felt. In short, the impact of television was extremely complicated and contradictory and difficult to characterize in simplistic terms.

2. Early Television: Effects on Family Life – Time, the Street and the Home

What difference did having a television as opposed to a radio (or having both)[2] make to family life, street life and home life in Milan in the late 1950s? This question is neither as simple nor as obvious as it sounds. Radio listening implied many similar effects to those of television. Listening was based around published programme schedules, the radio occupied a particular place in the home – usually

---

2. By 1954 the number of radio licences had risen to 5,281,495 from the 2 million of 1948. For television as opposed to the radio see Forgacs (1996: 282–3).

in the living room where, like the television, it was a prized possession – a consumer durable packed with social and cultural status. The important differences were threefold. First, television was new, rare and expensive, and thus carried far more status than radio. A set cost L.250,000 in 1954, amounting to around three times the average annual wage of a clerk (Mafai 1997: 80). By the end of 1954, only 88,000 television licences had been issued across the whole of Italy. Second, television had to be *watched*. The image-based medium carried a particular power and demanded a particular form of attention not asked for by radio. Finally, radio was not adapted to transmission in public places it was perfectly fitted to the private sphere (although Mussolini had made much use of public radio transmissions during his reign, most notably in crisis situations). Television could be watched by a number of people at one time. In a public place, it encouraged combined collective consumption.

In the initial stages of Italian television transmissions very few actual sets existed, and it was not until 1957 that most of the peninsula could pick up programmes. Thus, the classic image of the individual family unit watching their own television set *together* and alone was a rare one. Much more common was the public set – in bars, cultural circles, Church organizations and party offices. The decision to buy a set on the part of these different organizations was in part an attempt to attract new groups, in part a response to local demand and in part an attempt to control the use and interpretation of television.

A crucial form of television consumption in these early years was what I will call the public/private set. This usually consisted of the only set in a block of flats or street. Families would descend on the set-owning family in order to watch particular programmes. In this phase of 'public' and collective television watching, the medium often led to a temporary break-down of certain barriers, not their construction. The inter-class mixing implied by this collective watching role also implied some levelling and dissolution of class/space barriers within neighbour-hoods, streets and housing blocks. But, other hierarchies were also constructed or reinforced around the possession of and access to a set. One study goes as far as to indicate those with sets as 'opinion leaders' within the community (Eri 1968: 36). Not surprisingly, the first owners of sets were usually the better-off families, so this role was in some sense a natural one. Once again, television both strength-ened and weakened previous divisions – in different ways.

In certain areas of Milan, this phase was very brief. Already, by the early 1960s, the majority of families possessed a set (the total for the whole country was over two million) (Foot 1999e: 392, n.50). The Christmases of the late 1950s saw the sale of hundreds of thousands of televisions as consumers were tempted by special deals and huge advertising campaigns. Television sales techniques included swapping a television for a radio, generous credit deals linked to other consumer durables, dubious health claims ('Sight Savers which protect your eyes') and aesthetic design qualities. Televisions were also offered as money-saving devices. Phonola sold its sets as 'a joy for all the family – without leaving your home and without spending any money, you can watch fascinating sporting events, interesting theatrical shows, variety, films.' The link with the US was frequently underlined. A company called *American House* offered sets which allowed you to change channel 'without bending down' and had 'removable legs . . . thereby avoiding the use of costly and often anti aesthetic tables'. Families in advertisements for television sets appeared American and affluent (and happy and united), and even dressed like Americans in some examples.[3]

On the Comasina estate, to the north-west of Milan, 90 per cent of families had bought a set (presumably on credit) by 1962. This figure is far higher than any others we have for the same period (for example, in the whole of Italy, only a quarter of families possessed a set in 1962).[4] Milan, and especially its suburban neighbourhoods, had already accepted the priority of television amongst a group of key consumer goods, and also as a central part of their free time. The very isolation of Comasina from the centre of Milan – with its glittering attractions, cinemas, dance halls and theatres – encouraged this process of television purchase and use. The brief 'leadership'-factor phase created by the possession of a set had disappeared. At Comasina, therefore, the collective phase of television use was already over by the end of the 1950s. Surveys carried out in the early 1960s found television rooms in bars deserted. Television was being watched at home. Soon, the rest of Italy was to catch up with these Milanese neighbourhoods. By 1965, 43 per cent of Italians watched television every day, 17 per cent two to four times a week and 10 per cent once a week. Only one in five never watched television. Was 'Berlusconi' therefore, or the ideology he was later to represent, already hegemonic right at the start of the 1960s?[5]

But what about street life, bar life and face-to-face networks? One problem here is the assumption that these forms of sociability were dominant in the city before the 'arrival' of mass culture. In reality, the situation was extremely variegated and complicated. Some neighbourhoods did appear to be classic working-class communities, dominated by political parties, street life and bars. But, even here, this pattern of leisure and day-to-day life was confined to certain times of the day and marked by gendered use of time and space (the evenings and weekends for

3. All references are from the Milanese press in the 1954–5 period.

4. Eri (1968: 83). This figure relates to the number of television *licences*: the actual number of televisions was higher, both because of evasion and other situations.

5. This question raises a series of other historical problems, above all concerning the student and worker movements of 1968. If this answer is a substantial 'yes', then '1968' appears as a blip and not a sustained assault on consumerist values. If the answer is 'no', then these cultural shifts take place much later. Of course, the real response is much more complicated than either/or, and draws from the questions raised in Chapter 2.

workers, the mornings for housewives, the afternoons for children, Sundays for whole families). Other, newer, neighbourhoods, were host to a vast variety of time use and social relations. In any case, it is impossible to maintain with any certainty that there was a simple, idyllic, street-based cultural life waiting to be swept aside by the mass cultural forms spread by television. The picture that emerges from surveys carried out at the time is one of complexity within a city dominated by work, by the journey to work, by immigration and by the search for a house. Time was of the essence, and little was left for the commuter who left home at four in the morning and arrived back at 9.30 in the evening.

3. Early Television and Everyday Life: Furniture, Noise, Children, Schools, Volume, the Sitting Room and the Bar

Television had a whole series of micro-effects in the city that have so far escaped the notice of researchers. Within the home, the *salotto* or *soggiorno* (living room) began to be seen as the television room, used solely or largely for the activity of television watching. Previously, the *salotto* had tended to be a kind of no-go area, used only on special family occasions. Where there was no *salotto* in the home, the set was usually placed in the kitchen/dining room, where it inevitably began to dominate the semi-sacred meal times of the Italian family. As Leydi wrote:

> Our rooms have been changed to small cinemas and you only need to flick through the fashion papers to see how the architects insist in offering advice for the ideal location, in tele-visual terms, of the sofa, of the chairs and arm-chairs. But the table was a meeting place. The members of the family sat in front of each other, looked into each other's eyes, talked to each other. With television all this has disappeared. The family sets itself up in a line, so that everyone can see the screen and pass the evening in silence. (1964a: 48)

Televisions were sold as elegant additions to the furniture of the home, sometimes even with cocktail cabinets attached. An interesting feature of early sets were the doors attached to the front – almost as if the television had to appear as a 'normal' piece of furniture when it was not switched on. Chairs were arranged around the set, and some were reserved for certain family members. 'Sitting-rooms became real viewing-rooms, with seats, arm chairs, pouffes and footstools' (Ferretti, Broccoli and Scaramucci 1997: 186; Monteleone 1992: 302; Grasso 1996b: 767). Special chairs were sold as 'television' chairs. Often, in the early days (and in many Italian houses this habit continues to this day) the set was covered with a cloth, or protected in some way, when it was not being used. In part, this habit underlined the expensive nature of the object itself, but also there was a sense that the set was to be disguised as something else when it was not 'on', almost as if the owners were ashamed of their ownership of such an expensive item (Mafai 1997: 82; Ferretti *et al.* 1997: 185). Lights were arranged so as to best see the television, and in the early years the prevailing theory was that it was better to have all house lights switched off. In these cases, the watchers were lit by a strange blue light. The landscape and 'look' of the city changed accordingly, from the outside and the inside and from above – especially at night. In Petri's film *La classe operaia va in paradiso* (1972) a working-class family watch television in silence lit by only by the blue light of the set.[6]

In bars with televisions, the effects were more regulated, in part because of the rigid laws introduced to control the use of televisions in public places. The first set of laws (introduced in November 1954) were particularly harsh – lights had to be turned off, the set could only be inside and the television had to be of a certain size. After protests, these regulations were softened in February 1956, but others were introduced to stop the economic exploitation of these sets, such as the selling of tickets by bar owners or the use of higher prices during popular programmes (*Corriere Lombardo*, 21–22 February 1956). Bar-rooms, which had previously been arranged so as to facilitate conversation, or card games, were now organized as watching spaces, with the chairs turned towards the sets and many tables removed. 'The bar-rooms are transformed into small cinemas . . . with the seats arranged around the television set and the tables . . . pushed to the side' (Dallamano 1955: 8). Leydi noted that in the classic *osteria* (or bar/restaurant) there was now a room where older people maintained the form of the bar *before* television – with tables and chairs organized in the classic way. The noise of these places also changed. In the other rooms, conversation had ended, at least whilst the television was on: 'that which was once characterised by shouts, discussions and songs, now seems like a miniature cinema. High above a trestle the television set, in front all the seats in orderly rows' (Leydi 1964a: 42). Some commentators, such as Leydi (who had worked on early television programmes, including *Lascia o raddoppia?*) underlined the silence of the new bar going public. One bar owner was quoted as complaining that his clients 'they used to argue, play cards, sing and drink. I used to have a sore throat from talking and singing. Now they watch television. They make one glass last three hours'. The spectators were 'silent and immobile in front of the screen'. 'What has happened', asked Leydi, 'to collective life?' (1964a: 42). Yet, these new cultural forms *were* collective, but collective in different ways from before.

Silence was not the only reaction to television. Disputes and discussions began over volume, noise and control of the set, about lighting, about drinks to be ordered and, of course, about the content of the programmes themselves. People

---

6. Television was generally viewed in negative terms by the film-makers of the 1960s and 1970s. See Risi's *I Mostri* (1963) especially the episode entitled 'The Opium of the People'.

were forced to raise their voices to be heard, whilst others called for quiet. The television, and its controls, became *the* subject of conversation and debate, especially at certain times. Other organizations quickly gave in to television's power, and adapted their activities accordingly. Political parties re-arranged meetings, priests moved mass, dinner times were shifted forwards or backwards. Everyday life was also affected in other ways. Children's bedtime began to be determined by the timings of certain programmes. This link became especially strong with the introduction of advertising, in the peculiar Italian form of a series of short films, in 1957. These adverts, which were grouped together under the title *Carosello*, were especially popular with children. The end of *Carosello* became bedtime for millions of Italian children (Gundle 1986: 585–7; Giusti 1996). *Carosello* production was also based in Milan, making it 'a Milanese programme, in fact the most Milanese programme of all' (Grasso 2000: 57). Key decisions within the household were virtually taken out of parent's hands. But up until 1957, television schedulers had been very careful not to interfere with the normal daily lives of its spectators, and 'family life'. Children's programmes began after a time designated for homework in the afternoon (5.30), 'adult' programmes allowed for workers' to return home and there were no programmes at all between 7.30 and 8.45 pm, to 'allow' the family to eat. Television organizers were trying to limit the effects of their own product. These gaps in themselves, however, presupposed a regimentation of family life and family time. In any case, these concessions to the 'daily lives' of Italians soon disappeared, and the medium began to shape the habits of its public, at least in terms of control of time and family rules (Rizza 1986: 163–5).

The visual landscape of the city was also changed by television. 'In those years numerous aerials in the form of a T began to appear on house roofs, sign of wealth and prestige for the few people who actually owned a television' (Eri 1968: 71). 'A forest of aerials' (Marietta 1995: 436) sprouted above houses and the huge RAI aerial (in Corso Sempione in Milan) became a symbol of the power of television.[7] The television aerial was a visible and external sign of consumption and well-being. Whilst film director Visconti was making his nineteenth-century epic *The Leopard* in Sicily in 1962–3, he was hampered by the presence of numerous aerials on Sicilian houses. These forests of aerials also marked out the landscape and photographs as from a certain epoch. Television shops also began to emerge in urban areas, with their sets in the windows. By-passers stopped to watch certain programmes (in silence) through these windows, and crowds would often form at certain times. In 1963 Pasolini was able to indulge his ferocious irony with regard to the phenomenon of the aerials. 'You know what Italy seems

7. It is worth noting the (unintended) irony of the design of Berlusconi's *Milano 2*, without visible aerials.

to me? A hovel in which the inhabitants have succeeded in buying themselves a television and the neighbours, seeing the aerial, proclaim, as if reciting the paragraphs of a law, "They are rich! They are happy!"' (1995a: 58).

Milan was the capital of early Italian television – a position it was to lose to Rome in the late 1950s and then re-take with the explosion of private television in the 1980s (Grasso 2000; Ortoleva 1996: 194–7). In 1954 there were five television studios in Milan, and only two in Rome and Turin (by 1957 the figures were five, seven and one respectively (Parola 2000: 31). Studio TV3 in Milan was in 1954 the biggest television studio in Europe. The RAI in the city was housed in a modernist building in Corso Sempione, which was had been re-designed by none other than the architect Giò Ponti. The first transmissions in Italy were made from Milan in January 1954 (Grasso: 1996b: 22; 1996a: 369–70). Milan was also central in terms of the *production* of television *sets* and other material linked to the industry. Pirelli produced co-axial cables, glass factories began to mass produce screens, and six of the eight most important television production companies were located in the province of Milan – Magneti Marelli, CGE, Philips, FIMI, Geloso and Siemens (Monteleone 1992: 277).

Even in the schools and libraries of Milan, television began to have an important impact. One teacher in Milan installed a 'cabin' in his class in homage to the popular quiz *Lascia o raddoppia?* The teacher ran a mock quiz complete with cash prizes for his pupils. 'The material chosen is from the curriculum: in this way the teacher is looking to encourage interest in his pupils for those subjects that have been studied without enthusiasm during normal classes. The first experiments have shown that his students study much more willingly. Is this an example that should taken up in other Italian schools?' (*Corriere Lombardo*, 6–7 March 1956; Anania 1997: 26–7). Journalists discovered that in a new library in Milan, created by architects working on the *Triennale* architectural exhibition, there were a number of students who were working on material to present with their applications to appear on *Lascia o raddoppia?* (*Corriere Lombardo,* 19–20 January 1956; Anania 1997: 33–4). Early television was marked by a strong educational mission, and many television-users believed that their children would learn more than before because of the presence of a television in the home (Bettetini 1990: 17–19). It is also important to note that the early years of Italian television were marked by a complete lack of choice (the second channel was not introduced until 1961), few programmes (an average of four hours a day of programmes in 1954, and six in 1956) and a rigid control of the medium by the Christian Democrats and the Church (Morcellini 1995: 13).

Television was even given healing powers in the popular press. In 1955 a handicapped man made a public appeal for a television. 'Luigi Re's days would seem to be shorter and he might be able to forget himself for a while. In the door-keeper's offices . . . a television is needed in order to be able to live' (*Corriere*

Lombardo, 12–13 November 1955; 2–3 January 1956). Re's dream came true when an anonymous reader donated a set to the doorkeeper: 'he stayed in front of the set all day, forgetting himself and his terrible illness'. Some compared the popularity of television to a new religion, with the entrance of the mystical object of worship into the homes of millions of Italians. As Grasso has written, 'families were re-united in the evenings around the television set just as they were re-united before around the rosary' (1992: 8).

Television also began to invade and dominate other media, particularly newspapers and magazines. Some publications were created specifically for the television-watching market. In the popular press, the image of the set began to appear in various guises, television listings and reviews were published and the figure of the television critic emerged. Many humorous newspaper cartoons were based around television and watching. In July 1955 cartoons featuring televisions began to appear in the *Corriere Lombardo*. In one, entitled 'The telespectator's dream', a man is in bed with a television with an image of a young woman, in another called 'Efficiency of the . . .' a couple are kissing and ignoring the television altogether (*Corriere Lombardo*, 1–2 September 1955).

4. Early Television – The 64,000 Dollar Question: Thursday Nights

Rule One – The game is played on television, 'The rules of "Lascia o raddoppia?"'. (Cited in Ferretti *et al.* 1997: 178)

(It was) an incredible moment of tele-visual hysteria. It lasted a couple of years. It made television a fortune, increasing with great speed the number of licence-holders. (Leydi 1964b: 34)

The key programme during the early years was *Lascia o raddoppia?*, a quiz show which has become part of Italian history.[8] Produced, organised and transmitted from Milan, *Lascia o raddoppia?* changed the whole nature of the relationship between the city, its inhabitants and television. *Lascia* came at the right time for the RAI, with widespread reports of a television crisis and frequent complaints concerning the quality of the programming (*Corriere Lombardo*, 24–25 October 1955; 27–28 October 1955). Almost from the first programme, transmitted in November 1954, *Lascia* began to dominate the other media and public discussion. It was to run for a total of 191 'episodes', right through to 1959 (Grasso 1996b: 387; 1996a: 374). The form of the programme, with its personalities plucked from

---

8. The fact that this programme is cited in most histories of Italy and in school manuals, complete with photos of presenter Mike Bongiorno, is significant. Italy's history, and certain cultural processes, are explained through certain television programmes, and not vice versa.

the obscurity of the provinces and their constant presence, week after week, as they edged closer to a possible jackpot, was a perfect combination of real-life drama, gossip and quiz – with the added (and crucial) *frisson* of large amounts of money or the consolation prize of that ultimate symbol of the boom, a Fiat 600. As Gundle has pointed out, television played a dual role – being both a kind of 'rite of transition' as well as one of the 'factors behind the transition' (1986: 576). The quiz show became central to television programming (and has remained so over the next forty-five years).

So what were the effects on the city of *Lascia o raddoppia?* First, there was an enormous growth in the number of televisions watched, sold and installed. Second, television itself became a talking point for hundreds of thousands of families, and the dream of actually taking part in the programme led to applications from a huge number of Italians (over 300,000 during the first three years, Monteleone 1992: 297). There seemed to be a real possibility of becoming famous, if only for fifteen minutes. For the first time, unknown Italians became household names, and in a very brief period of time. Certain early participants made a particular impression, and remain famous today – more than forty-five years on. Third, television began to invade and even dominate the other traditional media – especially local newspapers. The *Corriere Lombardo* and national papers made *Lascia* front page news throughout 1954–5, publishing the full transcripts of the programmes, interviews with the protagonists and numerous comments from columnists. *Lascia* was interesting and 'news' *even for those who had never seen it*, such as in large parts of southern Italy, where the national network was not installed until 1956. One of the reasons behind the full publication of programme transcripts was this curiosity for those without access to television. Fourth, attendance at the programme (shot at the *Teatro della Fiera* in the centre of the city, close to the television studios) became a status symbol in itself, attracting thousands of fans (inside and outside of the theatre), politicians and celebrities. The link between the *Fiera* – symbol of modernisation and experimentation for the whole of Italy – and *Lascia* was an important one. Right up until the 1970s, the *Fiera Campionaria* week (opening on 25 April) was an attraction not just for residents of Milan but for millions of visitors from the whole peninsula, with their families. Other effects are more controversial, and some have entered into local folklore. Many histories speak of the streets 'emptying', but there is little evidence of this from contemporary reports. This myth continues to be repeated.[9] Certainly, *Lascia* had such a negative effect on cinema audiences that the cinema and theatre proprietors first tried to install televisions in the main auditoriums and foyers, and

9. See for example, Grasso (1989: 112), Forgacs (1992: 193) and, for the same myth from 1964, Leydi (1964a: 34) and for the myth as told by Bongiorno himself see Ferrari and Giusto (2000: 113–6). For *Lascia* see also Veltroni (1992: 141), Grasso (1992: 68–75).

later successfully lobbied the government for the programme to be shifted to Thursday nights (they tried for Monday) so as to leave free the biggest night for cinema and theatre – Saturday.

One final effect was perhaps the most important of all. Television began to be identified with 'Milan' and the 'north' in the minds of many poor southerners. In surveys carried out amongst southern residents in the 1950s and 1960s the image of the northern cities was an extremely positive one.[10] Of course, it would be a mistake to attribute this image to television alone, and there is little evidence which would allow us to make a direct link between these developments. Certain sociologists in the 1960s identified what they called forms of pre-socialization amongst prospective migrants. In short, these immigrants of the future were already well disposed towards northern society before actually migrating. I have criticized these theories elsewhere as simplistic and ahistorical (see Chapter 3 above). However, it is undoubtedly true that the glittering prizes shown by *Lascia* and other programmes were identified with the 'north' and certain northern cities in particular and contributed both to the extent and to the direction of the mass migrations that transformed Italy in the late 1950s and early 1960s. To cite one viewer from 1964:

> television shows me how people live, those who are not condemned to a life of poverty like us. I see beautiful houses, nice places, pretty women . . . it makes me dream and desire, but when a person dreams and wants something, it makes him think. He wonders why certain people have beautiful houses and pretty women, and we have nothing. And in this way I learn something . . . (Cited in Mafai 1997: 82)

The 'heroic' period of collective television and of *Lascia o raddoppia?* coincided with the short period when Milan was the undisputed capital of Italian television. Strangely, Rome was to take control of the television networks and production (but not of advertising) just as the economic miracle was about to begin – in 1958 (Ferrari 2000).

Finally, there are the most difficult effects of all to calculate and study – those over the longer-term – *cultural* changes. *Lascia* is often attributed with enormous powers within a general cultural shift towards cultural levelling amongst Italians during the economic boom. The prize of the Fiat 600 is also seen as 'evidence' of a direct link between the boom, mass cultural forms and certain television programmes. The debates over *Lascia* summarized all the debates over television itself – as Grasso has put it 'Commitment as opposed to Evasion, Ideas as opposed to Industry, Progress as opposed to Consumerism. The quiz would seem to

---

10. For example, nearly 70 per cent of those interviewed in a survey of the Gargano region in Apulia in 1965 agreed that 'life is better' in the northern cities (Eisermann 1971: 185).

encapsulate all aspects of the argument' (1989: 108).[11] *Lascia o raddoppia?* is often assigned a central role in the cultural transformation of Italy – the programme is frequently cited as an event which changed Italy, which united the nation, which 'Americanized' the peninsula, which gave birth to Italian television – as 'part of the national culture' (Dagrada 1996: 234; Grasso 2000: 55–61). Despite being one of the very first game shows on Italian television, no programme since has matched the popularity at a mass level of *Lascia*. Historians normally cite two or three programmes in their surveys of televisual history, with *Lascia* in the foreground. Critic Grasso's history of Italian television devotes a whole chapter to *Lascia*, as do other histories of the RAI (Grasso 1992; Ferretti 1997: 173–80). Mike Bongiorno, the presenter of *Lascia*, was *still* a key figure on Italian television in the year 2000, and played a key role in the transformation of the Italian media system from a state monopoly to a private-state duopoly in the 1980s.[12]

Obviously, a cultural levelling of sorts was implied by the success of *Lascia*. At the same time, on the same day, vast numbers of Italians sat down to watch the same programme, to discuss the same questions and answers, to debate the same strategic choices of the contestants. Yet, can we go any further? Can we draw the (further) conclusion that *Lascia* contributed to (or led to) a cultural assimilation of Italian workers or peasants? What proof is there of such a process resulting directly from *Lascia*, as opposed to a general climate of consumerism or mass transformation? Is it not simply too easy to 'blame' one (important) programme for a whole series of 'ills'? Could not *Lascia* be seen as much as a follower of other, important social changes (migration, for example, or industrialization) as of minor importance in comparison with these lacerating developments (Anania 1994: 158).

Additionally, what was the 'message' of *Lascia*, and how was it received? In reality, we do not know the answer the question. No sociologist has carried out any systematic research on the programme, or on the reactions to it. Much of the history is written as *folklore*, as a series of repeated popular myths. In reality, whilst *Lascia* was certainly inspired by certain populist sentiments, it was also organized by a series of intellectuals as a didactic exercise for the education of Italians. In fact, many of the popular debates over *Lascia* concerned the subject matter of the questions (for example, in one famous case, the use of specific musical instruments in Verdi's operas) as well as the more consumerist aspects of the programme. *Lascia* was clearly a mix of the old and the new, of the paternalistic

11. For the notion that the quizzes of the 1950s encouraged (or even created) the very idea of consumerism amongst Italians see Losito (1986: 187), 'the ethos of early consumerism was transformed into spectacle'.

12. For Mike Bongiorno see the classic article by Eco (1963: 30–5; in English 1993), Grasso (1996b: 83) and Gundle (1986: 318–9).

ethos of the DC towards the Italian people and certain consumerist ideologies linked above all to the American dream.[13]

It is thus a mistake to read *Lascia* in a simplistic and one-dimensional fashion, and to overload the programme with powers which it may not have had.[14] Gundle's important article on the effects of television in Italy, published in 1986, remains the most sophisticated and analytical piece that has appeared on the subject. Gundle attributes the power of television in Italy to four main factors: the power of the visual medium over other media; the importance of a home-based, private diffusion of consumerist values; and the coincidence of the arrival of television with an extremely rapid boom in a country without an 'integrated national culture' and the 'simplicity and immediacy of television pictures [which] seemed to link up perfectly with the traditional qualities of much popular culture' (1986: 576). All these arguments are important and worth further investigation, but we are still left with the main objections that have dominated this chapter – the construction of a mythical, golden age, which was supposedly destroyed by mass culture, and the exaggeration of the role of television in this process – and of certain 'key' programmes.

One further problem with the equation *Lascia o raddoppia?*-Fiat 600-consumerism-cultural levelling lies with the periodization of these events. *Lascia* was associated above all with the *collective* period of television consumption. In 1955–6 most viewers watched *Lascia* in the bars, cultural centres and party sections of northern and central Italy. As Monteleone writes 'television was watched with other people, mainly outside of the family unit' (1992: 302). In 1956 one sixth of television licences were held by public places, such as bars or party sections (Monteleone 1992: 285). By the early 1960s, television had begun to leave the public sphere and occupy the sitting rooms of millions if Italians. In 1959, 36 per cent watched television at home, by 1966 this figure had risen to 75 per cent. By then, the economic miracle was over. However, it is also important not to exaggerate the collective nature of television watching in this early phase. Most Italians clearly *wanted* to have a television of their own, in their own home, and saved up their hard earned wages so as to meet the L.10,000 a month payments. The very domination of *Lascia* – which lasted, after all, for just an hour a week – also made this collective phase into an extremely concentrated one. As Anania puts it television 'created moments, *but only moments*, of cohesion and socialisation' (my emphasis) (1997: 25).

13. For 'Americanization' see Gundle (1986).

14. See for example, for this approach, Losito (1986: 187). Television is increasingly seen by sociologists as a mediator of experience, Giddens (1991: 380) and see also Ortoleva (1996: 185–8).

5. Private Television, *Milano 2* and the Rise of Berlusconi

Berlusconi has won because he arrived after fifteen years of private television. The changes had already happened . . . the construction of a (new) common sense. (Manconi 1995)

They have damaged me in the area which I hold most dear, my image. (Berlusconi cited in Formica 1994: 4)

The age of *paleo-television* ended with the advent of private channels, with media entrepreneur Silvio Berlusconi, and with the *neo-television* of the 1980s. Berlusconi created his media empire in Milan, basing his first channel – *TeleMilano* – in the neighbourhood that made him his first fortune and encapsulated a whole Berlusconian lifestyle. The neighbourhood was known as *Milano 2*, and *Milano 3* was soon to follow. Berlusconi recreated the city and reinvented television within an integrated ideological and economic project that intervened within the social, virtual and spatial spheres. The processes which brought Berlusconi and his three national private television channels power and fame are complicated and contradictory, and this history in its entirety is still to be written (Ortoleva 1995; Livolsi 1998; Morcellini 1986, 1995). This short section will attempt to explain the rise of Berlusconi and the Milanese nature of the extraordinary 'American Dream' that he represents. Milan, by the mid-1980s re-took the role of capital of television, which it had occupied briefly (in the public sphere) in the mid-1950s. Milan's mixture of advertising and private channels became a powerful source of ideological and financial opposition to the monopolistic and clientelistic state/public axis based in Rome.

Berlusconi is almost a stereotype of the self-made man. Born to a modest family in a working-class zone of Milan in 1934, he began his career as a cabaret singer on ocean cruises. After graduating in law, he went into business during the economic boom. He built and sold his first house in his mid-twenties, and, after a second project for a massive out-of-town estate failed to make money, he began to plan a new kind of city, outside Milan to the east. Berlusconi managed to raise enough capital to build an enormous housing project (over a space covering 700,000 square metres) known as *Milano 2*.[15] The differences between *Milano 2* and other estates built in the 1960s were important.[16] Above all, *Milano 2*

15. For the shady dealings that have accompanied Berlusconi's whole career see Ruggieri (1994, 1995) and Sisti and Gomez (1997).

16. In part, however, the originality of *Milano 2* has been 'invented' as a key component of the Berlusconi myth. The *Milano-San Felice* neighbourhood, also in Segrate, was built and occupied before *Milano 2* and certainly pre-empted some of the ideas used by Berlusconi and his collaborators. For *Milano San-Felice* see Irace and Pasca (1999: 24–5, 74–5).

epitomized a new model of consumption – a 'city of number ones' as the slogan went. The whole project was built so as to enclose the residents within a model of wealth, a non-urban environment and space. *Milano 2* therefore was a complete way of life, a status symbol, and not just an ordinary housing project. Berlusconi made sure that the residents were isolated from the nasty aspects of urban life – traffic, crime, immigrants, workers, the city itself.

Milano 2 (1970–9: architects G. Ragazzi; E. Hoffer; G. Possa) was made up of a number of innovative architectural features, designed for young, well-off families and couples.[17] The housing blocks were neither too high rise, nor designed purely for single families. Each block was surrounded by green space (maintained throughout the year through the use of incongruous mountain ever-greens) and there was a small, central lake. Different routes were designed, using a series of bridges, for bicycles, pedestrians and cars, which travelled below 'street level'. The houses themselves were constructed in a reassuring brown brick, rejecting the hyper-modern white concrete associated with a series of failed projects around Milan. The neighbourhood was clearly marked off from the rest of the city, segregated by walls, bridges and roads. The houses looked *in* onto the rest of *Milano 2,* and rarely out onto Milan or nearby Segrate. Elaborate systems of night-guards and concierges completed the security features of the zone. 'I was convinced', said Berlusconi, 'that *Milano 2* would attract people, above all because it satisfied the desire for a different kind of lifestyle' (Ferrari 1990: 35).

In addition to these residential features, Berlusconi made much of the services linked to the area – hotels, shops, underground garages, sports clubs, schools, a church, a swimming pool, playgrounds, a conference centre and a residence for businessmen. In addition, Berlusconi had learnt how to sell such a project (and all the houses were quickly sold, at high prices, to more than 12,000 residents). His first step was to build a show flat with services, *before* the houses (thus reversing the classic order of construction for public projects, which often had to wait years for basic services). Berlusconi advertised widely for *Milano 2*, in the *Corriere della Ser*a and elsewhere, with slogans like 'a countryside house in the city', 'a city to live in' and 'a house in Milan without the smog and traffic-jams of Milan'. Many of the new inhabitants of *Milano 2* were to be the protagonists of the finance/advertising/fashion-led boom of the 1980s, as Milan shook-off its grim industrial

17. For the architecture of *Milano 2*, see the contrasting opinions of Vercelloni (1989), who praises the neighbourhood as an innovative project (and notes the influence of Le Corbusier) to the disparaging comments of Gravinelli (1990: 245) and the critique of Squarcina (1987). *Milano 2* also came under heavy attack from within the Faculty of Architecture at the University of Milan (Ferrari 1990: 44). Even Berlusconi's official biographer slips in some disparaging comments concerning 'bored housewives sitting by the artificial lake, feeding the swans' (Madron 1994).

image. (Fiori 1996: 35–42; Ferrari 1990: 33–48; Grasso 1996b: 68; 1996a: 383–9).[18]

One of the services included with a house at *Milano 2* was private cable television. This was, initially, an aesthetic decision, made in order to prevent the 'eyesore' of individual television aerials. At the time of the construction of the estate, private television did not exist in Italy, but before long this local channel was to provide the launching pad for the explosive entry of Berlusconi into the television market. Helped by influential political friends, especially in Milan (Craxi, above all) and in the media, Berlusconi began to organize the first private television channel in the city – *TeleMilano* – in 1974 (at first available only for the residents of *Milano 2*). After a slow start (the channel was initially run from a small shop) the impetus for growth was given by an unexpected decision of the Constitutional Court in 1976. Private television was legal, as long as it was local. In the absence of a proper regulatory law, channels sprang up all over Italy. Berlusconi began to build his media empire. His strategy, as Fiori has noted, involved four related tactics. One, advertising: Berlusconi built up specific advertising teams of salesmen. Berlusconi's television linked the medium, the message and the centrality of selling. As he put it 'I do not sell space, I sell sales'. The profits of Berlusconi's advertising company *Publitalia* rose seventy-three times between 1980 and 1984. Berlusconi's television 'overturned our way of looking at television. Instead of interpreting it as a series of programmes interrupted by some adverts, Berlusconi saw "free" and "private" television as a vast territory for advertising messages, an extraordinary vehicle of commercial communication' (Colombo 1990: 595). Two, programmes (above all American series) and films, often modified in relation to the sponsors' desires. 'The show exists to attract consumers' (Fiori 1996: 95). Three, stars willing to personally take part in advertising (see below). Four, the Milan base (the symbol of Berlusconi's company was a snake – symbol of Milan itself and of Alfa-Romeo, the Milanese car company *par excellence*. Berlusconi was often referred to as 'the snake' – *il biscione*) with a swift extension of coverage to the whole country. *Telemilano* began transmitting on the airwaves in 1978, after the installation of an aerial on the Pirelli tower in Milan.[19]

18. *Milano 2* became home to many of Berlusconi's employees, and was also close to the headquarters of Italy's biggest publishing company, Mondadori, which Berlusconi was to partly take over in the 1980s. Berlusconi used the neighbourhood as his headquarters for much of that decade. One of the problems with *Milano 2* was its proximity to Milan's Linate airport. Berlusconi used his influence to shift flight paths away from *Milano 2*. A third of *Milano 2*'s residents left the neighbourhood on a daily basis for work or other reasons.

19. For the details of the rise of Berlusconi within the television sector, see Fiori (1996) and the special issues of *Problemi dell'informazione*, XV, 4, December 1990, and 3, XI, July–September 1986.

In 1980 Mike Bongiorno again played a key role in the development of television in Italy and Milan. Signed up by Berlusconi on a huge contract, Bongiorno became the first star presenter to leave the state sector. The programmes themselves never had the same popularity as *Lascia o raddoppia?*, but the symbolic effect of Bongiorno's presence in the budding Berlusconi empire, as well as his enthusiastic acceptance of the primacy of advertising over all other considerations, was central to the acceptance and spread of the new private sector. For Grasso, Bongiorno

> was the first to understand . . . that it was no longer useful to promote programmes in order to support television, but instead create advertising spaces to see products, an area in which he showed himself to be a maestro, the real prophet of the Berlusconian creed. (1996b: 83)

Berlusconi and his Milanese power base was soon able to eat up all competitors, forcing through controversial legislation via Socialist Party support. Two programmes symbolized the early success of Berlusconi's television strategy. First, sport in the shape of the *Mundialito*, a friendly football tournament involving Italy which Berlusconi bought up and, after a long legal battle, was able to transmit on his channels in 1981–2. Second, there was *Dallas*. This hugely popular soap opera was the making of private television, setting up regular daily and weekly 'appointments' and creating a faithful public for the first time outside of the public sector. With *Dallas*, as Grasso has written, 'commercial television legitimated its presence in the Italian televisual imagination, identified and consolidated its public and traced out its editorial line' (1996b: 186–7). Berlusconi had 'understood perfectly the particular nature of that magic consumer good – television' (Murialdi 1990: 488).

The values of private television, without news programmes or documentaries and packed with quiz shows, films, American soap operas, talk shows and above all advertising both reflected and helped to create the hedonist years of the second boom in the late 1980s and 1990s. The withdrawal from politics that began to take definitive shape in the mid to late 1990s, with the collapse of the mass party system and precipitous declines in voting turnouts, was also a reflection of this type of media output and coverage.

> Through variety shows, quizzes, innumerable spot announcements, sponsored slots and imported soap operas, substitutes had been offered for the old reference points that were in decline: the Church, the parties of the left, the organised labour movement, values of parsimony and sacrifice. (Gundle and O'Sullivan 1996: 216)

Berlusconi was also a central part of the shift of political and media power away from its traditional centres – above all Rome – to Milan and the north.

Craxi's premiership cemented these alliances and this shift. Italian politics were Americanized, as Craxi invented new forms of political communication and used Berlusconi's networks to do so. The antipolitical and personalized campaigns of the 1980s and early 1990s, until Craxi himself was swept away by the corruption scandals after 1992, prefigured a sea change in the way Italian political campaigning was managed and marketed. Berlusconi himself was to take this style to a whole new level in 1994. He 'took the field' via a videotape transmitted on various televisions stations, he ran his political party like a business, and he manipulated his message to fit and transform public opinion (Grasso, 1993; Fiori, 1996; Ginsborg 1998). This ingenious and modern mixture of the old and the new, aided by the absence of any serious anti-trust laws in Italy, combined with Berlusconi's appeal as a self-made man (Gundle and Parker 1996: 9) and his economic and political power in Milan and elsewhere, all added up to a potent cocktail of populism, anti-communism and anti-political politics (Biorcio 1994: 162; Parker 1996: 120; McCarthy 1996: 130–7; 1997). As De Benardi and Ganapini have written, the success of Berlusconi-as-politician also reflected a whole series of epochal changes in Italian society and cultural norms

> through which the businessman-manager presented himself as an idealised model to follow within which civil society was seen as a collection of atomised subjects, no longer divided by class distinctions and carriers of conflictual values and interests, but levelled through consumption. This is the type of society which began to form in the 1980s and which had in the Craxian ideal its first formation. (1996: 511)

Berlusconi represented a model for the millions of small businessmen and self-employed of northern Italy – the *Berlus-clones* – who resented the combination of high taxes and poor state services and rejected solidaristic notions of society presented (weakly) by the left and the Church. He 'incarnated the private entrepreneur' (McCarthy 1996: 131).[20]

Berlusconi made specific use of his Milan image and relatively humble roots in his road to political power. His political organizers were all based in Milan, most from within the Fininvest and later Mediaset organizations. *Forza Italia!*'s first congress was held in Milan and Berlusconi consistently won its highest votes

---

20. Galli (1999: 853–8), Pieroni (2000). Of all employed Italians in the year 2000, 30 per cent were self-employed or had their own businesses, and 20 per cent worked in tiny businesses (with two to four employees). This figure, much higher than in other European countries, was also an indicator of social mobility (upwards, in two-thirds of cases). This type of social category, according to Pieroni, was naturally 'of the right'. 'A man who with his work has become a small businessman feels, rightly or wrongly, a capitalist. This type of man on the up has also been described as a *berlus-clone*.' His star quality was also important, exemplified by his omnipresent smile (journalist Serra calls Berlusconi the *sempre ridens*). For a brilliant analysis see Gundle (1995).

in the country in the 'moral capital' (26 per cent, 1994 (Parliament), 35 per cent, 1994 (European), 23 per cent 1996 (European), 30 per cent, 1999, European elections). Berlusconi's language also reflected the centrality of Milan in Italian political and economic history. In his very first broadcast as a politician, Berlusconi referred to a future 'new Italian miracle', a clear reference to the boom of the 1950s and 1960s (but also to that of the 1980s) and this became the slogan for the 1994 election campaign (*Il nuovo miracolo italiano*, 1994). These successes were repeated during the victorious election campaign of 2001.

One other key aspect of Berlusconi's cultural hegemony in Milan lay with football. In 1986 Berlusconi became President of AC Milan, a club with a glorious history that had been going through extremely lean times. The previous president was on the run after a corruption scandal and Milan, twice winner of the European Cup in the 1960s, had spent two separate periods in Serie B in the late 1970s and early 1980s. Milan had a huge fan base, in the city and right across Italy, rivalled only by that of Juventus, Inter and Napoli. Berlusconi set about re-building the team, playing a highly visible role in saving a club in crisis. The crucial television-football-politics link, spectacularized by the Fininvest channels in the early 1980s, began to take on more shape. Berlusconi usually attended matches personally, he became friends with the players and advised his managers on tactics. The *tribuna d'onore* at San Siro became the place to be seen in Milan. Berlusconi soon became a favourite with the fans. In 1987, Berlusconi appointed a little-known manager called Arrigo Sacchi. Within a year, and with the help of three brilliant Dutch players and two of the greatest defenders in the history of Italian football – Franco Baresi and Paolo Maldini – Milan had won their first championship under Berlusconi. The miracle-worker had done it again, in his own city. In 1989 and 1990 the club won the European Cup, and the city was paralysed by parties that went on for days. More than 20,000 Milan fans made the round trip to Barcelona for the 1989 final, using twenty-five charter planes, 450 coaches and a ship (Ginsborg 1998: 222).[21]

It was not just the winning, but the style of it. Milan played a spectacular attacking game, which bore no relation to the classic *catenaccio* tactics still used at the time by Italian traditionalist managers. Berlusconi was able to make football into family entertainment, not an activity for fanatical fans alone. AC Milan managed to sell 70,000 season tickets in the early 1990s, and the success continued throughout that decade, with five more championships and another European Cup. Many studies have underlined the ways in which Berlusconi's language is both televisual and sport based: he 'took the field'; his organization is a 'team'; he often explains political debates in tactical terms (Triani 1994). However, what has often been overlooked is both the territorial aspects of the link to Milan (as a

---

21. Ferrari claims that an incredible 80,000 fans made the trip (1990: 133).

Milanese team, but also one with a strong national following) and the symbiosis between control of the media – especially television – and the success of the club, combined with the political visibility of Berlusconi in the 1990s. In a country where the best-selling newspaper is entirely dedicated to sport, and mainly to football, and where refereeing decisions are discussed for years, and often lead to parliamentary debates, the control of one of the top three football teams in the richest league in the world, and the identification as president with that teams' (frequent) victories, has been a crucial factor in Berlusconi's rise to political power at a national and local level. Berlusconi himself claimed that his intention was to 'Milanize Milan . . . to import into the company those business-type methods and initiatives which would make the team represent our city' (Ferrari 1990: 136).

Berlusconi also began to build a local power base following his entry into politics in 1994. He managed to organize election victories for *Forza Italia!* candidates in the regional elections (Formigoni was elected in 1995 and again, this time with an extraordinary 62 per cent of the regional vote, in 2000), the Provincial Milanese elections (Colli, 1999) and those of the Milanese Council (1997, 2001). The latter case was a perfect example of Berlusconi's power in Milan. He personally chose the candidate – Albertini, an industrialist – and made a personal appeal to Milanese voters in a letter sent to the whole electorate. The letter was a classic example of the Milanese nature of Berlusconi's political appeal, and his widening of that appeal to the national stage. 'Our Milan', the letter claimed, 'must finally return to how it was, the hard-working Milan, rich of ideas and dynamism, the Milan of creative entrepreneurship and efficient administration.' Albertini was presented in similar terms to Berlusconi himself 'a man from the world of work, who has never been involved in politics, who was born and raised in Milan'. But it was clear where the real power lay; 'we Milanese are ready and willing', added Berlusconi, and 'I will be the top candidate for *Forza Italia!* in these Council Elections.' Albertini was Mayor of the city, but the important decisions were taken at Arcore, Berlusconi's sumptuous out-of-town villa, and any re-shuffles had to have the assent of the *Cavaliere*.[22] Once again, Milan's elite was based in the countryside around the city.[23] By 2000 then, Berlusconi was in control of all the key political institutions in the richest region of Italy (and one of the richest in Europe) – Lombardy. With increasing federalist powers being given to regions and local administrations, this power alone was enough to consolidate and build a hegemonic

22. One classic example of this kind of decision-making, very similar in content to the power exercised by Craxi over the city administration (where his brother-in-law, Pillitteri, was Mayor for a time) was the dispute between Councillor De Carolis and Albertini in 1999–2000. De Carolis would only resign after Berlusconi's written intervention, despite frequent appeals from Albertini. In May 2000 the 'non-political' Albertini described himself as 'a deep-hearted Berlusconian'.

23. This trend was also to be seen amongst those industrialists linked to the design industries of the boom, who paid important architects to construct villas in the Brianza region in the 1960s.

control over the political culture of a territory where Berlusconi was already a major economic player. The era of the Sforza and the Visconti families had long disappeared, but Milan had crowned a new king, with powers that rivalled those of the monarchs and lords of the past.

6. Conclusions: Television as an Urban Phenomenon

> Italy will be, in a certain sense, reduced to one single village, an immense *piazza*, the forum, where there is everybody and everyone can see all the others. (Luigi Barzini 1954)

> Over a period of 15 years, Fininvest networks . . . furnished Italians with a new set of values and aspirations. (Gundle and O'Sullivan 1996: 216)

Early Italian television contributed to the rapid push towards modernity in a series of subtle and complicated ways. First, the urbanization of Italy was both reflected in and helped by the spread of television. Television made and re-invented the city, and its spread coincided not with suburbanization – as in the US or the UK, but with urbanization and industrialization (Forgacs 1998: 203-94). Second, television contributed to the intensity of the two-post war booms. As Grasso has written, television 'sped up the rhythms of the social life of the nation in an extraordinary way' (1992: 22). In concrete terms, *Lascia* itself promoted the sales of both televisions and the Fiat 600 – symbol of the popular motorization of the years of the miracle. The key Milanese industries of the 1980s and 1990s – advertising, fashion, design – were either indirectly or directly reliant on television's cultural and economic power.

Yet, what was urban about television and the mass culture it supposedly transmitted? Here, the question becomes more complicated. Certainly, mass culture was in some senses modern, and the cities of Italy were obvious centre of industrialization, consumption and modernity. However, the urban mosaic and the changing urban landscape were not reflected by early television, which confined itself to educational and literary programmes and quizzes based in studios or the provinces. The 'urban' we are looking for was a much more ephemeral entity – more ideological than real, more mythical than realist. The 'typically urban values' mentioned by Gundle reflected the changing ideals introduced by the first post-war boom, but in subtle ways – the car-as-prize, the emphasis on money, the international transmissions, the film used in news programmes, the products advertised on *Carosello*. Later, private television, the television of Berlusconi, was far more obviously 'American' than before; It glorified in urban excess, consumption and glamour, and made a virtue of 'modernity'.

Public television was not Big Brother, as 1968 showed. 'The television generation was the generation of May 1968 . . . of the refusal to integrate' (Eco

1973: 11–12). The public had not been brainwashed, or had been brainwashed badly. Certain values were transmitted by television, but each individual put his or her own gloss onto each individual moment of transmission. The 1950s were a time of mass parties, of mass Catholic movements, of the beginning of mass education. A number of rivals to television presented themselves and offered up various interpretations of the pictures that 'invaded' homes, bars and party offices. And of course, the messages transmitted could not be simply condemned as propaganda. Television, as Anania has written 'undoubtedly opened up a new era for the individual use of free time and the greater possibility of choice of sources of information, as well as in terms of the pervasive and at the same time contradictory nature of the messages appearing on the screen' (Anania 1997: 187). But 1968 was also the year of the foundation bricks of *Milano 2* and the first steps towards the immense power base of Berlusconi. There are also strong continuities between the Messianic rush to watch early television and the popularity of Fininvest in the 1980s and 1990s. If we accept this version of ideological history, then 1968 seems more of a blip than the proof of any real revolt against capitalist values. However, there are also important differences between the effects of public and private television which should be taken into consideration. By the end of the 1990s the Berlusconian project had triumphed, above all in Milan, and Berlusconi himself was the richest man in Italy. He had even been elected Prime Minister for a short time in 1994 and again in 2001. None of this was bound to happen, but to explain why it did, and how it did, we need to go to back to the bleak housing estates constructed during the 'miracle'. The roots of *Milano 2* and *Telemilano* are to be found in the processes that surrounded the economic boom and the birth of television in Italy.

– 6 –

Capital of Design, Capital of Fashion

1. Capital of Design

1.1. Design and the City: Design is Everywhere

> All of our daily activities . . . from the turning-off of the alarm clock to the making of coffee, from taking the underground train to driving the car, from looking at our watch to sitting down to lunch or on a sofa, from the turning on of a television to using the computer, from working on a production line to following street signs, have been characterised, qualified and often improved by design. This term defines and concretises the relationship between product and project, or planning and production. (Pansera 1996: 15)

'Design is everywhere' (Hauffe 1998: 8; Forty 1995). Yet, the history of design – 'the drafting and planning of industrial products' (Hauffe 1998: 10) – has usually taken second place to the histories of architecture and planning. The external and visual aspects of the city have often dominated, at least intellectually, the study of the metropolis and lived space. Design, however, pervades daily life to a far greater extent than architecture or planning (even if the separation between these disciplines is not as simple or clear cut as it might appear).[1] Most of our lives are spent surrounded by, sitting on, sleeping on, drinking out of, driving in, working on or playing with objects designed by designers. Design permeates the city, and not just the city. It 'makes the world liveable' (Branzi in Bosoni and Confalonieri 1988: 8). The architects working in post-war Milan attempted to re-design the urban environment from top to bottom – as Ernesto Rogers famously put it – 'from the spoon to the city' and 'it is a question of forming a taste, a technique, a morality – all terms of the same function. It is a question of building a society' (1946; Sparke 1998: 145; Piva 1982). For Enzo Paci designers were placed

---

1. The blurring of the architect-designer role in Milan was a powerful example of this inter-disciplinary approach to the profession, from Magistretti (who designed chairs, book-cases, working-class neighbourhoods, churches and luxury villas) to Ponti (tower blocks, interior designs for ocean liners, chairs, coffee-makers) to Rossi (opera houses, monuments, cemeteries, coffee-makers). In Italy at least 'the history of modern architecture seems to coincide with that of the modern seat' (Branzi 1984a: 8).

'between art and society' and 'invented forms which had never been seen before and expressed new ways of living' (Pansera 1996: 43).

Nonetheless, design has never been produced in an economic vacuum, and the producers of goods have always been primarily involved in making profits, not producing art-work for arts sake. The compromise between markets, producers, creativity and society changes over time in relation to the developments in the economy and the cultural sphere (Forty 1995).

1.2. Milano as Capital of Design

> Italian design was born because here, and only here, there was a meeting in the 1960s between the producers and us. (Vico Magistretti, *Interview*)

With the end of the war, the Milanese authorities were occupied above all with the reconstruction of the city and the housing of thousands of citizens who had lost their homes through bomb damage after 1943. Yet, by the mid-1950s, Milan had become one of the world capitals of industrial design, a position it was to hold for the rest of the century. The reasons behind the rapidity and duration of this remarkable transformation lie in the particular combination of intellectual and professional *milieu* (especially in the realm of architecture), industrial innovation and concentration and market capabilities centred around Milan and Lombardy. Architects, designers, and architect-designers, were able to work directly within the rich fabric of small industry, artisans and workshops that characterized (and still characterizes) the vast productive region to the north of Milan. In addition, the showcase possibilities provided by the international *Triennale* exhibitions of the 1940s and 1950s brought Italian design (and Milanese design) to world attention. As Dorfles put it 'the *Triennale* provided the real basis for the interest and spread of design in Italy' (*Interview*). The opportunities provided by the historic market role of Milan and the reconstruction of the city, and later by the building and consumer boom of the years of the miracle, all contributed to the definitive and massive economic and cultural spread of the Italian look, Italian style and Italian design.[2]

Milan saw a vast concentration of designers, studios, services linked to the design industry, critics, showrooms, design magazines and other publications, exhibitions, trade fairs, awards and patrons of design (Pansera 1996: 40). The very absence and inefficiency of public attempts to organize or produce design left designers and industrialists with a kind of freedom to innovate and publicize that did not occur elsewhere. Italy also took advantage of its late entry onto the

---

2. In fact, the term Italian design is often taken to mean much more than just industrial design, but also 'an actual cultural category, a particular relationship with technology and industry' (Branzi 1994: 597).

scene to build links between established industrialists and professionals. For Branzi this development was marked by a kind of 'spontaneous negotiation' between small industry and designers (and the market). In some ways this system appeared as 'post-industrial' even in the 1950s (1999). Consumerism provided the market opportunities, at the same time, for sales and further production, as 'the world became washable, buildable, flexible' (Branzi 1999: 116). Design exploited the gaps left by an incomplete and imperfect modernity.

Over a short but heady twenty years, the city was to set itself up as a capital of design innovation and production. 'By the mid-1950s Italian furniture had become one of the major international symbols of an affluent, cosmopolitan lifestyle' (Sparke 1988: 99). This strong position was cemented at an international level by the exhibition in New York in 1972, *Italy: the New Domestic Landscape* (Ambasz 1972; Branzi 1999: 130). In many ways, the 1972 exhibition closed a specific phase of the history of design in Milan and Lombardy, and opened a new period marked by extensive and lengthy debates over the relationship between design, the market and the public. So-called 'radical design' also had its centre in Milan, but never managed to extend its impact beyond the intellectual circles interested in theoretical debates over the construction of the city and the world of goods within the modern metropolis. Strangely, it was the design that came before 'radical design' that had the most impact of the daily lives of Italian citizens and did the most to transform the city and the home. 'Radical design' confined itself to high-level debates and artistic (and often utopian) production available only to wealthy collectors and visible only in the richest of homes and museums. Post-war design reached millions of consumers and led to a metamorphosis in the interiors and exteriors of Italian homes. Its bedrock lay in the mosaic of industries that spread across the hinterland to the north of the city.

1.3. The Industrial District: Lombardy and Brianza

The Lombard region, throughout the last two centuries, has been able to develop an integrated economic system marked by strong specialized areas and districts. Lombardy was able to integrate 'agriculture, industry, commerce and finance; big, small and medium-sized industry; family firms and stock companies. All this within a complex whole marked by a pragmatic push towards innovation, by a prudent optimism and by the never-ending research for modernity sustained by a tenacious attachment to tradition' (Bigazzi 1996: 11). The road to industrial society here was one where links to the land were maintained over long periods. There was a kind of 'soft' industrialization 'based on the gradual interweaving of agricultural and industrial employment among workers' (Bull and Corner 1993: 4; Foot 1991, Chapter 2). Whole areas were industrialized without the wholesale expulsion of peasants and rural artisans.

Historically, the Brianza district to the north of Milan has been an area of small businesses, artisans and workshops – a 'vast artisan-based hinterland' (Gregotti 1994b: 239; Pansera 1996: 27–9) and 'the historic cradle of Italian design' (Branzi 1994: 602). This industrial district grew organically from rural society and peasant culture, presenting an alternative model of 'slow industrialization' to the 'rapid industrialization' that characterized most Italian and European regions.[3] Instead of the 'classic' groups of workers and peasants, myriad sectors of peasant-workers and worker-peasants continued to combine agricultural and industrial activity over long periods of time. From the early days of silkworm farming, where the worms were often cultivated in peasant bedrooms, a tradition of family-based textile manufacture evolved in the area. The furniture industry evolved from the wood-based artisan and peasant-traditions of the eighteenth century. A series of small businesses evolved to provide the furniture and fittings for the 700 rooms of Monza's Royal Villa, built between 1780 and 1848 (Ronzoni 1994).

Many of these businesses then, by the 1940s, were specialized in wood-based production and especially furniture (one third of Italy's furniture was produced in the area to the north of Milan in the 1950s). They had also begun to mechanize and adopt new technical and scientific approaches to production, whilst maintaining the artisan traditions which had marked their origins (*Le affinità elettive*, 1985; Bull and Corner 1993: 133–4). This area, therefore, was perfectly placed – being almost within the Milanese metropolitan area – to take advantage of the mass building and furniture demands of the 1940s, 1950s and 1960s, from mass-produced to quality-designed lines. 'High design' trickled down to these smaller, more popular firms. 'Even small carpentry shops very quickly learned to turn out bar counters that looked as if they had been designed by Giò Ponti' (Branzi 1984a: 45). They were 'learning from Milan', and Milan was learning from them (Branzi 1988). Thousands of new businesses were set up in the same area after the Second World War, creating one of the most powerful and extensive industrial districts in Italy (De Giorgi 1996: 581; Santini 1985: 47). Italy's design revolution and Italian style itself brought together elements of modernity, rationalism, craft skills and artisanship in a heady mix that allowed the survival of traditions of quality and of family-based work organization with large-scale production and innovative technologies.

3. This is not to say that this was a particularly enlightened region in terms of industrial relations or education. Many peasants were still suffering from diet-based disease in the 19th century (including *pellagra*) and children and young women were used in small factories and workshops across the region, Bull and Corner (1993: 20, 28).

1.4. Designers and Companies: Cassina, Giò Ponti, Vico Magistretti

Design was a phenomenon linked to the presence of progressive industrialists . . . and in general to a part of the upper bourgeoisie who considered business as an instrument of that bourgeois revolution which the Italian state never carried through. (Branzi 1985: 18–19)

Cassina was a firm with a centuries-old tradition of artisanship and production to the north of Milan. In fact, descendants of the Cassina family worked on the pulpit of Como Cathedral in 1795 (Santini 1981; Pansera 1990: 18; 1996: 114; Centro-kappa 1985: 106–11). In the late 1940s, Cesare Cassina, heir to the furniture business his father founded in 1927 in Meda just outside Milan, began to meet with architect-designers in Milan. Two relationships were to prove particularly fruitful for the company – that with Vico Magistretti and that with Giò Ponti. Ponti was already a well-established and famous architect by 1949. He had designed some of the first tower blocks to be built in Milan and was founder and editor of the important architectural magazine, *Domus*. In the 1950s Ponti began to work on furniture design for a number of transatlantic liners with Cassina (Sparke 1988: 95).

Following the success of this commission, which allowed Cassina to introduce mass production techniques for the first time, Ponti began to work on a simple, 'light' chair for the company. Inspired by the traditional chairs produced in the Ligurian town of Chiavari, but using modern production techniques, Ponti produced a design which was to become famous throughout the world, and is still in production. The chair (model 646, 1957, is the most famous, but a series of different models were produced from 1952–7) was known as the superlight – the *superleggera* – and combined clean elegance with a modern, stylish look. The chair's 'subtly tapering legs . . . rendered it unequivocally "contemporary"' (Sparke 1999: 67). It was also, as the name suggests, very light (it could be lifted with one finger) but also strong – combining 'maximum structural resistance with the maximum lightness of the sections' (Frateili 1995: XIX). The chair was tested by Cassina by dropping it from the fourth floor of the factory.

The piece was an immediate international and critical success, at a cost of only L. 50,000, underlining the possibilities opened up by alliances between individual businesses, designers, entrepreneurs and salesmen working around the Milanese markets. The *superleggera* was given pride of place in a celebratory exhibition of designer chairs, held at the *Triennale* (*100 forme del sedere, Italia 1946–2000*, May–July 2000). The chair remains 'one of the most celebrated and archetypal models of Italian design' (Santini: 1981: 20). In short, the chair became 'a classic' – 'a reference-point for Italian furniture design' (Gregotti 1994b: 349) 'one of the emblematic piece of modern design' (Pansera 1996: 114).[4] Ponti called the *superleggera* a 'seat-seat . . . without adjectives' and defended its simplicity and 'usefulness'. 'It is a normal chair – light, subtle, convenient . . . which cannot be labelled as rational, modern, organic, pre-fabricated'. 'Let us go back', argued Ponti, 'to the chair-chair, the house-house, work without a label – real, natural, simple and spontaneous' (Ponti 1952).

Following the success of items such as the *superleggera*, many small, previously artisan-based companies, whilst retaining the quality and craft aspects that had been at the basis of their work, moved towards modern sales and production techniques to keep pace with demand. Huge showrooms opened up in the Brianza region, and smaller, sophisticated shops were set up in Milan. Distribution networks were extended to the whole of Italy and Europe, local co-operatives began to form. Many firms 'saw the possibility of rebuilding within national and international markets an immediate "image" through the "Italian line"' (Centrokappa 1985: 19). New materials led to new design opportunities, especially with the introduction of plastics after 1956. Certain companies began to specialize in plastic production, including Kartell (founded in 1949), Artemide and Arflex (1950).[5]

Magistretti also began to work directly with Cassina after 1960, experimenting with ideas and production techniques in the workshops and factories of the company. Over thirty years, Magistretti's production with Cassina has produced a number of classics, from the 1960 Carimate chair (Irace and Pasca, 1999: 132) to the Maralunga sofa (1973). Once again, these items of furniture were inspired by an almost functionalist simplicity, combined with the smooth lines of Italian style that were to become so popular across the world. Like the *superleggera*, the Carimate was a best-seller for years and with its rural simplicity (the straw of the seat – 'it was a bit of a peasant seat' as Magistretti commented 'with urban sophistication'; there were the smooth lines of the wooden supports and legs, the colour'. 'The bright red wooden frame of Magistretti's chair was overtly "Pop" in inspiration' (Sparke 1999: 67) – and used elements of Scandinavian design.

The boom allowed millions of ordinary Italian consumers to purchase quality goods. After the boom, 'a chair and a sofa (were no longer) examples of culture,

---

4. For the importance of chairs for modern design see Sparke: 'because of its close affiliations with architectural space, its relative ease of manufacture and its potent symbolism, the chair, that "sitting object", was used by most of the architect-philosophers of the Modern Movement to articulate, in material form, their ideas about materials, construction and space' (1998: 47).

5. For Artemide see Gismondi (*Interview*). Another central area for design has been that of lighting. Magistretti's work for Artemide stands out – his lights and later plastic chairs (and his professional relationship with Gismondi, similar to that with Cesare Cassina), as does the production of Arteluce (Pansera 1996). Other areas not covered in this chapter include those of electric goods and cars, kitchens and bathrooms (increasingly design-led in the 1980s and 1990s).

Figure 1: The Pirelli Tower under construction (Archivio Storico Pirelli).

Figure 2: The Pirelli Tower nearing completion (Archivio Storico Pirelli).

Figure 3: City and countryside. Workers on strike outside the FACE factory in Bovisa, 1964 (S. Loconsolo; Archivio Storico Fiom).

Figure 4: Immigrants. *Rocco and his Brothers*, final scene. The workers return to the Alfa Romeo factory. Ciro and his girlfriend kiss (Luchino Visconti, 1960; BFI Films, Stills, Posters and Designs).

Figure 5: Industrious Milan. Alberto Sordi as a factory foreman, *Il Mafioso* (Film still; A. Lattuada, 1962; BFI Films, Stills, Posters and Designs).

Figure 6: Marcello Mastroianni, with the Pirelli skyscraper in the background (Film still; M. Antonioni, *La Notte*, 1960; BFI Films, Stills, Posters and Designs).

Figure 7: The old periphery. *Miracolo a Milano* (Film still; V. De Sica, 1951; BFI Films, Stills, Posters and Designs).

Figure 8: Clerks. Ermanno Olmi directs *Il Posto* (Film still; Ermanno Olmi, 1960; BFI Films, Stills, Posters and Designs).

Figure 9: Cinema and the City. Luchino Visconti directs *Rocco e i suoi fratelli* from the top of the Duomo, 1960 (Film still, Luchino Visconti, 1960; BFI Films, Stills, Posters and Designs).

Figure 10: The Pirelli Tower on completion, at night (Archivio Storico Pirelli).

Figure 11: Industrial Periphery. Sesto San Giovanni, April 1961. Workers from the Breda company at the factory gates (Archivio Storico Fiom).

Figure 12: Industrial Province. Workers leave a factory in Legnano, 1962 (Archivio Storico Fiom).

Figure 13: Industrial City. Workers leave the Pirelli plant, 1955 (Archivo Storico Pirelli).

Figure 14: Protest. Workers besiege the Pirelli Skyscraper during the 'hot autumn', 1969 (Archivio Storico Pirelli).

Figure 15: Protest. Pirelli workers sit in. *La Galleria*, 1969 (Archivio Storico Pirelli).

Figure 16: The 'old periphery'. Bovisa. Piazza Bausan, 1960s (Postcard Image).

Figure 17: City of Time. The Alarm Clock production line from the Borletti Factory (Milan, 1950s: Archivio Storico Borletti).

Figure 18: Fashion and Design. The *Superleggera* chair, Giò Ponti (Cassina. Model 699. 1957. Photo by Aldo Ballo).

Figure 19: Milan Today. Piazzale Lugano, 22, 2000 (Antonio Conese, Tam Tam Fotografie).

Figure 20: Milan Today. Piazzale Lugano, 22, 2000 (Antonio Conese, Tam Tam Fotografie).

but market objects, in the active sense of the word, elements of contact with the world of production' (Gregotti 1957 cited in Pansera 1978: 87). Magistretti's long collaboration with Cassina was based on the ability to experiment, to promote ideas, to work directly with artisans. The designer was a combination of consultant, friend, marketing and art director and planner. As Magistretti himself put it 'from the beginning . . . we worked together, in a way which is unique in the world . . . we discussed projects together from the start. I never produced finished designs . . . the design grew out of discussions, after looking at the technology available, the machines which the company used' (*Interview*). This kind of direct relationship, 'unique' according to Magistretti, was to typify the growth of Italian design companies around and in Milan during and after the 1950s.[6] Magistretti was part of a group of designers who in this period began to operate with 'a real new culture of interior design' which affected and shaped the living spaces of millions of people (Pasca 1999: 120). 'For some chairs the production reached tens of thousands . . . and this changes the landscape, changes the layout of offices, changes the landscape of many things' (*Interview*).

Magistretti's relationship with Cassina was close enough to involve the architect in the design of the Carimate golf clubhouse (1958–61), where the Carimate chair was first used in the restaurant, and Cassina's own luxurious villa in the same town (1964–5) (Irace, Pasca 1999: 58–9; 72–3). Magistretti was one of that rare breed of architect-designers who came out of the Milanese intellectual *milieu* around the Politecnico and the inspiration of architects such as Rogers. For Gregotti, this tendency to cross over lies at the heart of the success and originality of Italian design (1994a: 564).

Magistretti had participated directly in the reconstruction of the city through his work on public housing projects and the Pirelli neighbourhood at Cinisello Balsamo in the 1950s (Irace, Pasca 1999: 52–3). These estates stand out even today for the humanist qualities of their design, the quality of the construction and the availability of green space for the residents. Later, in the late-1960s, Magistretti was once again involved in the transformation of the city. His work on the first out-of-town middle class neighbourhood in Milan – *Milano San Felice* – with its hidden traffic, horseshoe form and garden city qualities – was to inspire hundreds of other similar neighbourhoods (often of a much-lower quality) in the rezonification of Italian cities, and in particular Milan, in the 1970s and 1980s (Irace, Pasca 1999: 74–5).

6. Other examples include the links between Sottsass and Olivetti, Castiglione and Flos, Zanuso and Brionvega.

1.5. The Triennale

The success of Milanese design, especially at an international level, was only made possible by the existence and success of a particular Milanese institution – the *Triennale*. Set up in the early 1930s and opened for the first time in 1933, the *Triennale* organized international three-yearly exhibitions of art, architecture, design and planning that coincided with a series of conferences and experimental architectural projects. These exhibitions were held in the extraordinary modern space of Muzio's *Palazzo dell'Arte* (1931–3) with its sweeping staircase, its huge windows and its marble floors. The position of the *Palazzo* within the *Parco Sempione* allowed exhibitions to spill over into the park and the city, creating a kind of open-air space that, on various occasions, was used to great effect. These events not only gave Italian production an international audience, but also set up creative networks of designers, architects and manufacturers who were able to exhibit and experiment in the creative years after the war (Pansera 1978; 1996: 37–8).

In 1947 the first post-war *Triennale*, organized largely by architect and Communist Pietro Bottoni, was based around the construction of an experimental neighbourhood to the north of the city – QT8 (*Quartiere Triennale Ottava*). Before QT8 experimental housing had always been demolished after the exhibition had been held. However, QT8 was intended to be a permanent part of the city. Working with the freedom to break normal building and planning regulations, the architects and designers were able to experiment in real urban situations. This was authentic urban design, on a grand scale, aimed at re-building with intelligence a shattered city. Sixty-six hectares of prime land were donated by the state for the original project, begun in 1946. The *Triennale* came under ferocious attack in the press and elsewhere, and was accused of politicization of planning. The whole event became known as the 'Proletarian *Triennale*', and the impact of the neighbourhood on the exhibition was never as dominant as in 1947, despite constant reports on its progress in successive *Triennales*. Nonetheless, the neighbourhood, which continued to grow throughout the early 1950s and involved hundreds of architects and designers in its construction, remains a shining example of illuminated planning in a city blighted by planning failure. The harmonious combination of low-rise housing; quality construction and an innovative hill park (Monte Stella) built from bomb rubble (in a city without hills) represents a rare moment of successful collaboration between the various professions and the local state (Pansera 1978; Rogers 1947; Bottoni 1947).

As the 1950s wore on, the *Triennale* made less and less impact on the map and layout of the city, but became more and more influential in the realms of interior design and architectural theory. Each *Triennale* was accompanied by extensive debates in the popular and specialized press and brought together (in a way unique to Milan) architects, architect-designers, artists, producers, planners and, later, fashion designers and urban theorists. The post-war Triennales 'turned into a necessary pilgrimage for enthusiastic young designers all over the world' (Sparke 1998: 149).

Design always had a central place in the *Triennale*. In 1954 the first international exhibition of industrial design was held at the *Triennale*, and from that point onwards 'the *Triennale* became . . . a place of critical debates around design at an international level' (Casciani 1991: 22). The *Triennales* were not just a forum for Italian design on a world stage, but also for the introduction of ideas concerning other schools of design into Italy. According to Magistretti, it was through the *Triennale* that he and others 'obtained information on Swedish and Danish kitchens, Danish furniture . . . one of the exhibitions at the *Triennale* allowed us to design our first pieces of furniture . . . furniture which contained the seeds of what was to become Italian Design' (*Interview*). At the IX *Triennale* (1951) a section was dedicated to the *Forma dell'utile*, with the first signs of modern design. The layout of the design section, however, lacked imagination and was similar to a kind of shop window approach to the discipline. This approach changed in 1954 (X *Triennale*) where whole interiors were designed for the show by Magistretti and others. In the park, other architect-designers built bars, libraries (which are still there to this day), and a childrens' game-sculpture. Whole houses were constructed within the 1960 exhibition. Yet, the *Triennale* and above all the design aspects of the exhibition came under heavy attack from the left and the purists in the architectural world. Canella, architect and professor at the Milan Politecnico, called the exhibition 'a Vanity-fair for those architects called to organise it' (*Casabella*, Sept 1960; Pansera 1978: 485–7).

The dynamic role of the *Triennale* was to last until May 1968, when the student movement occupied the *Triennale* on its opening day and destroyed parts of the exhibition (De Carlo 1998: 66–70 and the photos 81–92). The crisis sparked off by the occupation led to a suspension of the exhibition until 1973. The whole institution around the exhibition (and the whole idea of 'art' and 'museums') came under heavy attack for their supposedly 'elitist' and market-led management and outlook.[7] Often, design was rejected by these critics as mere 'merceologia' – 'the study of commodities'. Yet, these debates themselves were elitist and exclusionary, blocking any idea of coming to grips with 'mass culture' and the design of everyday objects.

After 1968, the *Triennale* lost its central role on the international scene for both design and architecture, and dedicated itself to internal wrangling. Design promotion and debate moved towards the abstract and artistic critique of *anti-design*, or towards the domination of the institutions and events organized by the

---

7. 'The Viet-Cong guerilla war is a creator of happenings which are much more meaningful than that which is shown within an exhibition of American artists' (protest cited in Pansera 1978: 112).

Milanese *Fiera* for traders and producers. Design became a subject to be studied in university, and various design institutes were set up in Milan and elsewhere. Design began to gain an autonomy from architecture for the first time, reaching a mass public for objects beyond the traditional furniture market, such as coffee makers and classic household objects (see the production of Alessi).[8] A design elite was formed, and the creative cross-over of disciplines so characteristic of the 1950s and 1960s began to disappear. Design's previous 'synergistic relationship to Italian architecture' went into decline (Branzi 1994: 599). The *Triennale* became a repository of the *history* of design, with its rich collection of design objects and its series of exhibitions celebrating and spreading the Milanese design tradition. After years of debate, a design museum was earmarked for inauguration in the ex-industrial zone of Bovisa in 2001.

1.6a. Urban Design: The Pirelli Tower

Designers did not confine their work to interior objects, but also attempted to 'design the city' through the same principles of quality, style and usefulness. The 1947 Triennale built one of the most interesting and (in the long-term) successful planned neighbourhoods in the city, designing everything from windows to chairs to parks to park benches. At the height of the boom Giò Ponti (with the structural engineering genius of Pier Luigi Nervi) gave the city a magnificent example of urban design – 'perhaps the first real project of design on an urban scale, a true monument to this new Milanese discipline' (Branzi 1985: 22; 1984a: 48; La Pietra 1995: 262–9; L. Ponti 1990: 186–91). The Pirelli Tower, finally opened in 1960, stands 127m high and towers over Milan's central station. Even the model for the project was 11m high, displayed at the Fiera (1955–6, Centrokappa 1985: 154) and a work of art in itself. The skyscraper is often the first building noted by new arrivals, especially immigrants during the heady days of the miracle or the second boom of the 1980s–1990s. The tower seems to be made entirely of glass, and has a smooth, thin shape. It glitters in the sun and the internal designs are spectacular, including a vast observation tower and specially designed furniture, lighting, clocks and lifts (Cevini 1996: 102–3). It was not just *a* skyscraper, 'but *the* archetype of a skyscraper – wanted by the Pirelli dynasty as a monument worthy of the company but also dedicated to the whole private Lombard business community' (Ponziani 1977). Over 2,000 people worked within the tower in the 1960s and 1970s, all for Pirelli itself.

8. As Mendini, who has worked for many years with Alessi, puts it, 'the home must represent the mind, the psychological space of a person, even if it is necessarily made up of little things, it must appear big and the objects must provide a lot of satisfaction in their use', Mendini (*Interview*).

Branzi has called the tower 'perhaps the first design project on an urban scale, a real monument' (1984a: 48). Ponti himself compared the transparency of the tower to a crystal. 'Architecture is a crystal . . . pure, clear, strong and lasting' (Ponti 1956). The *Pirellone* became the symbol of the modernity and audacity of the Milan of the economic miracle – 'of that euphoric spirit of economic reconstruction which confirmed the optimistic role of Milan as the "moral capital" of industrial Italy' (Irace 1988: 165; Cevini 1996). It was a perfect combination of the engineering capabilities of the city, represented by Nervi, and the design and modernity of Ponti. The Pirelli was also a symbol of power. Bianciardi's narrator in *La vita agra* comes to the city to blow up the tower. 'Every day I came to look at the *torracchione* of glass and cement . . . my mission was this, to blow up all four towers . . . and throw out the 2,000 people who worked there' (1995: 41). He never succeeds, taken in by the lure of the city, work and money. Lizzani's 1963 film of the book ends with the same character organizing a firework show at the tower. In 1978 Pirelli sold the tower to the Lombard regional government, but the skyscraper has continued to be known as 'the Pirelli' (Cevini 1986: 119–24). The tower, which had often been ignored by Italian architectural critics and historians, was celebrated abroad, becoming a symbol not just of Milan but of *Italian* modernity and the wonders of the boom years. A model of the Pirelli Tower dominated the massive *Italian Metamorphosis* exhibition at the Guggenheim Museum in New York in 1994 (Celant 1994).

1.6b. Urban Design: the MM

A different but no less important example of urban design on a grand scale came with the furnishings and layout of Milan's underground stations after 1964. For the first time, the planning of this type of project was conceived in a unitary fashion and the design of all the stations on the MM1 line (opened after many years of construction in 1964) was assigned to a group of architects under the guidance of Franco Albini (Albini, Herg, Noorda 1965). This studio designed a system of stations with similar signs (Noorda coordinated the graphics of the plan) stairways, shops, walkways, gates, lights, doors, ticket offices and platforms. The design settled on a system of curves dominated by the red of the MM1 line. This system was later adopted, with various modifications, for the second and third underground lines opened in the city in the 1970s and 1990s, and later for numerous other underground systems across the world (who often employed Noorda to design the graphics of the signs) including New York and San Paolo. Noorda and Albini worked together from the start of the project, so that the graphical and architectural sides of the project were integrated organically. Noorda also introduced frequent signs with the name of the station right along the platform, making identification of one's whereabouts much easier than before. The Milanese underground remains one of the best designed and simplest of networks amongst modern urban systems (Noorda, *Interview*). Certain stations contained innovative touches, such as the open air hole in the Central Station stop, or the elaborate system of exits and escalators at San Babila (Grassi and Pansera 1980: 210–11; *Guida di archittetura* 1990: 183).

Albini's functionalist work was received favourably, in general, as the 'only Italian example of the environmental definition of a public transport system through design' (Gregotti 1994b: 245). But critics at the time attacked the uniformity of the designs. 'In a city so lacking in sunlight, asked Fillippini, why not construct a station all in gold? In a city so far from the sea, why not use the sides of an acquarium? In a city with so few trees, why not have a forest-station?' (cited in Casciani 1991: 38). Later critics have concentrated on the 'static coldness' of the stations and the way the project has evolved in the city 'after years of use and lack of care we have the image of a dark and unsafe cave, ready for rapes and suicides' (Casciani 1991: 38).

1.7. Design for Mobility: the Lambretta

The new city of the boom – a bigger and more flexible city than ever before – created strong demand for new means of mobility. The first attempts to create cheap motorized transport came with the scooter. Milan's scooter was the Lambretta, produced in the vast Innocenti complex in Lambrate, to the east of the city (hence the name) using Fordist production techniques (100 scooters a day were being produced by 1948, although the first models were made without a production line). The Lambretta was Milan's response to the much more famous Vespa, produced by Piaggio in Tuscany. Early Lambretta models were built using aircraft technology and designed by Cesare Pallavicino with a 125cc engine and metal tubes. The scooters were created for family use, with space for up to four people on early machines. The horn was at first activated by a foot-pedal. These scooters were also cheap – costing only L.125,000 in 1948, less than the Vespa. The first Lambretta were produced in 1947 and mass production began in 1948. Four million scooters were eventually sold. Through the 1950s the Lambretta underwent various design transformations, becoming smaller and sleeker and losing its two seats. Production finally ceased in 1971, although the Lambretta remains a cult design object and has a place in most of the worlds' design museums (Pansera 1996: 156–8; Gregotti 1994b: 283; Tessera 1995).

This cheap but well-designed machine transformed the lives of millions of urban residents and changed the face of the city. The motor was hidden, allowing people to drive the scooter without covering themselves with dirt, and it was easy to change the tyres. Some parking places were needed, but in general the Lambretta could be left just about anywhere. The unmistakable noise of the scooter filled the days and nights of the city, and families used the bike to make day trips to the countryside outside Milan. For the first time, those without cars were able to move around the city without relying on public transport. This motorization or 'micromobility' affected above all the lives of young people in the city, but also made private vehicles available to the working class (and young people) for the first time. 'Once a means of transport had been obtained, even if it was a modest one, entire life-styles were transformed' (Piccone Stella 1993: 80). Networks of friends widened, as did the ability to cross the city without using inefficient public transport systems, especially on the periphery and late at night, outside of the commuting rhythms of the working day. Scooter ownership helped young people to break out of the suffocating circles of the family, the neighbourhood and the community (Piccone Stella 1993: 79–81). The Lambretta was also seen as a particularly Milanese vehicle (as were Alfa Romeo cars). The new 1962 model was launched by the Mayor of Milan at the time, Cassinis and, as in Turin with Fiat, many workers and Milanese identified with the company and drove Lambrettas in their city.

1.8. The Fiera: the City and the Market

Milan has always been a central market city, a place of exchange and finance dealing for buyers, producers and mediators. In the twentieth century, as we have seen, this role was concentrated in the key market institutions of the city – the Stock Exchange, the *Camera di Commercio* and the Fiera (Pansera 1996: 22–5; 29–34; 40–1). For design companies the *Fiera Campionaria* represented a key moment for the trade and display of new products and the exchange of information. After 1961 the *Salone del mobile* became a key part of the trade year as the great melting pot of the *Fiera Campionaria* began to give way in the 1970s to more specialized events. The *Salone del mobile* began to appear more and more as a mixture of an old-style *Fiera*, a series of artistic events and exhibitions and a huge media happening (Pansera 1996: 46). By 1999 the *Salone* was attracting over 170,000 visitors, 2,300 exhibitors (from 140 different countries) and companies with over 200 events and exhibitions being organized throughout the week and across the city (Cirillo 2000).

Throughout the 1950s and 1960s, the *Fiera Campionaria* (always held in April) attracted architects, designers, manufacturers and advertisers. The preparations for each annual event were elaborate and the results often spectacular. Millions of visitors were confronted with extraordinary exhibits and buildings designed by Italy's top architects (and destined for almost immediate demolition) (Centrokappa 1985: 200–5). Only photographs of these stunning constructions survive (see for example Luciano Baldessari's extraordinary Breda pavilions from 1951–5, Contessi 1995; Celant 1994). The *Fiera* presented itself as a 'city of marvels' and a place for the 'production of dreams' (Pansera 1990: 35; Pansera 1996; Grassi and Pansera 1980; Bigazzi 1996: 13; Centrokappa 1985).

1.9. La Rinascente and Il Compasso d'Oro

A further key factor in the success of Milan as international design capital was the role of the retail firm and department store *La Rinascente*. *La Rinascente* began life as the first modern Italian department store along American lines, opened in the centre of Milan (in Piazza Duomo) in 1918, the shop burnt to the ground only weeks later, and was re-opened in 1921. Damaged again during the war, *La Rinascente* (owned by industrialist Borletti) re-opened in 1950 and quickly became a central part of the retail and advertising sector during the years of the boom, with chains of UPIM stores across the city and the country (Amatori and Sillano 1996: 203–4). *La Rinascente* employed a whole series of designers (from furniture to fashion, including Munari, Gardella and Armani) and prided itself on its role at the heart of Italian consumerism – both setting and following market trends and trading in design products. Shop-windows were organized by top designers and clothes brought in from all over Italy and Europe, 'reflecting the changing conditions of millions of people who had begun to spend more and in different and newer ways' (Petrillo 1992b: 53; Centrokappa 1985: 210–11; 214–5).[9] *La Rinascente*'s profits increased at a greater rate than any other Italian company between 1955 and 1960 and its sales increased by 500 per cent across the whole 1950s (Petrillo 1992b: 48; Francesconi 1994).

In 1954 *La Rinascente* organized the first *Compasso d'oro*, a prize competition for quality design 'to encourage industrialists and artisans to better their production not only technically, but also in terms of form' (Casciani 1991: 22). The annual *Compasso d'oro* quickly became an important occasion for the promotion of design and the exchange of ideas – 'the emblem of the quality of Italian design' (Pansera 1990: 41). The *Compasso d'oro* was open to all kinds of design; from industrial goods and machines, to cars, to ashtrays and rubbish bins. The judges of the prizes were also top designers and often the winners and competitors were exhibited at *La Rinascente* and the *Triennale*. For the 1954 competition 470 firms submitted 5,700 goods, 200 were shown and fifteen prizes awarded (Gregotti 1994b: 284). Early winners included the designer of the Fiat 500, Giacosa, as well as many companies and designers working in the Milan area (ADI 1979). Much space

9. For the role of shop-windows in the consumer boom of the 1950s see the reportage of Baldini 'the city is set free here (in Corso Buenos Aires) with happy impetuosity and reveals all at once its possibilities and temptations: you have in front of you; two kilometres of shops, of lights and swarming pavements'. Baldini noted the importance of this shopping mecca for immigrants, the role of the shopper in the spectacle of the street, the importance of lights and large-size advertising and the absence of churches (1954 in Centrokappa 1985: 210–11).

was dedicated to the most important Milanese product – furniture. In fact, *La Rinascente*, as the last link in the production-consumerism chain, played a key part in the success of the industrial district to the north of the city. For Brustio, commercial director of the company in the 1950s, 'modern furniture was born in Italy with *La Rinascente*' (Centrokappa 1985; 215). For designer Munari the company was a 'school of marketing, of management, of design'.

1.10. Designers, Self-organisation and Publishing

Designers also began to organize themselves in the 1950s, forming the *Associazione per il Disegno Industriale Italiano* (ADI) in Milan in 1956, an organization that also included links to industrialists and critics. Milan became the undisputed centre of design and architecture publishing, producing magazines and publications that dominate the market, promote debate and provide a platform for new ideas and designs. Some of these magazines were linked to individual architects, designers or studios – such as *Domus* (1927–) with Ponti and *Casabella* (1929–) which became a centre of innovative debate under the editorship of Rogers after the war. Other important magazines based in Milan include or included *Il mobile italiano* (1957–60); *Stile industria* (1954–63); *Abitare* (1961–); *Casa Vogue* (1968–); *Modo* (1977–) and *Ottagono* (1966–). Others were produced by specific companies as house-organs (Bontempi 1991: 155–9; Pansera 1996: 45). These magazines, in very different ways, set up networks linking producers, designers, journalists, buyers, 'the public', students, photographers and historians across Italy but above all in Milan and Lombardy.

1.11. 1968 and the Birth of 'Radical Design'

The self-styled radical designers of the 1960s and 1970s paid great attention to the development of the modern city. A particularly influential project was that designed by *Archizoom* (No-stop city) in which 'car parks, residential zones, offices etc. were set up in layers, in an artificial space, as if they were dealing with goods exposed in a supermarket' (Isozaki 1984: 5). The *Archizoom* group, set up in Florence, broke up in the late 1960s and radical design took hold in Milan. All the protagonists of radical and new design projects set up studios in Milan. Andrea Branzi's theoretical work has gone furthest in its examination of the role of design in modern society, the importance of urban change and the study of design history, above all through a series of sophisticated historical studies on design and exhibitions (1996, 1999). Branzi was also behind the important centre for design study and formation, the Domus Academy, set up in 1983. Radical design undoubtedly produced important and innovative work over a long and fruitful period of study and production. However, the 'movement' tended towards an elitism that rejected the ramifications of mass culture. In fact, the pieces produced by radical designers have become expensive works of art, prized by collectors across the world. The push to change and improve the daily lives of ordinary people – as in the early and 'heroic' phase of mass quality design in the 1950s and 1960s following the influence of Rogers and others – was lost. In their disgust for the market and mass culture (and mass production), the radical designers lost all contact with 'the masses' and began to produce provocative work for small circles of collectors, exhibitors and critics whose influence remained entirely within this *milieu*. Their ideas remained (voluntarily) utopian – 'essentially intellectual and conceptual' (Sparke 1998: 202). The shift away from the architect-designer to the pure profession of design was another symptom of the trend away from a practical view of the city as an integrated system. The power of the integrated relationship with the small industrialists and artisans of Lombardy had been broken. But such alliances may only have been possible in the particular circumstances of the boom years.

1.12. Conclusion: Industry, Territory and Design

Milan's design revolution in the 1950s and 1960s and 'Italian style' itself brought together elements of modernity, rationalism, craft skills and artisanship in a heady mix that allowed the survival of traditions of quality and of family-based work organization with large-scale production and innovative technologies. 'Tradition and innovation stood side by side' and there were 'strong links with the domestic sphere' (Sparke 1999: 67, 70).[10] By the 1990s, Milan and its surrounding territory constituted a design *system*. This system was made up of private and public institutions, industries, magazines, designers and studios and a series of services linked to production and advertising of design goods and ideas. The centre of this system was the annual *Salone del mobile*, but design events took place in the city throughout the year, attracting international interest. Yet, the original project to change the city, organically, through a combination of planning, design, architecture and quality production had been lost along the way. Design in the 1990s had been completely detached from any idea of a common project, and was motivated above all by private interests and the large profits being made by design companies across the world. In addition, by the 1980s, the systems of design and fashion had become strongly interlinked as Milan quickly became one of the world's fashion capitals. The *industrial* qualities of design were forgotten as companies concentrated on advertising, image and a quality market, not a quality mass market.

10. Sparke (1999: 63, 70) also argues that this particular historical mix produced a more feminine style within Italian design.

2. Capital of Fashion

2.1. The Rise of the Milanese Fashion Industry: Milan as Fashion Capital

From the first shows in the city in the 1970s, Milan's rise to European fashion capital (with Paris and London) has been meteoric.[11] Over just fifteen years, a generation of designers emerged in the city who were to become famous throughout the world: Armani, Versace, Prada, Ferrè, Dolce & Gabbana. The city became a magnet for those associated with the fashion industry – photographers, models, magazine editors, critics, buyers, manufacturers, commercial traders, journalists. The economic output of the industry has been extraordinary. By the 1990s, fashion and design-based items were accounting for nearly 70 per cent of the profit side of Italy's national balance of payments (Branzi 1999: 7).[12] Six of the worlds' top ten fashion houses were Italian in 1999, and four of these companies were based in Milan (Dolce & Gabbana; Prada; Versace and Armani). There were 50,000 'cultural businesses' of all kinds operating in the city, many of which were linked to fashion (one third of all businesses) (Magatti 2000). Many of these businesses were so-called *micro-imprese,* tiny firms. In the key 'fashion zone' of Porta Ticinese, for example, 41 per cent of local businesses consisted of one or two employees. Many used vast networks of outside collaborators, services and traders to complete their everyday work (Rovati 2000). These micro-businesses were of a whole range of types, from traditional artisan workshops to modern computer-based services.

Fashion easily outgunned all other industries in the city in terms of export capital, and domestically was only rivalled by financial capital, advertising and the mass media. The various fashion weeks (four extended weeks by the end of the 1990s) began to dominate Milanese life. As ever, the political and social institutions were far behind these trends, but the Socialist administrations of the 1980s were the first to court the designers as potential economic allies in their plan to transform Milan into a post-industrial city. Attempts to manage and plan the fashion industry increased in the 1990s with the setting-up of a special fashion office and an assessor for fashion by the local council. Fashion began to be taught

---

11. 'Fashion' is defined after Breward (1995: 5) as 'clothing designed primarily for its expressive and decorative qualities, related closely to the current short-term dictates of the market, rather than for work or ceremonial functions', but it is also a much wider economic, social and cultural system involved in the creation and modification of tastes, habits and ways of living.

12. The fashion industry as a whole had a turnover of L. 35 billion in 1999, with exports amounting to nearly L. 20 billion. Over a million people were directly employed in the industry. Milan was described as the 'world capital of the clothing planet' by Regional President Formigoni in 2000. In 1971 there were 24,000 fashion outlets in Italy, a figure that was to rise to 82,000 by 1981 (Gastel 1995: 39; Ginsborg 1998: 38, 165, 578).

as a university subject in the city and the IULM private university even created a faculty entirely dedicated to fashion.[13]

Milan's rise to fashion capital can been explained in various ways. Milan certainly has a number of advantages over other European and Italian cities as a site for fashion production and commerce. It has strong links to European markets, it is the capital of advertising and private television, its private infrastructure allows for the provision of services so essential to the fashion industry and unavailable in other Italian cities, from photographers to drivers to studios and model agencies. Milan is also the centre of the fashion publishing industry, from *Vogue* and *Amica*, which began publishing in the city in the early 1960s, to the series of fashion magazines which began to proliferate in the 1980s. Moreover, the city possesses the institutional support to run fashion-based events – the *Fiera* (the 'Olympus of fashion') (Gastel 1995: 238), the *Camera di Commercio*, the *Triennale*. Finally, Milan has always had a fashion and clothing industry, based around the historic textile production of upper Lombardy and the silk industries of the Brianza – spark to Italy's first industrial revolution – and the elite seamstresses, hatmakers and tailors of the city itself (Bull and Corner 1993; White 2000: 20). Many of the industrial and strategic factors behind the success of design after the 1950s can also be applied to the growth of fashion (Branzi 1999). Milanese and Italian fashion was not invented in the 1980s and in fact was able to count on a strong tradition of production, marketing, design and an international reputation for quality. As White has written of Italian fashion 'by 1965 it was perceived internationally as of commercially viable high quality, and was already known for its stylish "casual elegance"' (2000: 171).

Milan's market and trading structure allowed for the exchange of sales and production information in the urban networks of trade fairs and special events. After 1969 an annual meeting of traders and producers was held in Berlusconi's *Milano 2* complex. In 1978 *Modit* began to organize two big annual shows at the *Fiera* (forty-five exhibitors in March, seventy-five by October 1978, 200 by 1979). In 1990 this organization was transformed into *Momi-Modit Milano*. The most important organiser of these events, especially in the early period, was the PR-man Beppe Modenese, who decided to create one centralized fashion show to launch Milan as a capital of fashion, and gave most of the key stylists of the 1980s their first opportunities (Vergani 1999: 529–30). The industrial and financial might of the textile manufacturers – most of whom were grouped together in a mega-organization known as GFT – also backed the move to Milan (Vergani 1999: 316). *Modit* became the 'catalyst of and driving-force behind the alliance between fashion design and industry' (Vergani 1999: 531).

---

13. However other projects, such as the so-called City of Fashion (planned for the derelict Garibaldi-Repubblica zone) and the Fashion Museum were suffocated by delays created by bureaucratic and political in-fighting and speculation.

After the boom and the later collapse of heavy industry in the 1970s and 1980s, a market was created both for fashion consumption and fashion production. The consumption of the 1980s was no longer on traditional consumer durables, but branched out into fashion items and status symbols. The post-industrial industry *par excellence* – high fashion – was closely linked to production of clothes for a mass affluent public. High fashion could not live without the ready-to-wear sector, and vice versa. The huge publicity and dream-like qualities of high fashion – with its glamour, its stars, its gossip and its obvious wealth – brought massive attention and publicity to the world of mass production fashion (Grignaffini 1987: 16–25).[14] 'High fashion lives on above all as advertising for everyday fashion' (Volli 1988: 131). Soon, the names of Armani, Dolce & Gabbana and Prada were to be famous (and worn) throughout the world. Labelled clothes (and shoes, bags, and sunglasses) became the status symbols of the 1980s and 1990s, and were copied shamelessly by contraband street traders. The rush to buy stimulated by the miracle had filled Italian homes with televisions and washing machines, and their garages with cars and scooters. The rush to spend of the second boom filled their wardrobes with designer suits.

Fashion also crossed-over into the well-established realms of architecture and design in the city. Fashion designers branched out beyond clothing, shoes and bags into perfumes, jewellery, glasses and sunglasses, watches and even cars. The new designer head offices were all planned by leading architects. By the end of the 1990s, some fashion designers had begun to produce complete ranges of furniture and open outlets completely dedicated to what had traditionally been seen as 'design' items.

2.2. Fashion, the Image of Milan and the 'Block of Gold'

The rise to fashion capital transformed Milan's image, especially abroad. Tourists came to Milan above all to 'see' the fashion and to buy it and Japanese tourist tours concentrated on the top Milanese fashion outlets. Guides distributed free at Malpensa airport concentrated on exclusive shopping and published translations in Japanese (*Shopping Milano* 2000). A *Milano Fashion Tour*, set up in 2000, took in the streets of fashion with the addition of a few art attractions. From a grey, industrial city, Milan's image became that of an exclusive, glittering and stylish shopping metropolis. Few of these tourists saw the bleak periphery of the city. Few were able to take in a tour of the monotonous small industrial districts of the Brianza and around Como, producers of much of the raw material for the fashion boom. Foreign journalists, so important to the image of Milan abroad,

---

14. For an unashamedly apocalyptic account of the fashion industry and the close relationship between mass culture, advertising and fashion see Volli (1988).

began to project the idea of Milan as a fashion capital, as the city of the future (Vargiù 1997: 125; *Life* 1 October 2000; 5 March 2000).

Fashion has an intimate connection with the layout of the city of Milan, and in particular with certain central zones. By the 1980s, the well-to-do area around the four streets of Via Montenapoleone, Via della Spiga, Via Sant'Andrea and Corso Venezia and had become known as the 'fashion block', or the 'block of gold'. These streets were dominated by over 500 elegant fashion outlets, with all the major designers opening stores in this area. The pavements themselves were also immaculately kept, with carpets, plants and other street-decorations (Dragone 1998: 390). This zone appeared and felt differently to other central zones, it gave off a strong image of wealth and (expensive) style. The shops themselves were unlike normal shops. They were unwelcoming and exclusive. They were not meant for 'normal' shoppers, or even for shopping – but for show, or for very rich tourists. The shop-window city of Milan found its perfect reflection in the shop-windows of the golden block, perfectly designed and unfeasibly expensive. This was a place of image above substance, the showcase of the post-industrial city, the heart of the capital of fashion. 'Abroad, everybody has heard of the "block of gold"' (Vargiù 1997: 128). Tourist guides directed people here with lists of shops and maps and the 'site' of the 'block of gold' became one of the most visited zones of the city, far surpassing Milans' rich art galleries. Many visits limited themselves entirely to the 'golden block' reducing Milan effectively to an exclusive shopping mall.

Via Montenapoleone has traditionally been seen as a fashion-dominated street (and the symbol of the Milan aristocratic zone – the city's 'drawing-room'): well-before the fashion explosion of the 1990s. In the post-war period the war Via Montenapoleone had begun to rival *La Galleria* as a zone where wealth was displayed and where the rich exchanged information and favours. This position was maintained and reinforced throughout the 1980s and 1990s, as the street became the 'backbone of the consumerist circuits of fashion' in the city (Vergani 1999: 538–9). In Via Sant'Andrea the shops lining the street read like a litany of fashion history – on the right Missoni, Doriani, Marisa, Chanel, Costume, National, Moschino, Lang, Fendi, Scavia, and so forth, and on the left Marisa, Pasquali; Trussardi; Armani, Kenzo; Fusco; Ferrè; Guidi; Prada: Hermes (Alberoni in Vergani 1999: 690–1). In fact, very few shops *not* linked to fashion remain in the street, which was once dominated by antique-dealers, as property prices have reached incredible levels. Via Della Spiga became a fashion street before Via Sant'Andrea, with the first modern boutiques in the 1960s. Since then, 'the invasion, here, has been total' (Vergani 1999: 203–4), with the inauguration of at least thirty-eight stylist and fashion outlets. This particular part of the city remains a showcase for the fashion industry, and a concrete example of the wealth and urban power of that industry in the Milan of today. As the 1990s wore on, the 'block of gold' began to spread beyond these streets to the whole historic centre of the city, to *La*

Galleria itself and the Brera zone. Central Milan was well on the way to becoming, exclusively, a fashion centre at the cost of all other economic, social and cultural activities.

2.3. Fashion, Design, Politics and the 1980s

> Fashion is the first metaphor of power . . . Fashion has designed a victorious political-economic-social system, above all in the symbolic realm. (Volli 1988: 138, 142)

As fashion began to dominate the city, economically, in the 1980s, links began to emerge between *la moda*, politics and the urban scene. The Socialist administration of the 1980s, inspired by the post-industrial politics of Bettino Craxi, embraced the disappearance of heavy industry from the city and formed strong alliances with the fashion industry. Political style was placed above substance in the Socialist Milan of *Milano da bere* (see Chapter 8 below for a full discussion of this period). Many fashion designers worked directly for PSI politicians and in return received the go-ahead for a series of economic and urban projects, and permission to hold fashion shows in a wide range of urban institutions, from *La Scala* to the *Triennale* to the Stock Exchange to the Racing Track to the Central Station.[15] This alliance worked at all levels, from the design of clothes for the opening night of La Scala, to advice over political presentation and congress organization.

The most lasting link at this level was that between Trussardi and the Socialists in Milan. Trussardi designed a series of gadgets and outfits for PSI events. In the 1980s the designer was allowed to build a huge temporary arena on the north-west edge of the city. This arena became known as *PalaTrussardi* and was inaugurated with perhaps the most famous event of the *Milano da bere* years, a Frank Sinatra concert attended by the Milanese political and economic elite in all its glory. This concert is often cited as a kind of peak of Craxian kitsch (Dalla Chiesa, 1995: 39, Stajano 1993: 55). Trussardi was also one of the first designers to create a kind of cultural space in the centre of Milan – opposite *La Scala* in *Piazza della Scala* – with the inauguration of his *Marino alla Scala Palazzo* in 1995. This multi-functional building played host to exhibitions, fashion shows, congresses and meetings, as well as an exclusive restaurant and bar. The idea of 'fashion' as part of an elaborate and elitist life-style was encapsulated in the elegant rooms of the Marino Palace, visible to almost all visitors and residents of the city of Milan and extremely close to the seat of political power in the city – Palazzo Marino. Even the choice of name for Trussardi's Palazzo seemed to indicate the

---

15. Trussardi's shows used spaces in the city which had never been used before. He attempted with some success to free fashion from the elitist and business-dominated arenas of the *Fiera*, giving the industry a high public visibility in Milan for the first time, see http://www.trussardi.it for the full chronology of his shows in the 1980s and 1990s. Trussardi was also one of the first stylists to branch out from clothing to gadgets, tiles, bicycles and interior design.

political weight he held in the city in the 1980s and 1990s (Borioli in Vergani 1999: 774–5).

An even more direct link between fashion, design and politics was that between designer Filippo Panseca and the Socialist Party. Panseca became, over time, the official designer for the PSI and his most famous work was for the Party at the height of its powers, especially the organization of the 1989 PSI Congress in Milan. This congress saw the Socialists embrace the end of Milanese industrial society through a combination of high-tech glamour and choice of location. The congress was held in one of the most famous ex-factories of the city, the huge Ansaldo factory complex which had been purchased by the city council after its final closure in 1986. In the 1950s the factory still employed around 5,000 workers.

The PSI intended the congress to symbolize the birth of a 'modern' post-industrial city and the creation of a political style to fit with that new epoch. For the occasion, Panseca designed a huge pyramid-television screen which projected the speaker at any particular moment. Panseca had also been behind the new symbol of the PSI, a red rose, which replaced the former hammer and sickle. The pyramid captured the attention of journalists, supporters and critics of the Party. The congress, attended by over 1,100 delegates, also continued the personalization of Italian politics around the figure of Craxi. His two-and-a-half-hour speech, projected onto the pyramid behind him, was interrupted ninety-eight times by applause. The congress lasted for six days. Most contemporary and later accounts of both this specific congress (whose short-term political decisions have all but been forgotten) concentrate on the pyramid and the design of the congress itself. Image had not just overtaken substance, but completely replaced it.[16]

The rise of Milanese fashion in the 1980s has been depicted by historians and commentators in two extreme ways. Some link the decline of Milan to the success of the fashion industry and its links with the 'rampant' capitalism inspired by the 1980s boom and the Socialist Party. In this version, corruption, the decline of communitarian industrial society, the abandonment of socialist ideals and the frivolity of fashion go hand in hand. This disgust for *Milano da bere* was particularly strong amongst certain groups of intellectuals and journalists, many of whom participated in the periodical *Società Civile*. The other version of Milan's transformation was diametrically opposed to this one. Milan had triumphantly moved, without trauma, from an industrial to a post-industrial society through the rapid growth of industries based around fashion, services and finance capital. This version was carried forward, of course, by the Socialist administration and its supporters, but also by large sectors of the Milanese bourgeoisie and middle classes,

16. See *Panorama*, 25 June 1989, Biagi (1989), the daily papers from the period of the congress (May 1989), *La Repubblica*, 20 Jan. 2000 and Stajano (1993): 18. Later administrations have built even closer links with the world of fashion and design. Mayor Albertini was persuaded to dress up in designer flip-flops and even in underpants by stylist Valentino in the late 1990s.

who benefited from the short-lived but heady boom of the 1980s, and from the much longer boom of the 1990s.

In reality neither extreme version captured the complicated truth about the city. Milan had been able to overcome the closure of a series of traditional industries through rapid re-employment and growth of other forms of industry. Thus, the city never experience the scorched-earth de-industrialization of many other urban areas. This process was due to many different factors, from the historical mixed-industry role of the city (Milan never was an *industrial* city *tout court*), to its regional and European strategic role and its ability to provide services and capture the role of fashion capital, for example, at a time of enormous growth. However, this change also brought with it a decline in solidarity and old-style communitarian values, however mythologised these may have been. The Socialists *did* govern through systematic corruption (which involved all the major and minor political parties) and their embrace of fashion was, at best, in extremely bad taste and at worst the promotion of greed, conspicuous consumption and individualism. Nonetheless, the administration was also, and perhaps above all, a *reflection* of Milanese culture and society in the 1980s, and the success and power of post-industrialism was above all a mass movement which corresponded with dramatic and wholesale cultural changes in the city and Italy as a whole.

2.4. Five Milan-based Designers: Fiorucci, Armani, Versace, Prada, Dolce & Gabbana

With the meteoric rise of Milan to fashion capital, certain key designers and companies came to be associated with the city and based their work in Milan. The first designer to break with the suffocating traditionalism of the Florence show-rooms was Walter Albini, who held his first show in Milan in 1971 (Vercelloni in Vergani 1999: 14–17; Morini and Bocca 1987: 70–7). In Florence (at Palazzo Pitti), which held shows only twice a year, only twenty companies were able to participate and the whole event lasted for a mere one-and-a-half hours. Albini and others broke with Florence and with the fixed calendars and rigid rules of the Palazzo Pitti shows. They experimented with new arenas and new marketing methods away from the exclusive styles of the elitist fashion of Florence.

The ground for the success of pop fashion and youth fashions had already been laid in the late 1960s by an innovative entrepreneur, Elio Fiorucci. Fiorucci's anarchic central stores sold a huge variety of goods at low prices, basing their trade on the shops of London's Carnaby Street. Quickly, Fiorucci's often bizarre outfits became popular with Milanese youth (although ignored and despised by all those involved in the student movements after 1968) and his shops (particularly the large three-story store in the central Corso *Vittorio Emanuele*, with its bright lights, rock music and beautiful shop assistants) were a magnet for visitors from the whole region. Fiorucci broke with traditional specialized shopping, providing the opportunity for fashion stylists and other designers to reach a much wider and younger public. The whole experience of shopping was revisited, becoming an occasion for meeting people and social behaviour, not a chore. After opening his first shop in Milan in 1967, and a second massive store in the city in 1974, Fiorucci enjoyed huge economic success, and was able to build a chain of 600 stores in ten years. Fiorucci was also the forerunner of the stylists of the 1980s, designing his own pair of signed jeans and other garments.[17]

The new breed of designers in Milan came to prominence in very different ways, and created a new kind of economic entity – a mixture of designer, artist, film-star, businessman and celebrity. The first stylist to make his name internationally via the Milan scene was Giorgio Armani. After moving to Milan from his home-town of Piacenza in the early 1950s, Armani worked in the fashion department of *La Rinascente* from 1954–60, helping at first to organize the shop-window collection, and then as a fashion buyer. After working on his own designs with Cerutti, Armani went solo in 1974. His 'classic' 'postmodern' jackets and suits became a by-word for Milanese style throughout the world and Armani himself became famous, appearing on the cover of *Time* in 1982 (Codeluppi 1996).[18] By the mid-1980s, the Armani corporation had become one of the top five fashion companies in the world, with luxurious head offices in Milan and the production of glasses and sunglasses, perfumes and furniture. Armani never played the political role of Trussardi, preferring the 'pure' arena of business to the dirty realm of day-to-day politics. His alliance with the textile giant GFT in 1978 cemented his role at the centre of the vast and complicated mass production quality fashion industry (Vergani 1999: 30–4). Armani also occupied parts of the city as almost permanent promotional spaces. A vast wall close to the central Corso Garibaldi was host to Armani advertising, and the frequent changes to this 'exhibit' achieved a high level of visibility within the city, symbolizing the fashion-image of post-industrial Milan. Armani has often criticized the 'spectacular' aspects of the fashion system and fashion shows, often preferring to concentrate on more simple and popular designs which reached a wide audience (Giacomoni 1984: 65–71).

Gianni Versace came to Milan as far more of an outsider than Armani. Born in the southern city of Reggio Calabria (in a family of tailors), Versace represents in some ways the antithesis of the cool style of Armani. Versace's designs are

17. Grecchi Ruscone (1987: 50–3). Fiorucci's influence on a whole generation of designers has been immense, such as Dolce & Gabbana.

18. The film *American Gigolo* (1980), where Richard Gere's suits were designed by Armani, was extremely important for the stylists international success: 'the unforgettable elegance of Gere imposed in the collective mind the Armani style' (Mereghetti 1997: 80). By 1997 Armani's companies had a turnover of nearly 2000 billion lire with 2000 shops and outlets worldwide.

borderline kitsch, inspired by a whole range of cultural references none of which owe anything to understatement. Versace's first trip to Milan in 1972 led to various designs for Milanese companies. In 1976 the Versace family formed a company in the north carrying Gianni's name. The first collections were shown in 1978, and within twenty years the company had an annual turnover of 1,700 billion lire. Versace based much of his success on the astute use of publicity campaigns and the star system. The rise of the 'top model', in fact, is closely associated with the organization of Versace's collections. Versace also appeared on the cover of *Time*, in 1995. Much more than Armani, Versace's production emphasized his massive wealth (as in the re-designing of a number of Milanese and American palaces) as well as that of his clients and cultural circle (Carloni 1999a: 798–801; Giacomoni 1984: 25–8; Morini and Bocca, 1987). Versace's funeral in 1997 saw a whole range of the rich and the powerful turn out in Milan's Cathedral to pay homage to the man who had symbolized the city's role as fashion capital of the 1980s and 1990s.

Dolce & Gabbana represent the new breed of fashion designers who broke through in the 1990s. Interested above all in 'youth' fashions, the *D & G* label conquered world markets in that decade. Following their first show at the *Fiera* in 1985 and the opening of their first shop in the same year, Dolce & Gabbana had surpassed both Armani and Versace in terms of turnover and profits by the end of the 1990s. *D & G* can claim to be true post-modern designers, borrowing from a whole host of half-remembered cultural references, many of which originate in Italian cinema and art, and producing cheap but stylish clothes for the young and the very young (Asnaghi 1999: 219–20). The 'new Mediterranean style' of *D & G* quickly became hegemonic not just amongst Italian youth, but also that of Europe and America. Like Versace, *D & G* became part of the world star system, centred on the fashion, music and film industries and encapsulated by their designs for Madonna's world tour in 1993.

Prada, unlike Dolce & Gabbana or Versace, has its origins in the pre-war Milanese fashion industry and have long-term links with the city's historic production of quality fashion goods and luggage. As with many successful fashion companies in the city, the status of the Prada label enjoyed a exponential rise in the 1990s, especially in Japan. Prada, concentrating on minimalist shoes and bags, had built up an empire encompassing eight factories and sixty shops by the end of the 1990s, as well as links to over 120 shops outside of Italy. Prada's success signalled something of a turn away from the extravagant fashions of *Milano da bere* towards classic and lasting items, although it was also the result of an aggressive marketing campaign (Carloni 1999b: 625–7). Prada's shops, especially the store in *La Galleria*, became the focus of mass buying and the first port of call for most fashion tourists. However, Prada's meteoric rise from a small artisan luxury good producer to a world fashion leader began outside of Milan itself, especially through shows in New York. This trend perhaps signalled, at its apparent height, the beginning of a long decline in the centrality of Milan within the world fashion industry.

2.5. Fashion and the City: the Impact of Fashion Week

The impact on the city of the rise of fashion can be seen in a number of ways. The landscape of the city has changed above all the centre of the city around San Babila and the *Duomo*, areas now dominated by fashion shops and outlets to the exclusion of almost all other industries. But fashion has also had dramatic effects on the rhythms of the city. The fashion industry does not work on a nine-to-five basis, like other industries, or from September to September. Fashion is based around a series of launches, shows and events, which are concentrated into particular moments of the year. For Milan, there are at least four such moments in any one twelve-month period – male and female summer fashions and male/female winter fashions. Other, lesser events, are scattered throughout the year. Most of the vast and variegated services which go towards the production of a collection and the organization of a show are concentrated in these particular weeks or days.

During the busiest periods – womens' and mens' 'fashion weeks' (the week lasts nine days) held in February and at the end of September and January and June respectively – at least 100,000 models, critics, buyers, tourists and producers descend on the city. Three-hundred-and-fifty shows are packed into each 'week'. The hotels are booked months in advance and traffic is often gridlocked right across the city. These city users and business users (see Chapter 8) bring vast resources into the city, but also cause problems for the everyday activities of those not involved directly in the fashion industry. Fashion shows have, in recent years, spilled out from the traditional trade fair halls into a variety of locations, from the top of the Pirelli tower to the *Triennale* to the Labour Union offices. *La Galleria* was host to a vast, televised fashion show on the final day of the 'week'.

In general, the city was being used as one vast fashion hall, with spaces opening up and closing for short exhibitions and displays which then moved on for another year. All this underlined the 'post-industrial' nature of the fashion industry – no fixed times, no fixed places, no gates, no clocking on or clocking off, no (obvious) uniforms, no fixed pay day. Fashion remains an industry built around a few huge businesses – the big designers, the big photographic agencies the most important retail distribution networks – and thousands of tiny businesses, working to flexible times and hours and geared up towards these vast displays of fashion, or to the quieter production of varied goods throughout the year (Bovone 1997, 1999). Milan's economy and rhythms were dominated by fashion as the new millennium began, and the political, social and cultural effects of this industry had permeated into all levels of Milanese society.

The Milanese Urban Periphery: Myth and Reality, 1950–2000

Milan today is the periphery. (Motta and Pizzigoni 1991: 11)

The future is peri-urban. We must stop considering the hinterland as a indescribable horror, as an illegitimate and residual part of the city. (Martinotti 1997)

The periphery points us towards a new reflection on society, on its habits and changes, on our capacity to represent it, understand it and predict its developments. (Secchi 1992)

Much contemporary debate on the city concentrates on what is known in Italy as *la periferia urbana* – the urban fringe, the suburbs, the outer city. In fact, it is almost impossible to study urban history without a deep understanding of the periphery. Milan's urban fringe has always occupied an important place in the image and the daily life of the city. During Italy's first industrial revolution, the periphery saw the first real working class neighbourhoods develop next to metalwork and engineering factories. In the 1950s and during the economic miracle, these older peripheries were surrounded by massive public and private housing projects that re-shaped the landscape. Over the last twenty years, the city has changed again – with the growth of the *città diffusa* (spread-out city), the closure of most heavy industry and the increasing individual mobility of residents, city users and commuters. Throughout this whole period, the periphery has largely been seen as a problem, as a crisis, in negative terms. Political and planning discourse has put the periphery at the centre of its proposals and considerations. Debates over the future of the city (and not just Milan) have focused on the 'recupero' of the periphery, on its 'requalification', on its 'socialization'.

This chapter aims to examine these debates, and the changes in the Milanese periphery over the last fifty or so years, through an analysis of a series of descriptions of the periphery, of ways of looking at these areas, and of the various diagnoses put forward for the cure of the illness which supposedly afflicts the urban fringe. Two arguments lie at the heart of this work. First, the exposure of a fundamental confusion over the meaning of 'the periphery' – for Milan but not only for Milan. Second, the deeply problematic ways in which peripheries – and their problems – have been represented and various solutions proposed. Above all, I will argue that many of the critical analyses of the periphery conform to stereotypical and simplistic representations of these complex areas and that most of the solutions to the 'problems' of the periphery adhere to a ideal-city-type image which is both antiquated and unrealistic – which is both out-of-date and never has been 'in date'. Furthermore, these problems (and the periphery itself) are not as 'new' as they are depicted, and many were in fact already present in the peripheries of the early twentieth century or even before.

The main bulk of this chapter will be destructive – breaking down existing and deep-rooted depictions of the periphery. The concluding section will point towards the construction of new methodological approaches for future analysis of urban territory.

1. Definitions of the Periphery: Where is the Periphery?

A first confusion concerns the *location* of the urban periphery. Taken literally, we are dealing with a zone at the edge of city centres – in Milan's case an urban 'belt' – an area that is *not* the centre. Yet, this banal definition captures little of what is meant by 'the periphery' within political debates or at the level of everyday perception and experience. In fact, the periphery can be defined in a whole series of ways (few of which are incompatible with the others).

1.1. The Periphery as a Well-defined Urban Zone

This is the technical definition of the periphery – but even here, and even for one city, there is no agreement. The periphery moves around. In the 1970s a well-known book (Boffi, Cofini, Giasanti, and Mingione, 1972) identified the Milanese zones of Isola and Garibaldi as 'peripheral'. Today, nobody would make a similar claim. The gentrification of the city centre (and these zones) and the expansion of the 'urban' territory, plus the shorter travel times introduced by mass public transport have pushed out the physical periphery to more external zones. In the 1960s Milan's local administration carried out a detailed survey of fifty-two zones that were termed 'peripheral' – many of these would not be seen as being so today. When the Comasina housing estate was completed in 1958 it was surrounded by fields and lacked basic road links to the rest of the city. Today, the zone is part of an extensive and unbroken urban sprawl, and has fast accessibility to 'Milan' itself.

The periphery is a historical and continually changing formation, not linked to any specific distances/measurements. It can be (and has been) argued that the whole idea of the periphery is meaningless in a situation of extended urban form and changing territorial patterns right across northern Italy. This remains to be seen, but does not alter the centrality of debates over (and experiences of) the periphery in contemporary Milan. In addition, we can make useful historic distinctions between different forms of periphery. The classic distinction here is between the *old* periphery and the *new* periphery, where the former contains those zones linked to the first industrial revolution (early 1900s) and the second encompasses those zones which were created during the miracle (1950s and 1960s). Already, we are starting to break down the concept of the periphery (and it is a good moment to start talking about *peripheries*) into constituent parts. Certain well-defined characteristics have traditionally been associated with these two types of peripheries. The old periphery (in Milan) is the classic, mythical, working-class neighbourhood, where residence and workplace were tightly linked, where a community existed, where the typical housing form was *di ringhiere* (courtyard blocks with long shared balconies and small flats). The new periphery is the classic, mythical 'self-sufficient' public housing project, where residence and workplace were totally separated, where no community existed, and where the typical housing form was the anonymous tower block.

1.2. The Periphery as Way-of-Life

Thus, as well as being associated with certain images and geographical locations, the periphery can also be seen (and has been seen) as encompassing certain *ways of life* – as an anthropological state. Most positively, this association is linked to those features of the old peripheries I have outlined – community, face-to-face daily relationships, solidarity, resistance and (in a particularly Milanese context) hard work, honesty, simplicity and thrift. More negatively, the link is with the 'typical' features of the new peripheries – desocialization, emptiness, unemployment, familism, crime. In the 1960s and especially in the 1990s, the link between the periphery and crime solidified in the public mind. Hence our third possible characterisation of the periphery.

1.3. The Periphery as Bronx/Badlands/ 'Zona a Rischio'

> Here the desolation of the people can be touched and is at the same level as the structural decline of the buildings. (*La Repubblica*, 18 February 1993)

Certain zones, over time, have gained a reputation as crime-ridden no-go areas, as dangerous places. This is true for every city in the world (and sometimes for *whole* cities – Naples, New York, Los Angeles, Bogota for example). These reputations, justified or not, have an immense power over citizens both from these zones and from elsewhere. People's residence choice, their movement around the city, their day-to-day and minute-to-minute activities, the way they move around and through the city are all conditioned by these reputations and stereotypes. It is often difficult for people from these zones to gain employment if they give their correct address. Taxi drivers will often not take passengers to the zones in question. Housing prices will be lower in particular streets and blocks. Of course, there is nothing new about the stigmatization of certain zones of cities – as Booth's maps of London from the early twentieth century show (1902) or the novels of Dickens (1987) or the studies of social historians White (1986) and Stedman-Jones (1971). There is often a strong link (within the reputation or stereotype) made between immigration (usually fairly recent immigration) and the problems of these zones – here an ethnic link is made between crime, decline and urban space. Sometimes these zones will actually become nicknames, or labels attached to their residents. Concrete examples of such zones in Milan are Quarto Oggiaro (from the 1960s onwards) and 'Via Bianchi' in the 1990s.[1] Similar 'ghettoization', both physically and in terms of status distinctions, was discovered by Virciglio in his work on Sicilian immigrants at Asti (a medium-sized town near Turin), where the poorest ended in the 'Casermone' (literally 'very big house'), 'an enormous space' in the centre of town a 'ghetto for thousands of immigrants'. Later, in the 1970s, many of these families were 're-ghettoized' in a peripheral quarter known as Praia: 'even today the label "praiano" . . . often takes on negative and prejudicial connotations' (Virciglio 1991: 88–96).

The eight tower blocks in Via Artom were built in 1965–6 next to the largest car factory in Western Europe – Fiat Mirafiori in Turin. By 1966 most of the 780 flats were occupied. At first, there were no streets, only mud. With time, the social situation hardly improved. There were no shops, no bar and most of the doorbells were burnt by vandals. By 1996 the council was planning the demolition of the towers and the re-housing of their 45,000 residents. The residents felt marginalized: 'we are simply "those from Via Artom"' said one, 'they call it the "Bronx"' complained another. 'If we want to find work, we have to put another address on our identity cards.' A local councillor summed up the desperation not just of the residents, but also of the administrators, in the face of Via Artom – 'here what is needed is dynamite' (Meletti 1996).

Such a depiction of the periphery leads us down certain paths. First, there is an absolute dislocation between the actual 'peripheral' (in the literal sense of *non-central*) nature of the area involved and its characterization *as* peripheral. Given, this definition, a peripheral area could easily be in the city centre. The peripheral nature of the space is no longer linked in any way with a sense of spatial isolation or distance (and perhaps we are closer here to the constructions of 'inner cities' familiar from British debates). Second, these situations are obviously historically

---

1. For the concept of the Bronx and the stigmatisation of neighbourhoods and their residents see Wacquant, (1993). See also, in no order of preference, Simon (1991), Davis (1990) Wolfe (1987), Lemann (1991: Chapter 4) and for the UK Campbell (1993 and 1984) and Hudson (1994). For Paris, Masperò (1994) and the film *La Haine* (Mathieu Kassovitz,1995).

determined and contingent. A zone can be dangerous, or be seen as dangerous, in one historical moment, and be transformed, image-wise or in reality, in another.[2] This transformation is often associated stereotypically with gentrification, but can also be linked to a series of sociological processes or simply to economic change. There are a whole series of shifting mental and physical borders (or frontiers) at work here which come into play and which map out the city for every citizen. The urban mosaic is rebuilt every day and every journey through the city, every local news report, every overheard anecdote is a contribution to that rebuilding process.

1.4. The Periphery as Other

The negative image of the Milanese periphery – especially the so-called *new* periphery marks these areas as places to avoid – on a daily basis, to live in, to drive through. Nobody willingly chooses to live in any city's 'Bronx'. This is the periphery as Other, as the negative twin to the good urban stereotype of the tranquil, well-to-do neighbourhood or the classic working-class quarter. This Otherness is not only a result of the presumed or real dangers originating from the periphery, but also physical, real and visual – an Otherness that can be touched and smelt. Hence, the decline of certain neighbourhoods – which sometimes originates with their very birth – is symbolized by real features of the houses, the inhabitants, the roads: burnt-out cars, graffiti, rubbish. Others are marked by actual buildings with names – the tower blocks at Quarto Oggiaro, the no-go streets of Via Bianchi,[3] the wastelands of Villapizzone near Bovisa in Milan. One of our main tasks in the rest of this chapter will be to flesh out this Otherness, to try to understand its character, content and development over time.

2. Images of the Periphery – Stereotypes and Reality

One of the best ways to understand the periphery is through photographs and film. In the 1960s a series of photographers visited the new peripheries of Milan to record the city as it expanded. Very few were able to avoid the rhetoric of the city/ country contrast in their work: of which a classic example is the shot by Carrieri taken through fields towards towerblocks (and see the whole of Carrieri 1959 and Chiaramonte 1995: 37–49; Zannier 1994: 323). More interesting work takes in

2. For the creation of danger and moral panics, located in the Britain of the 1970s, see the seminal work of Hall, Crichter, Jefferson, Clarke, and Roberts (1978).

3. In 1991 this no-go neighbourhood ('the illegal city . . . a neighbourhood where the state is absent') was 'discovered' by journalists on Milan's periphery. The residents were being forced to ask permission to enter and leave their own homes and a tram stop had been moved after a series of attacks on drivers, *Corriere della Sera*, 9 June 1991. 'Via Bianchi' dominated the Milanese press for the rest of June.

the people of the periphery, but even here, much of the material is purely critical, more interested in shock value than description or analysis. Film and the periphery have never had an easy relationship in Milan, but with *Rocco and his Brothers* (1960) the Milanese periphery began to be given a visual identity. Visconti's meticulous research picked out a series of extraordinary urban settings for some of the most important scenes in the film. These spaces had never been filmed before, and many Milanese were simply unaware of their existence. A key architectural moment in the film is the scene that looks at the southern migrant's first house in the city. This building is at the same time a stunning visual creation and a bleak, monotonous block. Visconti's periphery was still a badlands, but it was also something more, something beautiful and stark, as in the white light of the final scene. *Rocco and his Brothers* opened the way towards a more open aesthetic approach to the periphery.

3. Constructions of the Periphery: What is the Periphery?

We need to delve deeper into the various ways in which the periphery has been analysed to understand the place of this difficult but essential part of the city over the last fifty years. The periphery has been seen in manifold ways by different writers, planners, architects and historians. Most of these representations take their cue from an ideal-city form against which the periphery is contrasted.

3.1. The Periphery as Anti-city or Non-city

There is nothing remotely geographical about the place. (Masperò 1994: 20)

Often, the periphery is described as an 'anti-city' or even a 'non-city' (De Rita 1990: 55–62). Why? First, because of the supposed lack of the classic features of most modern cities – squares, shopping streets, cobbles, order, monuments. Second, because of a kind of lack of identity and history that is applied to the (especially new) peripheries. These new neighbourhoods are analysed as rootless – without the traditions, cultures and landscapes of the traditional city. Third, because of yet another lack – of boundaries, of signs, of recognizable monuments or buildings.[4] Here surveys are used to prove that peripheral residents (although many argue that they do not actually live *in periferia*) are divided over where the borders to their neighbourhoods are and where the centre is (Bianchi and Perussia 1988; Bianchi 1990; Guiducci 1993). Guiducci argues that these neighbourhoods 'do

---

4. The lack of boundaries label is also applied to the whole of Milan, see for example Macri (1995: 227). For Camagni, 'most citizens do not know where Milan ends (or begins)' (1994: 9). Secchi, in contrast, writes of a proliferation of boundaries, 'a thousand frontiers' (1992).

not possess on the whole their own centre, a characteristic monument, an important church or anything which distinguishes them' (1993: 16). The main limitations with this kind of critique lie in the lack of analysis of the past, and in the model of an ideal city used. It is assumed, almost without argument, that we all should aspire to a kind of clearly bordered neighbourhood-community ideal with an agreed centre – a kind of peripheral (ancient) Athens.

A number of questions emerge: first, *why should this be the model for a neighbourhood or a city?*[5] A more interesting question would be not why do people not agree on the boundaries of their own 'neighbourhoods', but why should they agree? There seems to be the image of an ideal neighbourhood here which appears more like a village with a central *piazza* than a modern city (or as a non-industrial city like Naples) This model is not even Fordist but pre-industrial. Second, did this type of neighbourhood ever exist? Why should people know where the centre is? Why should there be a centre at all? In reality there are a series of different and competing city/neighbourhood models, not just that summarized by these theorists/ sociologists (who make no attempt to demonstrate that this ideal past was ever there, or argue that their model is a preferable one).[6] It is also clear that the whole concept of 'boundary' being used here is defunct. These surveys only talk about physical, obvious, visual boundaries – and yet the subjective experience of every citizen creates and recognize a series of semi-invisible micro-boundaries that are not necessarily linked to physical forms of signs with words written upon them. They can often be seen, but they can often only be heard or even smelled, or just dreamed. As Amendola has written with regard to urban fear:

> the inhabitant of New York or London is able to understand immediately from the state of doorways or light-fittings, from the speed of taxis and from the expressions of by-standers, from micro-signs present on walls and in shop windows if s/he has gone through one of the numerous invisible boundaries present in the city and has entered a dangerous neighbourhood. (1995: 16–19)

As one moves through the historic centre of Naples, it is very simple, as a stranger, within a distance of ten yards, to move from a situation of absolute safety (subjectively) to one of fear/danger.[7]

---

5. It seems to me that this kind of model also emerges from the influential work of Rogers (1997).

6. For example, Melis and Martinotti (1998: 16) state simply that 'once upon a time there was a city . . . with a precise social, cultural and architectural identity'.

7. It is perhaps this very unpredictability of the city – this identity of difference – which gives urban dwellers not only a constant sense of excitement/danger but also a constant reinforcement of their own identity in confrontation with a myriad of Others, see Solà-Morales (1994: 184–9) and Sennett's (1990) walk through Manhattan, as well as Benjamin (1971).

Finally, the term *anti-city* (Tonon and Consonni 1976) has been used – with regards to the old and the new peripheries – as a way of indicating a kind of latent or actual opposition to the values of the 'bourgeois' city. This definition is reinforced by classic photographic images contrasting city and countryside and by the evocation of the countryside in memories of urban residents who recall peripheries as borderline zones. Many residents born in the 1960s or urban immigrants from those years can remember horses being kept in courtyards and farm animals being driven through the streets. But *anti-city* also signifies specific sets of sub-cultures – both for working-class neighbourhoods in the early part of the century as well as for the youth/immigrant movements of the new periphery in the 1950s and 1960s. Here we are also dealing with a political construction – a *red belt*. Both before and after fascism the periphery voted massively for left parties.[8]

Thus we have a four-pronged non-cityness of the periphery. The first is visual and historical, the second is historical and anthropological, the third is visual, the fourth is political and social. The periphery is a place where it is easy to get lost, where everywhere looks the same, where there is no connection with the 'real' history or identity of the city of which the periphery is formally part (and the part where most urban inhabitants live). This is also the periphery-as-labyrinth, as a maze of identical houses and streets where road signs indicate *Milano Centro* but only lead you further around the ring roads. There are no signs reading *Milano Periferia.*[9] In some hinterland towns, vandals have destroyed all the signs indicating entry points. In Bollate, for example, you only know where you are 'through a process of exclusion'. It is 'neither a city, nor countryside, nor periphery. Neither an industrial area, nor a village, nor a town' (Ferrante 1982: 36). Masperò's *Roissy Express* is the most original recent example of a personal (railway-based) exploration of the history and image of the urban periphery – taking as its subject the massive urban fringe of Paris. Here the sense of subjective disorientation and emptiness is compounded by photographs and personal testimony (1994).

Of course, this picture of the city contains well-known elements of truth. Clearly, there is a vast difference between the centre of a historic city like Milan and its forty-year-old new periphery. But we can only accept the idea of a non- or anti-city as a provocation – as a useful indicator of some ways of looking at the periphery. The first three indicators all suffer from a centralized and static idea of the city – almost as a walled space or as the classic medieval urban centre. The peripheries have failed to live up to this model, and thus they have failed to become either parts of the city, or cities themselves. Yet, there is no reason why our urban

8. Politically, some radical geographers have attempted to apply underdevelopment theory to the city, with the peripheries as the potentially revolutionary and underdeveloped parts of the system Lacoste (1976).

9. The image of the labyrinth is a constant in the journalistic accounts of, for example (Bocca 1997a). For the concept of the labyrinth see Dematteis (1990: 127–36).

models can't be different ones, and why the centre itself can sometimes be seen as failing to keep pace with newer urban models.

3.2. The Periphery as Ex-city or Ex-community

Similar criticisms can be made of the idea of the periphery as *ex-city*. This representation applies above all to the old periphery of Milan, and concerns the supposed disappearance of a certain kind of working-class neighbourhood with the boom of the 1960s and later the de-industrialization of the 1980s and 1990s. Yet, in some ways this description applies to the whole of Milan and emerges from many of the interviews and inquests into the city carried over the last twenty years. Milan (with its peripheries) is accused of having *failed* to become a certain kind of city – usually defined as a modern metropolis – and also of having *lost* the urban-village-community features that tend to emerge in certain phases of industrial development. The idea of ex-community is linked to the disappearance of the working class from the city, but also to the spread of consumerist values and a 'desocialization' associated with late capitalism. Again, the main problem with this critique, as with those analysed earlier, is the comparison. The assumption that there had been a 'community' in Milan is far from proven (and there is often no attempt to prove anything of the sort). The evocation of various golden ages is a permanent feature of analyses of changes in Milan – from the pre-industrial era evoked by the Catholics in the 1920s, to the pre-boom era summoned up during and after the miracle, to the golden age in vogue today – the industrial society of the 1950s. In contrast, the idea that Milan has failed to become a 'metropolis' relies on a theological and ahistorical view of urban development and national difference.

3.3. The Periphery as Non-place

The idea of 'non-places' has assumed great importance within debates over changes in the urban and peri-urban territory over the last twenty years. A non-place, according to Augé, is 'a space which cannot be defined as relational, or historical, or concerned with identity' (1995: 77–8). This identification relies, clearly, on precise ideas of place ('relational, historical and concerned with identity') and of identity. Usually, Augé-type classifications are applied not to the lived-in periphery, but to areas like shopping centres, airport lounges and motor way services stations. In the first place, these so-called 'non-places' cannot simply be crushed into the same category. It would be difficult to deny the historical role, for example, of the Central Station in Milan. In the second place, many of the attributes attached to these areas/constructions, can also be applied to the lived-in periphery. The only important difference is the residence-factor – the presence of the 'home'. From the outside, however, or from a visual/landscape point of view, there is no reason why the new (or even some of the old) peripheries could not also be seen as non-places. The real problem with the non-place category is a reification of the idea of 'place' – the link made between identity and the older city. Too much weight is given to the non-city elements of 'non-places'. As Boeri has shown for the Milan area, these zones are still (and increasingly) urban zones – *different* kinds of cities – not 'non-cities', and not in opposition to the historic centres but in close connection with them.

In addition, this common use of the concept of non-places is a simplification of the original theorization used by Augé and others. As an anthropologist of the everyday, Augé actually sees non-places as anthropological categories, whose function and meaning are not set in time but depend on the relationship of individuals with these sites. Thus we cannot simply divide *places* and *non-places* but only sort out a series of complicated and ever-changing relationships between places, non-places, workers and users of these areas that create and recreate meaning and identity. To cite Licata 'the historic centre becomes a non-place in terms of mass tourism while an airport becomes a place for those who work there, on a daily basis' (1996: 200). This clarification of Augé allows us to use the concept of non-places in a much more sophisticated fashion, but perhaps the extreme individualiztion introduced by Licata also empties the concept of much of its clarity and usefulness in terms of analysis of urban change. A series of useful distinctions can also be made between public and private space and semi-public and semi-private spaces. These typologies, applied above all to the edge city constructions so important in the US but increasingly central in Europe allow the theorization of the sophisticated systems of exclusion and inclusion in areas such as shopping malls and also the inclusion of electronic spaces (Cenzatti and Crawford 1993: 34–8; Graham and Marvin 1996; Castells 1996).

3.4. The Periphery as Failed City: Planning and Architecture

From the point of view of the growth of Milan, particularly during the boom, the new periphery has often been seen as a failed city. The obvious planning disasters, the illegalities, the ugliness and poor quality of many of the new developments are blamed for having destroyed the coherence and landscape of the Milanese periphery. A great opportunity to plan and build a new city for the thousands of immigrants who arrived in the city in those years was lost. What was built was chaotic, empty, brutal and often unplanned in anything more than a minimal sense. In reality, this condemnation of the periphery *tout court* is a simplification. Certainly, many neighbourhoods were built that failed both on their own terms and in the sense of historical and practical links with the city. The grand plans of 1953 (Milan) and the inter-communal plans agreed with the whole province and beyond were destroyed by a thousand small changes (variants) and by the power of the speculators. Yet, much of this failure is not architectural, or to do with planning, but social. Many of the great public and private projects on the periphery were well planned and integrated (Comasina, 1954–8). Famous architects worked on a series of public projects – Rossi, Canella, Aymonino. Yet, the inhabitants of these neighbourhoods were usually (and inevitably) from the poorer sections of the community, and many quarters became centres of unemployment, crime and drug dealing. This immense 'failed city' was (and is) the habitat for the vast majority of Milan's residents. The 'failed city' *is* the city, and its failures are not so much aesthetic, but cultural, political and social.

4. Constructions of the Periphery – Keywords/Dualisms: Order, Disorder, Chaos; Light/Dark

> The streets are dark, there are no squares with services, there are few shops, social centres are badly run or empty. And all around the processes of desocialisation abound – individualism, drug use, micro and macro criminality. (Guiducci 1990: 38)

> The bourgeoisie doesn't house its workers, it stores them. (Left slogan, 1970s) (Masperò 1994: 159)

In order to draw out the content of the concept and the reality of the Milanese periphery, we can analyse a number of dualisms or keywords applied to the centre/peripheries distinction, or to the golden age/modern epochs.[10]

The city centre, or the old walled city (with or without its walls) is seen as a paragon of order, the periphery is linked to disorder. Other sets of dualisms and keywords fit into this same pattern – planned/non-planned, monuments/non-places. Hence, Milan-centre has its ring-roads, its *Galleria*, its Cathedral Square, its canals. The periphery lacks monuments, signs, recognition, history. Many of these peripheral belt-regions sprang up almost overnight in the 1960s, and here is where the 'disorder' is seen to be greatest. This chaos (a more extreme term) is also characterized in other ways – illogical road networks, piles of rubbish, darkness. In recent years, this idea of chaos has been extended to the hinterland, to the peri-urban area, to the vast tracts of urban space which extend from and towards Milan in all directions (especially to the north and north-east). Yet, there is a different way of looking at this distinction. We can see the periphery not as representing disorder, but as *new* forms of order with new rules, new ways of building, living and moving. This may require new analytic tools, and even a new language – but some progress is being made, and new rules and typologies are being created

---

10. For an alternative set of dualisms see Boeri *et al.* (1993: 74–6).

(I refer here in particular to the work of Martinotti and Boeri). It is necessary to reject the hegemonic 'model' of the old city, the historic city, in order to recognize and discover these transformations.

A second set of keywords/dualisms encompass far more 'social' categories. Social peace/crime, poverty/wealth; Bronx/Garden city; ghetto/neighbourhood. This is, once again, the periphery-as-badlands stereotype looked at earlier. Here the dualisms are less strong because its is clear that the centre of Milan is neither a garden city nor a collection of homely neighbourhoods. Perhaps the most powerful of these keywords is danger or insecurity. The centre is a place where people know where they are, they feel safe to shop, talk, walk, work. The periphery has a different image, as a dangerous wasteland with pockets of space which are to be avoided, even by those who live there. Here the much-used term 'dormitory' – applied to many of peripheral neighbourhoods – is appropriate. The periphery is a place where the street is only to be used for getting from your car to your house (or avoided altogether – the Milanese place great value on garages, which are bought and sold separately from houses and are known by the appropriate term of *box*) which is to be used only for sleeping in. Other terms are much more extreme – often using wartime language – for example, *Quartiere Lager* (concentration camp).

A third set of dualisms fits into a hybrid visual-social category. The first are to do with perception – black-and-white/colour; light/dark.[11] Invariably, the centre of Milan is seen as a colourful, decorated space; the periphery in black-and-white, as monotonous even in this sensual sense. The most important photographic documentars of Milan and its hinterland in the post-war period – Cerati, Lucas, Beregno-Gardin, Nicolini, Basilico – have all worked almost exclusively in black-and-white. The vast majority of the photos in the important collection/archive financed by the Province of Milan from 1987–97 have been in black and white (Sacconi and Valtorta 1997). The film director Luchino Visconti said he had made *Rocco and his Brothers* in black and white because that was how the city would have appeared to southern immigrants. This contrast *within* Milan thus coincides with one between Milan and elsewhere – where *Milan itself* is black-and-white. Here the relationship between the city and its trademark fog is central. Many 'golden-age' arguments speak nostalgically of the fog 'that there was'.

Two further dualisms are a mixture of social, physical and visual features. Full/ Empty and accessible/isolated. The former sums up both a state of mind and an image – the dormitory neighbourhood, the bleakness written about by so many

---

11. See for example the images in Bocca (1993) or Fantini (1994: 10) who describes a journey from centre to periphery as becoming 'increasingly dark and gloomy'. In terms of colour, Ramona (1992: 1) has written about the *red* periphery (politicized and rebellious), the *black* periphery (such as the Bronx), the *white* periphery (middle class residential suburbs), the *yellow*, industrial, periphery and the ex-industrial, *green* periphery.

commentators, the concrete jungles. But it is also a 'golden-age' image, symbolizing the shift from an industrial to a post-industrial landscape, from an environment full of workers and factories and bars to a series of new empty spaces, the so-called *aree dismesse*.[12] The architectural/planning debates in the ex-industrial cities over the empty spaces left by the end of Fordism are illuminating here. The shift is also one from a sociable, or visibly sociable environment – from a community – to an *ex*-community, a home-based society. This shift is also physical – from the street to the living room, from the political demonstration to the national lottery. Peripheral places are also seen as isolated – from the city, from free time centres, from transport links. Centres are accessible – socially and physically.

There are a number of contradictions that emerge from these dualisms. First, the distinction between cultural levelling – a process supposedly brought on by the pernicious influence of mass culture and the decline of traditional cultures – and the chaos attributed to the urban periphery. On the one hand the periphery is pictured as a great, unending series of unchanging landscapes. Everywhere looks the same, and feels the same. Inhabitants are reduced to faceless figures taking early trains or cowering behind reinforced doors. On the other hand, we are presented with a picture of the chaotic development of the periphery – its lack of order, or planning, of rigidity. The periphery is chaotic, but is uniform in its chaos. There is a kind of generalization of chaos, to reverse Arendt's famous description of Nazism, 'the evil of banality'.

5. New Ways of Imagining the Periphery

It seems essential to try to formulate some new ways of imagining the urban periphery. Here I will look at two attempts which have been proposed in recent years in Milan.

5.1. Fragmentation and Micro-analysis

The city is a non-ordered block of fragments, separate parts which have no link between them on the whole, and which belong indifferently to the ancient city or to more recent developments. (Motta and Pizzigoni 1991: 20)

The first idea is an attempt to reduce urban analysis to the micro-level. This is designed as a reaction to both the failures of big planning and to the restraints

12. This image is reinforced in the above mentioned project of *photographic documentation* organized by the Province of Milan, where the photographs taken very rarely show anything other than spaces emptied of people. See also Basilico (1999). For an analysis of empty spaces see Gregotti (1993: 2–4), Secchi (1993: 5–9).

imposed by industrial society, as well as an attempt to bring architecture and analysis back to a human level. Motta and Pizzigoni (1991) argue that analysis should be reduced not to the neighbourhood, or the street, but down to individual building blocks or pieces of the city. 'Every piece presents itself as closed in itself, without links or relationships with the others. We need to start to talk about fragments and to recognize in the single fragment the only real possibility of change: the fragment is the basis for the construction of the city' (1991: 37). The city is seen as a combination of a series of smaller parts, not as a coherent whole – 'it is this attention to detail which characterizes the contemporary representation of the city; a pavement, a window, a flight of stairs, a balcony, a bench in a park, the four walls of a room – these are the images which have allowed us to represent the city most convincingly' (1991: 70). Fragment analysis is not trying to recreate a 'coherent whole' that has been lost but accepts, and even celebrates, a complex situation. This methodological shift is similar to that in other disciplines – with the reaction against big analysis found in micro-historical work in the late 1970s and 1980s. Language is important here. We are talking about fragments not parts. There is no big picture, but only a small picture – on a human scale. Of course, the attempt to 'rebuild' a mosaic-like whole is one possibility that follows from fragment analysis. Motta and Pizzigoni reject this. Their approach is intensely realist and concrete – to study what is there, each stairway, each courtyard, each side-street – and to work with that reality. Every building is an exception, every feature is original, every change is important. The grand (and often unrealized) plans of the past are thus abandoned in favour of intense local development and are (in this case) combined with a detailed historical approach to the growth and shifts in each street and neighbourhood.

This approach also allows us to escape from some of the problematic dualisms we have discussed in this chapter – the periphery is not studied even as the periphery, and certainly not as a 'negative' 'problem' but simply *as it is*. Implicit within this analysis is an alternative vision of the growth of the city – not as a kind of living organism but as a series of isolated blocks, buildings or spaces. Finally, fragment analysis also rejects the image of the periphery as a uniform space, as a unending and homogeneous series of neighbourhoods. The proponents of this type of analysis see themselves as urban archaeologists, excavating and classifying the buildings and spaces of the periphery.

5.2. The Changing Territory and the Eclectic Atlas

The image of the metropolis is the image of society. (Branzi 1995: 116–19)

We must destroy a myth: the periphery no longer exists. (Boeri, Marinoni, Zardini, Zucchi, 1995: 161)

A second new analysis takes as its starting point the immense changes in northern Italy over the last twenty years. Here the exception is the centre, and the periphery the norm: 'the contemporary city is not a degeneration of the historic city, it is something completely different, rich of new potentiality, to understand and use. In the contemporary city new life styles are asserting themselves, linked to a different relationship with nature and to new forms of mobility across the territory' (Boeri *et al.* 1995: 161). These changes are underpinned by a series of epochal social and cultural developments that have transformed the landscape – deind-ustrialization, increased living standards and massive private mobility. This new form of analysis is multi-disciplinary, sensitive to photography and film studies, and close to micro-historical approaches (Boeri, Lanzani, Marini 1993). So, what has happened and how can we analyse the periphery and urban space in the 1990s? First, there has been a decline in the centrality of the old 'city' – in terms of population and the bordering of urban space ('many central places are outside', Boeri 1997c: 9). Second, there has been a massive extension in the space covered by 'urban' landscapes of various types. Urbanity is now 'a potential quality of all inhabited places and no longer a dimension based upon the link between buildings and a certain geographic area' (Boeri 1997c: 9). You can now pass through the whole Milanese region 'without ever losing sight of an urban landscape' (Boeri *et al.* 1993: 18). Third, the breakdown of visual boundaries means not so much the death of the city, but the decline of the traditional image of the countryside. Traditional maps cannot represent these changes, and these theories tend to use alternative means – photographs, remote sensing, mental maps (an 'eclectic atlas' in Boeri's words).

Classic maps are simply too static to capture forms of territorial change linked to movement. For example, many of the signs and advertising hoardings that dominate the peri-urban landscape are designed to be seen on the move. Motor way service stations – visited by 200 million people at least once in Italy every year – are absent from cartography, yet represent a key and familiar part of the urban landscape – the new urban *piazze*. These are hybrid landscapes, with new centralities and categories (Zardini 1996). Fourth, these attempts to analyse changes in urban territory are sensitive to morphological developments. Martinotti has analysed the populations that gravitate around urban centres and adopted a flexible analysis to deal with a complicated urban world.

5.3. Four Populations: Urban Space and Morphology

> The old urban residents are pushed around and threatened by new populations who are not only those immigrants from poorer countries but peaceful invaders who arrive daily in their millions; commuters, visitors and metropolitan consumers. (Martinotti 1994)

Martinotti has mapped out four urban populations who gravitate around the city on a regular basis (Martinotti 1993a: 137–98; 1993b: 112–85). First, there are legal *residents*, around whom most of the debates concerning the future of the city take place, who vote in local elections and who live in the city and use it on a daily basis to live, shop, work or as students, children and pensioners. This group dominates all the available statistics – and yet represents a minority both in numerical terms as well as in terms of its impact upon the city. In an earlier phase of the industrial city, the sleeping population and the daily population were far more similar, although there were always complicated and shifting relationships with the countryside and rural work. The demolition of the city walls (Milan's were removed in 1873) represents a key moment in the shift towards differing populations and institutionalized commuting (Martinotti 1993b: 151).

The second group can be termed *commuters* – those who use the city (usually daily) for different forms of work. Of course, commuting is not a new phenomenon. In the early part of the century, thousands of building workers came into the city to work every day. In the 1950s and 1960s, commuters were a common sight on the early morning and late evening trains that run from the city to the hinterland. Certainly, over time, the nature of commuting has changed – both in terms of the transport used (from public to private) as well as in terms of the type of work involved. In the 1960s, estimates of the number of commuters stood at more than 300,000. Between 1950 and 1960 the number of passengers using the urban network every year rose from 632 million to 768 million (Bocca 1980: 84–90; Petrillo 1992a: 64). In the 1990s, up to one million commuters were coming into the city every day (in trains, buses and 600,000 cars) via the 250 entry points to the city (Bocca 1993: 14). One of the key characteristics of the commuting category (which often distinguishes them from city-users, see below) is that the vast majority enter and leave the city during the classic working day. Many city-users enter the city at night (Leonini 1998; Dal Lago 1997). The days of the week are also different, often Monday-to-Friday for commuters, Saturday or Sunday for city users. City users can often be residents as well, as with the young people from the vast urban periphery and province who come to Milan to shop, to meet people, or just to sit around. This centre-periphery divide is particularly strong in Milan.

The third group described by Martinotti is a much more disparate group made up of those who enter the urban area to carry out a series of functions not linked either to residence or to work (in the narrowest sense). These people can be termed *city users* – and include shoppers (and window-shoppers, ninety-five per cent of consumption in the Province of Milan takes place in the city of Milan itself (Foti 1993: 21)), theatre, film, exhibition, nightclub and concert goers, football fans, tourists, 40,000 students (who could also be characterized as commuters) and those who need to visit one of the bureaucratic centres located in the city (motor administration, local government, business centres). Also included within this category are a whole series of more shady, even 'underground' activities that are nonetheless highly visible – clients for prostitutes (an activity which extends right around the vast ring-roads that surround Milan), drugs and those who just drive in and around. Here, the city becomes similar to a vast, illegal and exciting theme park (or video game) where the city user is always one step ahead of the police in his or her attempts to exploit the pleasures offered by the urban 'services'. Obviously, it is extremely difficult to measure the extent of 'city use', despite the fact that more and more research on urban morphology is moving away from a resident-based analysis of the city. It is worth noting the frequent and complicated interchanges of the populations we have identified thus far. During holiday periods vast numbers of Milanese residents leave the city for holiday homes. In August, up to 75 per cent of the residents are absent – becoming 'city users' of a certain type in other cities or simply tourists or residents elsewhere.[13] In these periods, the resident population is even more marginalised and marginal. The urban populations we have discussed are thus marked by extreme and complicated levels of mobility, and not just across the borders of the city of Milan. The advent of mass private motorization is one of the central factors behind the shift towards differing urban populations, and has been crucial in the shape and landscape of the new urban territories outside the city (Boeri *et al.* 1993). In 1987, it was calculated that, every day, nearly five million trips were being made in the area of the Province, with over 60 per cent being entirely within the city itself. Nearly two million daily journeys were made into Milan and out again. Half a million return journeys were made from the city to the province and beyond.

Finally, following Martinotti, we come to a fourth urban population – *business users* – those people who visit the city for business reasons but who, unlike commuters, do not come in on a daily (or even a regular) basis. Business users are a mix of commuters and city users, with specific consumption (and business) needs and often with high disposable incomes. New research has estimated that 300,000 Japanese businessmen pass through Milan every year. This 'invisible' group – forgotten or ignored by city planners and politicians – represents an important resource for the city as well as an interesting part of the urban morphological landscape. Business users generate a whole series of services – which are necessarily flexible and efficient and often seasonal (based, for example, around certain trade fairs). Milan's fashion weeks – when up to 70,000 business users and city users descend upon the city (buyers, models, journalists) – represent the peak moments for these categories, the moments when they dominate the urban space economically and visually (see Chapter 6). One of the key problems

13. On 15 August 1997, only 320,000 of Milan's residents were still in the city, *Milano in Comune*, III, 2, June 1997.

concerning both city and business users is their lack of responsibility towards the city – as non-residents. Residents have some responsibility towards their environment imposed upon them by their continuing presence there. They pay taxes, and elect representatives to run the city. To generalise, they prefer some sort of long- or medium-term strategy towards the city. City and business users (and, to some extent, commuters) have different needs and a far more short-term view of the city and its problems. Martinotti has identified a form of disenfranchisement of residents due to the increasing weight of city and business users. It is also true the latter may well be forgotten within the more parochial, bounded and electoral strategies of local politicians. Finally, certain problems have an impact on all four populations – albeit in different ways. Traffic jams affect everyone – the drivers stuck in them, the children who breathe the fumes, the bus passengers who cannot reach their destinations, the pedestrian who cannot cross the road, the pensioner who cannot get past the cars parked on the pavement.

Clearly, this separation and identification of urban populations allows a far more flexible and nuanced analysis of developments in the city. Evidently, these are not hard and fast categories whose boundaries are distinct and immutable. A person can be part of all four populations, or none, or one, or two, or three. There is scope for a critical approach to the divisions imposed by Martinotti, and for the opening up of new types of 'population' categories. These divisions could also be looked at in different ways – such as via the terms 'the city that works', 'the city that consumes' or through the analysis of various time periods (the city at night, the city by day, the city in August) or places (the street populations, the in-car population, the static population) It is worth noting at this point that many of the debates on the crisis of Milan concern (above all) its residents – as with the panics over depopulation and deindustrialization. Very few analysts have taken a wider view – beyond the city's boundaries, beyond the population statistics – which is the only way to understand the dynamics and workings of any modern city.

5.4. Populations and the Shape of Urban Territories

The mobility and inter-changability of these different populations has rewritten the form and shape of the landscape. Where once space was measured by the distance between work and residence 'today', for Boeri, 'this space is rewritten . . . by extremely mobile lifestyles'. Some city users, for example, 'use the historic urban centres as discotheques' (Boeri *et al.* 1993: 14). For Boeri and others who have begun to look in detail at these new urban landscapes, we are not dealing with a chaotic development, but one closely linked to the social, familial and cultural developments in Italy in the 1980s and 1990s. 'A country rich in terms of individual family choice, small builders and single investors, but poor and backward in terms of collective provision, has finally constructed a landscape in its own image' (Zardini 1996: 14).[14]

The actual content of this territory is made up of a series of repetitive structures. First, the family house or groups of houses, often linked to small or tiny factories. Second, there are big commercial centres. These regular features (architectural, artistic) are usually mixed with profoundly local characteristics. We thus have a complicated mixture of sameness and variety, of repeated content and changes in form (as Folin has written 'buildings which are always the same but always different' 1997: 146–7). Much of this development is linked to arterial routes and key transport links (almost always car-based) – forming spiderlike settlements radiating out from and into the old city, or around totally new, nodal, commercial and productive centres.

These forms of analysis share certain traits with those of fragment analysis, and are certainly not incompatible with the latter. Both make a virtue of the micro, and look closely as individual buildings, roads and spaces. The new territorial analysis, however, takes a far wider view of urban space, and attempts a global analysis of landscape change. This is obvious from the large slices of Italy used by Boeri and Basilico. Yet, there are a number of problems with these two original and provocative methodological approaches to the study of the urban territory.

5.5. Problems with 'Extreme Fragment Analysis' and the Eclectic Atlas

Extreme micro studies are not usually the best way to understand changes even in the micro-elements studied. Comparisons are often the only way of isolating the unique and repetitive elements in each construction. What we have here is a useful but over-reductive 'building materialism', which must be combined with other methodologies and is best adapted to architectural planning. In addition, Motta and Pizzigoni not only give up any idea of the city, but seemingly any idea of 'the urban' at all, and of studying global change. We need a wider lens to see what is really going on in the cities and across the territories of Europe and elsewhere. Finally, Motta and Pizzigoni have (rightly perhaps) abandoned any idea of big (or even small-scale) planning for micro-solutions based on the actual form and content of spaces used, inhabited by and seen on a daily basis by urban dwellers and visitors. This approach has the great advantage of overturning all the utopian dreams not just of an ideal city but even of planning at the level of the neighbourhood or street. It is also perfect for a city like Milan in an epoch like the 1990s, where the

---

14. For the habits of the Milanese see Martinotti (1988). The vast majority of 'city users', it seems, do not actually spend any money during their 'use' of the city. This surprising conclusion appears to alter the image/stereotype of the high-spending consumer, replacing it with groups of (mainly young) people who use the city as a backdrop for their social behaviour Boeri *et al.* (1993: 132).

vast majority of people spend the vast majority of their lives at home, in the office or in their cars. This hyper-realism is refreshing and allows us to escape from the reams of superfluous plans produced by architects' studios in their hundreds, but never realized. Motta and Pizzigoni come to their fragments without aesthetic preconceptions, like urban archaeologists 'our work, they write, has been to design it [the urban periphery] without worrying about ugliness or beauty' (1991: 110).

Moving on to Boeri *et al.*, whose approach is far more wide-ranging and 'revolutionary', there are moments when the interpretation of the landscape appears to be reading off building and urban form from developments in Italian society. In other words, Boeri sometimes makes a simplistic link between supposed familist economic and social trends in Italian society and the shape and distribution of 'urban facts'. This type of analysis – popular in, for example, work on edge cities in the US, seems to veer dangerously close to a kind of orthodox territorial Marxism – where the economy and society can be read off from the shape of the houses (Garreau 1991).[15] Base and superstructure are perfectly matched. In reality, and Boeri would agree, this process is two-way (society and culture create the territory, but the territory also creates and modifies society and culture), complicated and mediated.

A second problem is of a different kind. Boeri makes much of the supposed newness of the developments they analyse, photograph and document. Sometimes, this 'newness' is placed within the arc of a vague 'last twenty years', sometimes it is pinned down in the 1980s (Boeri *et al.* 1993: 73). Yet, as with some of the 'older' analyses of the periphery I have looked at in this chapter, Boeri and his co-authors do not really demonstrate (nor do they make much attempt to demonstrate) that all this really is so very new. From my own work on the 1950s and 1960s in Milan, it appears to me that some of these processes identified by Boeri as 'beginning' in the 1980s were already in embryo in the 1960s. If this is correct, and at least we can claim that there is an element of doubt about the historical reconstruction of events, then the determinism of individual car-based mobility, cited by Boeri as central to the territorial developments he studies, is also in trouble. The car was important in the 1960s, but not central, yet the urban landscape had already begun to resemble that which Boeri links to the widespread 'mobility on four wheels' and the post-industrial society of the 1980s and 1990s. Here, a real, through, documented historical research is needed – *when were houses and roads built? Who built them? Who owns their own home and who does not?* With this information we could draw up another map to add to the rich collection in Boeri *et al.* (1993) – which would show us clearly the historical process behind the construction of the peri-urban territory in the Milanese and Lombard regions.

15. Garreau (1991: 7) calls edge cities 'the culmination of a generation of individual American value decisions about the best ways to live, work and play – about how to create "home"'.

6. Possible Solutions to the Problems of Milan's Periphery

Analytically, the work of Boeri, Basilico and Martinotti allows us to understand the periphery, and the use of the urban territory by various types of populations. We need further historical research to fully comprehend the origins of these processes of urban change and urban sprawl. The situation is, to say the least, a complicated one – and only by escaping from many of the stale dualisms identified above can progress be made in the analysis of the peripheries of Milan and elsewhere – where the vast majority of Europe's peoples now live. Obviously, the most important set of problems in some of these regions are social – and can only be solved by social change. Culturally, however, what is to be done? If Boeri is right, a US-type car-based mobile society is already in place in Lombardy – and is creating an urban landscape in its own economic and cultural image. If we accept this as largely correct, is there any point in attempting to create a community in this 'rich' periphery. Are old forms of collective space dead, or merely useless? Can we reverse this process by building small and beautiful parks or *piazze*, and do we want to reverse it from above – through the state, or architects? Can we really rebuild community through architectural and planning decisions? In the city of Milan, at least, there are huge opportunities to change the urban landscape – given the massive open spaces left empty by deindustrialization. The debates here are important and crucial for the future of this urban centre. The future of the metropolis which now spreads right across to Venice, Turin and Genoa is far less debated, and far more important for Italy and its peripheries.

–8–

From Boomtown to Bribesville: The Images of the City, 1980–2000

> Milano mia, portarmi via, ho tanto freddo schifo e non ne posso più. [My Milan, take me away, I'm freezing cold and I can't take anymore.] (Roberto Vecchioni, *Luci a San Siro)*

This chapter will look to analyse the momentous changes in Milan during the 1980s and 1990s, above all through the mapping of the changing images of the city within a period marked by a succession of crises. We have seen how Milan was the 'capital of the miracle' during the economic boom of the 1950s and 1960s. The 1980s saw Milan at the centre of Italy's so-called 'second miracle', based upon the transformation away from heavy industry and towards a series of post-industrial activities. This period was marked by a specific kind of political domination and cultural change in the city, with Craxi's Socialist Party at the helm from 1976 to 1993. Massive and deep-rooted systems of political and economic corruption were unmasked by the dramatic 'clean hands' investigations in the city, which began with the arrest of a mid-level Socialist official in February 1992, and led to the disappearance of the Socialists from the political scene that they had controlled for so long. In 1993, the regional Northern Leagues won a crushing victory in the Mayoral elections, but this relatively new grouping was unable or unwilling to attempt a revolution from above in the city, in part because the channels of mediation that had been constructed by the previous administrations had been broken, and in part because of blocks on public projects imposed after the scandals began to spread to the higher levels of Italian politics. In 1997 the *Lega*'s Mayor was removed and an industrialist (Gabriele Albertini) was elected with the backing of a right-wing alliance of post-fascists and Berlusconi's *Forza Italia!* grouping. This whole period of political upheaval saw rapid territorial and industrial changes to the city and its hinterland, and a series of moral, economic and cultural crises rocked the city and its (declining) population.

In order to have any success in outlining and analysing the changes in the city over this complicated period, we need to try and understand what we mean by 'Milan' and to adopt some conceptual and morphological tools.

1. Images of the City

What do we mean when we talk about the image of the city? First, it is essential to move into the plural. There is never one image of any one city, but a whole series of competing and complex images that are never fixed and are continually being created and re-created. Second, it is obvious that these images are subjective images, mediated through language, the mass media, memory, photographs, films and the environment. It is not necessary to have lived in or even visited a city to have an image of that city in one's mind – on the contrary. Often, these images are stronger in those who have never seen a city first hand. The examples of Naples, or of the Bronx, are classic instances of cities (or neighbourhoods) that have extremely strong images amongst those who have never seen them. Given these premises, we can now attempt a sort of typology of city images drawing on the work of architects, planners, urban theorists, sociologists and historians. First, there is a strong connection between the images of the city and identities (of the city, of each individual). Daily experiences, local events, the habitat, the media all combine with personal interactions and meetings to help produce a system of symbols, signs and reference points. Mental maps have been particularly useful here in identifying the variety and complexity of subjective views of the city (Lynch 1960; La Pietra 1973). For Lynch, the mental image of the city 'is the product both of immediate sensations, and the memory of past experience that is used to interpret information and as a guide to action' (1960: 26). Concretely, people are identified with their neighbourhoods and their identities linked to the dominant images of certain areas This process is particularly strong with negative images (see Chapter 7).

Secondly, more positive images can be linked to a myriad of events, structures and morphologies: physical space (upper and lower parts of the city), wealth, cleanliness, building types, views, light, and, of course, the kinds of inhabitants present. With positive images, there is often a real attempt to link personal identities to place and space – as with the gay quarters of San Francisco, or the ethnic (public) tourist-based identities associated with many US cities – Chinatown, Little Italy, Greektown. Builders and planners make conscious attempts to impose their own image of the city upon its residents. This can be at a tiny, micro-level – a park, a road, a statue – or at a mass, macro-level – town plans, monuments (Harvey 1994: 200–28; Dickie 1994a; Berman 1993: 287–348). For hundreds of years the Catholic Church has rebuilt and redesigned the territory in its own image – dominating the skylines and the backstreets of many Italian cities. Mass tourism is crucial to the sedimentation of certain images and to the connection between key 'attractions' and places. Certain buildings are set up as (or simply become) the symbols of certain cities, or of certain epochs in certain cities – Canary Wharf in London for the Thatcher era, the revamped 1980s centre of Birmingham side by side with the classic symbol of 1960s planning – the Bullring, or the *Piccolo Teatro* in Milan as (negative) symbol of *Tangentopoli*. Organizations are formed to promote cities, to reinvent their images – with logos, slogans, research projects, festivals and conferences.[1] Films and books also become associated with certain images and certain urban areas – for example, *Blade Runner* with Los Angeles, *The Bonfire of the Vanities* for New York. All of these images and the physical and mental constructions linked to their promotion are contested, are never fixed and are continually being reformed and deconstructed (Mela 1996: 149–63; Gasperini 1982; Martinotti 1996: 153–72).

2. The Identification of 'Milan': Forms of Space

It is useful at this point to divide our answer into a series of different (but overlapping) forms of space.

2.2. Geographic Space

> It is not possible any more to pick up on historic and geographic signs, or even social ones, you pass close to enclaves of poverty without realising it, you brush past rich neighbourhoods without noticing them . . . the megalopolis has no maps, it is impossible to find your way by following churches or monuments which have been buried or have simply disappeared. The urban form no longer exists. (Bocca 1993: 10)

Milan is a city without clear boundaries and with no river or hills (apart from one artificial hill, the Monte Stella). Its flat landscape is filled with a myriad of urban forms, landscapes, buildings and open spaces. Concentric (traffic-dominated) circles radiate out from the centre of the city that is dominated by the Cathedral – its huge *Piazza* and the glass-covered *Galleria*. Some images of the city and its hinterland are linked to this flatness, to the unending and monotonous nature of the landscape, to the ubiquitous nature of the Milanese climate – especially its fog – and with the labyrinth-like character of the hinterland. Mountain ranges should be visible from many balconies in the city – but rarely are – due to the smog that

---

1. In the 1980s a number of organizations were formed in Milan to promote varied and conflicting images of the city (and for other, more political, reasons), for example, *Società Civile* (1985) and its civic electoral list 'Per Milano Mani Pulite' (1992), the Associazione degli Interessi Metropolitani (1987), Amici di Milano (1997) and MeglioMilano. Davis's work on Los Angeles is essential for an understanding of the contradictions between growth, growth limitation, crime, order and public space (1990).

hangs over the city. This 'lack' of a view increases the sense of *anomie* for many Milanese and immigrants. Many commentators note that even locals get lost frequently on their way into the city, that newcomers are disorientated by the sameness of the urban environment – its lack of landmarks – that streets lead nowhere, or turn back upon themselves, or simply take you round the city but not towards the intended destination. This alienated/alienating nature of the urban landscape is a reflection of and a contribution to the declining image of the city, and Milan's constant crisis of identity.

2.2. Political Space

Political space is far easier to pin down. We can identify three political spaces each with their own resident populations and clearly marked cartographic boundaries. In the year 2000 the city administration – the *Comune di Milano* – took in the city itself (18,000 hectares; a boundary running to 94 km) the shrinking Province encompasses 188 local *comuni*, 3.7 million residents and 1980 km^2, the Lombard *region* stretches for 23.857 km^2 and over 1,500 *comuni* and can count on nearly nine million inhabitants.[2] All these political spaces contain elected local governments, electorates, different powers and governing offices – Palazzo Marino for Milan, Palazzo Isimbardi for the Province, the Pirelli Tower for the Region. Further boundaries mark the edge of Italy itself (Switzerland is a mere 40 km from Milan, France lies 180 km to the east, Slovenia (325 km) and Austria (150 km) to the west, Germany less than 300 km to the north) and, looking further afield, those of the EU, the European Free Trade Area and the Schengen Agreement. Each different political organization has various responsibilities concerning the management and administration of the territory, the city, traffic, immigration, housing, industry and planning. These clear political spaces begin to break down when we begin to look at actual policy and urban behaviour, which often makes no distinction between province, region and city. Tensions between the various political bodies controlling the vast semi-urban territory of northern Italy make co-ordinated planning and policy-making an extremely difficult task.

Bureaucratic political spaces are not the only frontiers that occupy the minds of those who live, work or just visit the areas at the centre of our discussion. Many other borders are constructed and reconstructed over time. The Northern Leagues have, at different times (and often at the same time) built political alliances on the basis of borders dividing the 'north' and the 'south' and those dividing the

2. The Province of Milan is the second biggest Province in Italy (after Rome), but in recent years a series of areas have created their own provinces, such as Lodi, leading to shifting boundaries. For the statistics from the 1970s see *Italia 70* (1971).

region of 'Padania' from the rest of Italy (Biorcio 1997). The 'red belt' around Milan saw the Left dominate politics in the zone just outside the immediate urban periphery for most of the post-war period. Catholic parties controlled large parts of the 'white' territory around Bergamo, Brescia and Como for decades both before and after 1945.

Milan as a political space can also be looked at in more parochial terms – as a power-base for politicians and parties working at a national level, and as a source of financial and political resources, as well as industrial and financial influence. Milan became a key player in the 1980s with the rise of Craxi – a politician who had made his name in the city and who was the local power broker for the ruling coalitions from the mid-1970s onwards. Craxi's four years as Prime Minister saw him use Milan as a source of votes, contacts, finance and local prestige. For the first time since unification, Milan's political weight began to rival that of Rome. Craxi used Milan as his political space, living only in a hotel in Rome whilst maintaining offices and contacts in the former city. This political weight continued throughout the 1980s, with the formation of the regional Northern Leagues (the only big city they have controlled is Milan), the anti-Craxi movements of *Società Civile* and *La Rete* and, in 1994, the birth of Berlusconi's *Forza Italia!* organization – with its power base in Milan (Berlusconi won over 49,000 preference votes in the 1997 local elections, over eight times more than the next candidate). Finally, the far-left Rifondazione Comunista grouping can mark Milan out as one of its strongholds and the same is true of the main trade union federations. Almost all the new political forces of the post-*Tangentopoli* era originated in Milan (apart from *La Rete* at Palermo) or have had their first real impact in the city. It would be no exaggeration to describe the city as an intense and dynamic political laboratory in the 1990s.

2.3. Urban Space

Aren't you afraid to enter the Bronx? (Children to journalists, Milanese periphery, *La Repubblica*, 3 April 1993)

It is here that many of the most interesting changes have taken place in the 1980s and 1990s. It is crucial to analyse 'Milan' as a diffuse urban area that can be looked at in a series of different ways – moving (without creating hierarchies) from the city centre to the urban periphery to the metropolitan area to the urban sprawls across to Turin, Genoa and Verona and Venice on to huge urban networks which stretch from, for example, London through the Rhine Valley (the so-called 'blue banana') or from Barcelona through southern France and Munich (the 'sun-belt')

(Revelli 1997: 7–13). Little advantage is to be had by choosing one of these spatial interpretative forms over another. There is no reason why we cannot employ a whole series of different ideas and views of urban space, and in this way escape from the suffocating centralism of much analysis of Milan. This is an urban space without real boundaries – a peri-urban area – where new forms of territory and spatial identification are mixed with older, more traditional places and spaces 'in a series of forms of settlements, airports, shopping malls, residential neighbour-hoods, leisure-based structures, and simple bundles of buildings of various types around streets, motorways, stations and other service centres' (Boeri and Martinotti 1997). It is also clear that any understanding of the Milanese or Lombard economy needs to place the territory at the forefront of its world view. Whereas, in the 1960s, Milan film directors and writers waited patiently outside fog-bound factory gates in order to understand the city, it is now clear that this centrality has disappeared. Only through a more flexible analysis can we begin to draw out the contradictions and complications of economic development and urban change in the 1980s and 1990s. As we have seen the variety and spread of new urban forms also makes comparisons between 'cities' extremely difficult – the very definition of The City is forced into crisis by territorial developments. The various peripheries which make up the peri-urban area around Milan have been analysed in detail in Chapter 7.

If we think of this overview of geographic space as a journey into Milan, from the peri-urban zones we pass into the 'new' urban periphery – with its swathe of public housing estates, wastelands, open ex-industrial space and road networks. The next 'stage' towards the city centre is constituted by the ex-industrial peripheries, characterized by famous ex-cathedrals of work, big and small – Breda, Falck, Pirelli, Montecatini – traditional working class housing and older public projects. The ex-industrial areas – all recognizably 'neighbourhoods' with some residual sense of belonging – are all undergoing transformations or awaiting projects. Finally, within the original circle of canals, we have monumental Milan, with its shopping streets, its fashion district, its night life and bars. This voyage has been towards the centre, but it is only by looking beyond the centre, and even the city, that we can begin to understand and explain the economic, social and political changes that have transformed Milan in the 1980s and 1990s.

The image of Milan takes in not just the city, and its monuments, but the whole Lombard region at times. Political power, especially in the 1980s, was often greater on the peripheries. An apparent promotion to a Ministry in Rome could be seen as an insult, or a demotion. The ability to control and regulate the rich territorial industries of some Lombard regions can signify more than governing the declining resident populations in Milan. Economic and urban thinking (if freed from the banalities of day-to-day politics) has become far more oriented towards the peri-urban, the city user, the commuter – than to the static and conservative solutions imposed by the residents and a city-central vision. Space is much more flexible and regional (and international) than it appears on the political or geographical map – as with the ill-defined yet powerful ideal of the 'nord-east', or the 'north-west', or Lombardy, or the north, or 'Padania'.

2.4. Economic Space

This is a varied and variegated concept. Bonomi's recent analysis of northern Italian capitalism has identified *seven* economic norths – and even these categories are broad brush strokes (1997). Here, two conclusions can be drawn. First, the region is an economic powerhouse. Lombardy claims 40 per cent of Italy's businesses and half her jobs in the information sector, and 30 per cent of all research and development. The economic area of 'Padania', identified by the Fondazione Agnelli in 1992 and made up of eight northern regions, produced 54 per cent of Italian GDP in 1990, attracted over half of all investment and contained 80 per cent of Italy's individual businesses. Three quarters of exports and 64 per cent of imports either originated from or were directed towards this area, whose living standards are amongst the highest in Europe – behind only Hamburg, Ile de France and Brussels.

These broad statistics mask huge variations, specialization and changes over time in terms of individual industries, the territory and the other forms of space identified in this chapter. Pockets of poverty exist alongside huge tracts of wealth, small and tiny industries are often prisoners of financiers and banks, public squalor and inefficiencies affect most Lombard citizens and immigrants (Guidicini 1990; Dal Lago 1999). In addition, the dynamism of the 1980s and 1990s has not been a linear process, and masks traumatic changes in identity and production – above all the rapid and unrelenting deindustrialistion (of big industry) which hit the city of Milan and its hinterland in the 1980s and 1990s, a process that is discussed in more detail below. The claim that unemployment in Milan is close to zero is true statistically, but false in real, human terms. The presence of young people within the family home until, in many cases, they reach their early thirties, is common – and masks a kind of unemployment. In addition, the poverty of many pensioners in an ageing city is not connected to their role in the productive process. Finally, the exploitation and uses of immigrant labour over the last fifteen years – the vast majority of which is missed by official statistical methods – represents a vast reservoir of un-and-underemployment at the level of the everyday in the urban fabric. A final form of space was analysed in detail in Chapter 7, the *populated* space of Milan with the four populations identified in the work of Martinotti and others.

3. The History of Milan and its Images: 1976–2000

3.1. 1976–1992: Milan as Bribesville (Tangentopoli)[3]

Politically, and culturally, this was the period of 'Socialist hegemony' – Craxian mayors. Socialist Party mayors linked to Craxi ran the city from 1976 onwards (Tognoli, 1976–86); Pillitteri (Craxi's brother-in-law) 1986–92; Borghini (appointed by Craxi); January 1992 – February 1993). Craxi himself was Prime Minister of Italy from August 1983 – March 1987 and Secretary of the Socialist Party after 1976. This period was characterized by the full functioning of *Tangentopoli* – bribesville or kickback city – but not the judicial inquests which exposed *Tangentopoli* after 1992. *Tangentopoli* can be defined as an almost scientific system, involving all the political parties and many other civil organizations, whereby public contracts and funds were divided between their intended destination and kickbacks to the parties, and local contracts, building permits, and so forth, were awarded via a system of party funding via bribes (which were distributed according to well-defined percentages). This system was just that – a well-oiled *system* – which the politicians saw as 'normal' and even essential to the functioning of political life.[4] To cite two politicians involved in *Tangentopoli*: 'this system, even if it was negative, allowed for a certain kind of survival in economic terms'; 'through the system of kickbacks and voluntary contributions from businessmen, the party system discovered the only way, at least with regard to us in Milan, to survive'.[5] Newcomers to various public posts accepted what they called the 'environmental situation' in place, and worked the system to their own advantage. Personal as well as political fortunes were made, in an extra-ordinary mix of pre- and post-modern corruption – sacks of cash were transferred by hand whilst elaborate Swiss bank accounts were created.

---

3. It would perhaps be more accurate to divide this period into two, or three. In reality, the exposure of the system of corruption that became known as *Tangentopoli* began in March 1985 with the arrest on corruption charges (for which he was later absolved on a technicality) of Natali, Socialist head of the Milanese transport authority, continued in 1986 with the Ligresti building scandal, and ran right through the late 1980s and 1990s with the so-called 'Duomo Connection' affair, which reached right up to the higher echelons of Milanese politics. Undoubtedly, February 1992 marked the beginning of the end for the system, but the connection between the Socialist-DC (and Communist Party, in Milan) ruling axis and corruption, in the public mind, was well in place before 1992.

4. Some writers have highlighted this 'Milanese' aspect of the system – as corrupt efficiency or *efficient* corruption (Pivetta 1995). For Barbacetto and Veltri (1991: xv) the system of corruption was 'scientific, well oiled, automatic'. Balzani, Socialist and town planner, admitted in 1987 that 'the bribe is automatic' cited in, Barbacetto and Veltri (1991: 58).

5. Both politicians were part of the DC, but the system involved all parties. The quotes are from Maurizio Prada, ex-president of the municipal electric authority and Roberto Mongini, cited in Nascimbeni and Pamparana (1992: 142, 129).

Yet, despite the widespread acknowledgement of and participation in this illegal system (or perhaps because of this), the dominant image of the city of Milan in the 1980s was *not* one of a corrupt city. This was the period of *Milano da bere*, an advertising slogan for an after-dinner drink which became the symbol (at first positive, later negative) of a whole epoch and political style.[6] There are various theories as to why the system of *Tangentopoli* was able to survive and flourish for so long. First, because of its ability to co-opt most of the political and economic ruling class in Milan – and not just the ruling parties but most of the opposition. Those who spoke out were usually isolated mavericks, such as the entrepreneur and politician, Radice Fossati and a group of intellectuals, academics and journalists around the pressure-group *Società Civile*, formed in 1985. For most politicians, there was no 'choice' involved – to be a politician meant to accept *Tangentopoli*. Often, money was not even asked for, but offered as if of right. A second type of explanation centres on the so-called 'southamericanization' of Italian politics – symbolized by Craxi's authoritarian leadership of the PSI (and of Parliament), and the clientelist and nepotistic culture prevailing in cities like Milan in the 1980s and 1990s (Sapelli 1994; Marcoaldi 1994). A third explanation emphasizes the co-option (or tacit agreement) of civil society into the system, right from the 'daily bribe' up to the enormous 'maxi-tangenti' paid directly to the political parties (Vuillamy 1993). Much of the mass media was also part of the system, and managed to keep the lid on the scandals which began to hit Milanese politicians in the mid-1980s. This hegemony of *Tangentopoli* was reinforced by various external factors – economic prosperity, the cold war, the politicization of Italian civil society – from hospitals to sports clubs to public housing. What was in place was a powerful political *machine*, with deep economic and cultural roots. Della Porta's persuasive study of *Tangentopoli* picks out as one of the unique *Milanese* aspects of the corruption system its 'capacity to extend corrupt practices to almost the entire array of political parties, thereby creating vast complicity across the board' (1993: 106).

These theories go some way towards an explanation of the success and pervasiveness of the *Milano da bere* image in the 1980s. We need, however, to map out the content of that image to understand its hold on the public imagination in that period. What was *Milano da bere*? What kind of city was projected by that image? The buzz-words of that period can help us here – modernity, development, European-city, 'the post-industrial lift-off' (Finetti 1985). Craxi often returned to Milan in his speeches in the 1980s (texts that were to take on a whole new meaning after the explosion of the scandals in 1992). In 1985, he spoke of a

6. The slogan was invented by Marco Mignani, the drink was Amaro Ramazzotti. There are very few analyses of *Milano da bere* that go beyond mere description, or the simplistic link between *città da bere* and 'city to be consumed', but see Zucchetti (1995: 13–29) and above all Mora (1995: 164–78).

new spontaneous and silent 'miracle' . . . a new model of development . . . made up of widespread entrepreneurship, of convinced professionalism, of specialisation . . . a new metropolitan reality which we can call 'post-industrial', or, if we prefer, 'different'. (Craxi 1985: 434–43)

More negatively, Milan was described as a yuppy-city dominated by money. Some commentators identify *Milano da bere* as a period of euphoria

when even the masses and housewives bought '24 ore' [the Italian *Financial Times*] to check the share prices as they shot up . . . when Craxi came from Palazzo Chigi [the presidential residence in Rome] to Palazzo degli Affari [the Milanese Stock Exchange] to receive applause. (Petruccioli 1992)

The comedian Paolo Hendel's brilliant satirical creation – a businessman who believes that every park should be covered in asphalt, in a 35-hour *day* and in a voting *gold card* linked to income – fits perfectly with the *Milano da bere* ideology.

This image was a mixture of two strategies – on the one hand, a celebration of wealth, of consumption, of form over content – as in the key 'moments' (and places)[7] of the image's construction – the Socialist Party congresses (especially that of May 1989 held within the ex-Ansaldo factory in Milan, discussed in Chapter 6 above) the opening night of La Scala, the construction of the new Piccolo Teatro (which later became a symbol of scandal), the adaptation of the PSI's symbol from a hammer and sickle to a red rose. These occasions made a virtue of kitsch, of vulgarity, of new wealth, of power – values often in symmetry with those of the consumer-led boom of the 1980s, and the changes associated with that period in its capital, Milan. The *Milano da bere* image attached itself, triumphantly, to the deep economic changes taking place in the city. It made a virtue of deindustrialization and of the 'new' industries which were becoming dominant – fashion, advertising, private television. Milan was presented as the city of the future, the cutting-edge of transition away from an 'old' industrial society. *At the time*, this image was received favourably, often by those very people who were scandalized by the extent of the scandals uncovered after 1992. I would argue that, notwithstanding its corrupt underlying character, the *Milano da bere* image captured the essence of the social and political changes underlying the 1980s and 1990s in Milan and Lombardy – the shift away from big industry, and the deep crisis of the

---

7. Stajano mentions a 'geography of scandal' – a map of the key places in the city linked to *Tangentopoli* (or a map of *Tangentopoli*) including Craxi's office and house and various bars and restaurants (1993). The link between the urban territory and the control of political and economic power should not be underestimated. Craxi's office looked out upon Piazza del Duomo (Stajano 1993: 18). See also the reflections in the architectural magazine *Lotus* (1994: 108–31).

traditional left.[8] It was this which explained the image's success in the city (and in Italy, if the 'Craxi Project' is viewed more widely) and explains the subsequent support not for the forces of opposition to Craxism (if we exclude the specific circumstance of the *Lega* victory) but for right-wing parties displaying strong political and ideological continuities with that period (above all *Forza Italia!*). Very few spoke out as Milan was 'sacked', and a whole series of projects were begun that were either later abandoned, or that took years to finish.

It was only after 1992 that those isolated voices who had identified and condemned the reality behind *Milano da bere* began to have an audience (but not power). Almost immediately the image of *Milano da bere* began to take on negative connotations. History was written, and re-written. A whole epoch was condemned as 'vulgar' – as if these features could be removed simply by the removal of a group of corrupt politicians. Craxi, leaving aside the system of corruption he used and helped to create, had understood what was happening in Milan before anyone else. He understood the importance of the media, the non-importance of traditional party structures, the power of the local over the national and the centrality of public resources even in a city like Milan (Della Porta 1995). Despite the obvious break in Milanese political life after 1992, the underlying processes (which I discuss below) were transforming the city and its territories. *Milano da bere* is now the object of scorn, but its legacy is immense.

3.2. The Tangentopoli *Scandals and the Lega Administration. 1992–7*

In February 1992, as Italy lived through its most dramatic election campaign for years and the city of Milan was covered in huge posters of Craxi with the slogan, 'Milan at the centre of Italy's progress', a relatively unknown Socialist Party official was arrested immediately after taking a bribe of seven million lire. Nobody could have predicted the portent of that arrest – but since then the names involved have become household ones. The arresting public prosecutor was called Antonio Di Pietro, the arrested official, Mario Chiesa. Within months, after a succession of confessions and arrests, the whole *Tangentopoli* system in Milan had begun to unravel. Within fifteen months, the Socialists, the Christian Democrats and the ex-communists had been humiliated in local elections. A political ruling class had been removed (with a few exceptions).[9] A relatively new political grouping, the

8. Looking at one Communist Party 'section' in the centre of Milan, the Sezione Togliatti in the Garibaldi Zone, this crisis has been a long time coming. In 1947 there were 1,800 members in this section, by 1978 478 and in 1994 less than 100 (Fantini 1994: 159).

9. The language linked to this phase is revealing, combining a sense of the end of a regime (or a monarchy) with that of the end of a war. Thus, we have the image of the 'ex-building *king*' (Ligresti) of the *Liberation of Milan* represented by the inquests (invoking both the Resistance of the Second World War and the fall of the Eastern European regimes) see the title of Dalla Chiesa's interview-book (Calderoni 1993) and of the post-Tangentopoli *reconstruction* of Milan.

Northern League, was running Milan by June 1993. Italy's 'quiet revolution' had begun, in the what was to become known as its 'ex-moral capital' (Barbacetto 1996).[10]

It is worth taking some time to examine the origins of the 'moral capital myth' in the light of the events after 1992. The myth of Milan as Italy's moral capital began to take concrete shape with the industrial exposition of 1881. This huge explosion into the public sphere – the Expo (*l'Esposizione nazionale delle arti e delle industrie*) covered an area of 162,000 square metres and over 8,000 businesses were represented in rooms of 'new machines' and 'galleries of work' – was a conscious attempt to demonstrate and spread this 'myth'. Huge volumes were published to coincide with the Expo – most notably the comprehensive survey of all aspects of the city and its industry in *Mediolanum*. But what was the content of the idea of a 'moral capital'? On the one hand, Milan was the true capital because Rome was not – the myth was a negative assessment of the contribution of Rome and the south to Italy's industrial progress. Milan was modern, industrious, hard-working, honest, productive; Rome was corrupt, unproductive, lazy and pre-modern. Rome was the political capital, Milan the real driving force of the nation, its moral heart (Rosa 1982; Legnani 1984: 123–7; Dickie 1999: 85–7; 173; Riccardi 1991). Yet, the myth was also a celebration of these values in themselves – a series of character traits and concrete realities pertaining to the Milanese worker, entrepreneur and industrialist – modernity, hard work (as in the proverb 'Milan dis, e Milan fa' – Milan says and Milan does), thrift, legality, the self-made man (Pirelli was the ultimate example, his first small factory was opened in the city in 1872, by 1920 his plants occupied a vast sector of the northern urban periphery). In Milan 'here by day there is always much to do: people go, come back, rush, make themselves busy, they study and they work' (Papa cited in Rosa 1982: 42). In addition, Milan was a moral capital because of its cultural strength and its intellectual classes – the *Corriere della Sera*, the publishing houses, the writers and poets – and its scientists, its universities, its engineers (F. Colombo 1998). Milan was the city of urban planning, of order, of productive intellectuals, the only real Italian *city* and the only *European* city in Italy – a city not of *no government*, but of *good government*. Not everything was reduced to money and work and the moral 'correctives' introduced by the most powerful urban socialist reformist movement in Italy – with its vast network of welfare and educational institutions such as the *Società Umanitaria* – meant that capitalism, it was argued, had a human face in Milan. The moral capital ideal was thus an organic mix of dynamism, modernity, *Gesellschaft*-values, paternalism, collective enterprise and humanity. For all these reasons, and despite the dark side of Milan revealed in

10. By the start of 1997, 2,346 people had been investigated by the 'clean hands' team, 890 had been sent for trial and 713 sentences had been passed, with only 4 per cent being acquitted.

journalistic inquests such as *Milano sconosciuta* (Unknown Milan)[11], 'Milan, twenty years on from Unification, was secure that it really was the "moral capital of Italy"' (Rosa 1982: 21).

Since the 1880s, what Spinazzola has called 'the only serious ideological myth, not empty and rhetorical, elaborated by the Italian bourgeoisie after unification . . . the myth of Milan, the myth of the "moral capital" – has entered into crisis on numerous occasions' (1981: 317; Decleva 1980: 181–211). Fascism, although born in Milan, made Rome the centre of its political and planning projects. A variant on the myth was put forward again during the war, when Milan became the 'capital of the resistance' and later a model of reconstruction and honest local administration. As the 'capital of the miracle', the myth became reality for hundreds of thousands of migrants who flooded to the city in search of work. Milan's moral elements – dynamism, hard work, innovation – were once again at the centre of Italy's development. The *Tangentopoli* scandals brought the whole question to the centre of political and intellectual debate. The loss of industry and its proletariat had already left many of the virtues of the myth in tatters. The 1980s Craxian boom was the reverse image of that of 1881 – a boom where money took precedence over work, where form was far more central than content, where waste was exalted and 'greed was good'.

Milan as *Tangentopoli* was, as many commentators have pointed out, an ex-moral capital (Montanelli and Cervi, 1991: 213; Barbacetto and Veltri 1991: xiv, xv, 47). The values of 'Milanesità' had been crushed by those of the protagonists of *Milano da bere*. With the judicial inquest and the scandals themselves, the situation became more complex. Some saw the origins of the clean-up in the city as confirmation that the moral capital's values – at least amongst a virtuous elite – were still in place. Other analyses detected the final death of the myth in the arrests of leading Milanese politicians and businessmen, and the exposure of systems of corruption in the city. In reality, the myth lives on – and is not linked to one industrial epoch. Milan is hard-working, productive and innovative – and is seen as such by commentators and most Italians despite the end of industrial work in the city. Milan is certainly an ex-industrial centre, but many of the myths which began to take shape more than a hundred years ago are still going strong, and represent important reference points for any analysis of the city and the changes in its image.

Despite appearances, therefore, the relationship between the *Tangentopoli* scandals and the image of Milan is complicated one which has changed over time.

11. 'Nobody could possible imagine that they would find in this moral capital, small streets where the sun never signs . . . where the air is terrible, alleys where you are forced to roll up your sleeves, which are covered in rubbish and in solid and liquid excrement.' (Valera 1880 cited in Rosa 1982: 57)

One indicator of this change is the word itself – *Tangentopoli*. Dictionaries published in 1991 only carry the word *tangente*, defined as 'a benefit extorted following benefits or illicit favours' (*Lo Zingarelli* 1991: 1958). By 1992 the word *Tangentopoli* was in circulation and in daily use – in newspapers, on television, in conversations. The first journalist to use the word was the Milan-based crime correspondent of *La Repubblica*, Piero Colaprico, who prided himself on inventing the term (Colaprico 1996). At first, the word seemed to be linked to Milan itself – to the territorial nature of the city and its system of corruption. Milan *was* *Tangentopoli* (with a capital T). Very quickly, however, the word's meaning began to shift. Other scandals began to break out across Italy – in Rome, in Naples, in Turin. *Tangentopoli* now began to lose its capital letter. It now signified a more dislocated system of corruption, a period of time, or (later on) the specific period of the inquest and its domination of public opinion. Thus the phrases 'uscire [exit from . . .] da *Tangentopoli*' or 'dopo [after] *Tangentopoli*' or 'durante [during] *Tangentopoli*' became possible (*Lo Zingarelli* 1995: 1795; Istituto Deagostini 1995: 2037). Dalla Chiesa, one of the first to condemn the corrupt system, has written of Milan as the 'capital of *Tangentopoli*' (Calderoni 1993: 163).[12] For Turone there were 'other Italian Tangentopolis' (1993: 356). With time, the 'opoli' began to be used in a similar way to 'Gate' in the US – as 'the mother of all scandals'. Thus, in 1996 we had 'affittopoli' linked to rent-controlled politician's houses (mainly in Rome) and in 1997 'medicopoli' associated with a massive 'false prescriptions' scandal in Milan.

At first, therefore, and for more than a year (until July 1993) *Tangentopoli* was associated with Milan. But the messages transmitted about the city *as Tangentopoli* were contradictory and confusing. On the one hand, the city was identified with corruption – with a system of bribes – and with the arrests and humiliation of its political and economic élite – Craxi, the ex-mayors Pillitteri and Tognoli, the building tycoon Ligresti, the heads of all the major municipal corporations, from the airport authority to the transport administratiohs.[13] The key Milanese institution here was San Vittore – the ancient and crumbling prison near the city centre – where most of the arrestees were taken and where a number of interrogations took place (it may be too early to assess the long-term influence of these repetitive images on the corruption-Milan-Bribesville connection in the public mind). On the other hand, however, Milan was taking a lead in cleaning up the widespread corruption that all Italians knew was to be found right across Italy. Here the image was a different one – the investigating prosecutors Di Pietro and his colleagues –

12. Barbacetto and Veltri (1991: 124) had used the phrase 'the capital of *tangentilandia*' in 1991, before the *mani pulite* inquest began to have a national impact.
13. For an extraordinarily prescient map of these structures of power *before* the scandals see Andreoli (1989).

and the stock footage of the huge and imposing fascist-built *Palazzo di Giustizia*, with its permanent group of journalists and television cameras outside. At one time or another, from 1992 onwards, the most powerful figures in Italy were to pass through those offices or courtrooms in Corso di Porta Vittoria, two minutes walk from Piazza del Duomo.

The shift from the importance of the first image – Milan as *Tangentopoli* – to the second – Milan as centre of the 'Clean Hands' investigations – had other contributing factors. First, much of the blame was laid at the door of the parties – particularly the PSI and DC (who were effectively destroyed by the scandals) – and not at that of 'Milan'. Hence, the demonization of the *Milano da bere* period as a negative one, often by those who had been enthusiastic supporters or at the very least passive adherents to the myth. Second, many intellectuals began to argue that Milan was the only place where such an inquest could have been begun and had so much effect – that *mani pulite* proved the extent of *legality* in Milan compared to the rest of the country and the strength of the virtuous elites there (Foa and Ginsborg 1994). Third, the central role of the Northern Leagues in both the downfall of the old system and the management of the new tended to shift the blame again away from Milan. The *Lega*'s insistence on 'Rome the thief' (*Roma ladrona*) moved the focus of attack away from Milan and the north towards the capital and the south. The ethnic aspects of the League's propaganda and mobilization are not to be underestimated. In some cases, the Leagues attempted to link the incidence of scandals to the ethnic origins of those involved. Finally, with time the focus of the scandals shifted away from Milan to other, more stereotypically 'corrupt' cities. The particular nature of the enormous personal corruption involving health officials De Lorenzo and Poggiolini was an important moment, as was the indictment of seven times Prime Minister Andreotti for Mafia links in 1993. By 1994, *Tangentopoli* was no longer identified in the public mind either with Milan or even with specific territorial phenomena, but with a generalized system of corruption linked to specific personalities and certain political parties.

Certain militants, journalists and intellectuals took a different view. Groups like *Società Civile* attempted to paint a picture of a corrupt *city* and an urban region controlled by the Mafia. According to these critics Milan was (and is) a sinister place, an *ex-moral capital*, which rejected the chance of real change (specifically in the 1993 Mayoral elections, where Dalla Chiesa lost heavily to a Lega candidate) in favour of continuity and closure. The most eloquent exponents of this position are those who first identified and spoke out against corruption in the mid-1980s. There is no doubt that these analyses contain elements of truth. The attack against corruption began in the *Palazzo di Giustizia*, not on the streets, and those ready to demonstrate against their politicians were, even at the height of the scandals, very few. The inquests did not represent, or create, a political shift to the left. Milan is a right-wing city (and this includes all of its four populations) – and it has become so in response to deep economic, social and cultural changes that have taken place since the mid-1970s. The backing for the judges, which had not been demonstrated via 'left-wing' forms of political protest – such as demonstrations – was clear from the voting patterns after 1992 which saw the near-disappearance of the PSI and DC (and the decline of the moderate ex-communists the PdS, later DS).[14] There had been no real moral or political revolt, from below, against corruption. The failure of the Milan-as-Mafia image to make any impact on public opinion derives partly from a particular view of the Mafia linked to the south, and partly from the everyday experiences of Milan's four populations. The deep crisis of the traditional Milanese left, triggered by the precipitous decline of its main social reference point – the industrial working class – was not halted by the corruption scandals of after 1992. The *Milano da bere* period was not just about corruption but also represented a sea change in values, society and culture in the city and its hinterland. These changes could not be reversed by the removal of a class of corrupt politicians.

Politically, the *Lega* was able to achieve very little in its four years in power in Milan (1993–7). The end of the *Tangentopoli* system had seen the breakdown of the networks which, within the logic of that system, channelled resources towards public projects (and the parties). Political corruption continued, albeit at a greatly reduced level, and illegality at lower levels of civil society and within public and private institutions remained endemic. No real attempt was made to push through any kind of regionalist or separatist project from the power base of Milan, and the *Lega* administration concentrated on clean government, continuity with previous public projects, some privatizations and political campaigns against immigrants, youth centres (*centri sociale*) and 'Rome'. Certainly, the legacy the *Lega* inherited was not an easy one – economically, socially or culturally – but the only sense in which the post-1993 administration represented an alternative was as 'honest' government. Since the *Tangentopoli* system had quite obviously collapsed, and there was no basis for its reconstruction, this 'honesty' was in many ways inevitable – and not necessarily a reflection of the merits of the *Lega* and its administrators. The removal of mayor Formentini from the run-off in 1997's elections, which represented one of the very few cases of a sitting mayor from 1993 not being re-elected, was further evidence that the 1993 result had been a generic vote for the right and against the left and not an indication of any deep-rooted shift towards regionalist politics in the city.

14. In the 1993 local elections, the PSI vote fell to two-and-a-half per cent (it had never been lower than 14 per cent since 1945). Before long, the central offices of the Party and another thirty-seven party sections had been closed. In the same elections, the voters also deserted the PdS (formed out of the old Italian Communist Party in 1990), who won just under nine per cent of the vote, being overtaken by *Rifondazione Comunista*.

3.3. Third Phase: June 1997–2000

Milan is a car park. (Bernardi, 1997)

The Milan of the 1980s finally got the administration it had sought for years in 1997, a mixture of the hard-line, law-and-order right and a free-market liberal industrialist wing linked to the most popular figure in the city – Berlusconi. The centre-right coalition led by the ex-leader of the metalwork industrialists, Albertini, won 53 per cent of the votes in the second round run-off, easily beating the centre-left coalition headed by another industrialist, Fumagalli. Crucial to this result were deep divisions on the left. *Rifondazione* leaders called the two candidates 'clones' and invited their supporters (nine per cent in the first round) to spoil their ballot papers. The right was also divided, and *Lega* leader Bossi called on his supporters to 'go to the seaside'. As a result only 65 per cent of the electorate voted and it was estimated that up to 15 per cent of *Rifondazione* voters actually supported the right, with one in five leaving their ballot papers blank (*La Repubblica*, 12 May 1997). Yet, the programmes of the two candidates were very different and represented two alternative views of the city and its future. Albertini's slogan 'we will run the city like a business' struck a chord with those who had suffered under *Tangentopoli*, and his alliance with Berlusconi made sure that Milan would not be left out of national power-games and negotiations. The right-wing *Alleanza Nazionale*'s concentration on criminality and its determination to 'deal with' illegal immigration in a Giuliani-type 'no tolerance' programme appealed to large sectors of the middle-class electorate. Meanwhile, the centre-left programme underlined the values of solidarity, tolerance, multi-racialism and integration, and promised support from within the *Comune* for the weakest sections of Milanese society. Albertini supported a *laissez faire* approach to the traffic crisis, Fumagalli a much more hard-line approach coupled with innovative solutions such as collective taxis (Fumagalli 1997; *La Repubblica* 23 April 1997).

Both coalitions, however, were in broad agreement on the economic future of the city and its vast hinterland. The big factory was gone, forever. Milan was a technological city, a fashion city/capital, a service sector city – it was no longer (nor had it ever been exclusively) an industrial city. In fact, its ex-factories represented, for both coalitions, the key to the development of the metropolis. The fifteen million square metres of *aree dismesse* are where the topology and morphology of the city's damaged urban space will be rewritten (Bocca 1993: 15; *Progetto Bicocca* 1998). If the model of the management of the city in the 1950s is followed (or that of the 1980s), Milan will continue to have the lowest level of green space per person of any European city, but there were signs of change in the innovative plans for the Bicocca zone or the vast and popular park known as the Parco Nord.

4. Year Zero: Social, Economic and Cultural Change

How do I feel today? Like I am at a funeral. (Gasworker on day of closure of last gasometer, *La Repubblica*, 12 July 1994)

When I go back to Bovisa, today, I feel like I am visiting the tomb of a friend. (Olmi 1999)

As the film director Paolo Virzí has written, 'the crisis of the factory is also a crisis for the form of cities, of their landscape, of their make-up' (*L'Espresso*, 25 March 1994). The most important, traumatic and dramatic change to Milan – its landscape, its identity, its rhythms – has been the rapid and complete deindustrialization and industrial decentralization. The latter process began in the 1960s, the former in the 1970s. By the 1980s all the historic factories in the city and its hinterland had closed or employed tiny fractions of their former workforce. The names are like a litany (and their founders are all buried in that extraordinary temple of industrial achievement – Milan's Monumental Cemetery) – Pirelli, Falck, Breda, Alfa Romeo, OM, Innocenti. In the 1950s the biggest employer in the city was Pirelli, today it is the *Comune di Milano*.[15] Bovisa, the working-class neighbourhood *par excellence*, saw its last big factory close in 1996. Industrial jobs in the Province of Milan fell by 280,000 between 1971 and 1989. Those employed in factories with over 500 employees fell to 163,991 by 1991 (the figure in 1981 had been 272,507).[16] Employees in businesses employing between two and nine employees rose from 496,003 (32 per cent of the total) to 656.805 (41 per cent) between 1981 and 1989.

Sesto San Giovanni, a suburb of Milan that was once known as the 'Stalingrad of Italy', represented the extreme end of this trend – with two million square metres of ex-industrial space, a third of the whole area of the town, (*La Repubblica*, 27 November 1997). Industrial workers at Sesto fell from 40,000 to 3,000 in just over a decade, wiping out a history of factory work that went back to the early years of the century. One newspaper reported that young children were heard asking their teachers at an exhibition on the Breda, once an enormous and famous engineering plant at Sesto, 'were there really factories at Sesto?' (Melone 1994). By the end of the 1990s, Sesto had taken off as a technological and service centre and much of the legacy of industrial capitalism had disappeared from the landscape

---

15. In 1985 in the Province there were 70,000 teachers, 32,000 people were employed in health services and 66,000 in local authorities (and in Milan itself 26,000). In addition there were 11,000 railway employees and 16,000 postal workers (Foti 1993: 64).

16. Yet 75,000 jobs were created between 1971 and 1989 in the Province, and by the 1990s there were 450,000 small and medium-sized businesses in the city and its province (Foti 1993: 10, 30).

and the political make-up of the zone (Bull 1996; Ravelli 1994). By 1989, the main union federation in Milan – the CGIL – could count on only 90,971 members, a fall of over 40 per cent from 1981. In 1997, in an initiative heavy with symbolism, Fiat, the owners of Alfa-Romeo, offered its factory for sale – with one proviso, for every 200 square metres bought the purchaser was obliged to employ an ex-Alfa worker (*La Repubblica*, 1 October 1997).[17] In 1994 Sesto San Giovanni voted in a representative from Berlusconi's *Forza Italia!*

Many of these factory closures were accompanied by heroic rearguard struggles, in which the formerly militant working class went through the motions of opposition without any hope of success. Symptomatic of these moments of loss for the city and for those employed in these famous industries was the dispute at Innocenti. Here a worker, Ubaldo Urso, climbed to the top of the huge factory chimney and threatened to throw himself off if a number of sackings were not withdrawn (Paolozzi 1992; Stajano 1993: 88–102).[18] In reality, most of those laid off by these closures were re-employed or promised re-employment. Many ex-workers have formed extremely successful small industries and service businesses, often in co-operation with their ex-colleagues. Nonetheless, it is clear that the end of so much large-scale Fordist production, which had dominated the physical and economic landscape in the city for so long, represented a difficult moment. No longer would the streets be dominated by thousands of blue-suited workers on a shift change (even street signs – with their warnings of *uscita operai!* (workers' exit) – became redundant). No longer would Milan be associated with Breda, with Pirelli, with Alfa Romeo – with smoke and chimneys and the factory gate. A new identity was in construction. As Turani (1998) has written, Milan is now

> a city in which nobody really produces anything (not bolts, not saucepans, not bicycles, and certainly not cars) . . . they produce thoughts, opinions, shows, legal cases, advertising campaigns, finance . . . a city of talents . . . different from a city of tens of thousands of blue collar workers . . . Milano was something precise, well-defined: it was a great industrial centre, with a strong working class and a strong ruling class. Both were proud of their own work and their own missions.

For the traditional left, and for the ex-working class, the period 'of the big factory' began to be viewed with nostalgia. In a strange ideological shift, the same critics who had stigmatized the Fordist factory as a dark Satanic organization

---

17. Union militancy, unsuprisingly, fell to a new low and the relationship between hours worked and hours on strike in Lombardy dropped from 2.15 in 1983 to 1.08 in 1990 (Foti 1993: 11).

18. The apocalyptic terms used by these workers are understandable, as they saw a whole world disappear before their eyes – to cite one such ex-worker 'as the old environment has disappeared, the species has become extinct' (Paolozzi 1992).

where men were reduced to beasts, now pined for the return of those factories.[19] A kind of 'new apocalypticism' began to take shape on the left, which started to characterize the '1980s' in the same way as critics had stigmatized the boom thirty years before. This romanticization of the positive effects supposedly produced by big industry – community, production, even legality – was accompanied by a reappraisal of the first economic miracle (see Chapter 2 above). Where once the immigration of the 1950s was described as a disaster for the country and for the immigrants, it was now seen as an example of virtue, of naive productive honesty. The contradictions of the momentous changes of the 1980s and 1990s were largely ignored in favour of a conservative, nostalgic and myopic view of the past and the present.

The Milanese ruling class was transformed, as its famous working class disappeared. Media barons (Berlusconi), fashion designers (Armani, Ferrè, Versace, Dolce & Gabbana), advertising companies (800,000 television advertisements are produced every year in the city) and financiers (Milan is host to 30 per cent of the national head offices of all banks with a presence in Italy) replaced the old industrial classes (for this transformation see Sapelli 1996). A whole series of new jobs began to dominate the city – most linked to the arrival of city and business-users and to the mass media. By 1987, Milan could call upon 800 DJs, 1,200 make-up artists and 4,700 film dubbers (Foti 1993: 113). The landscape of the city changed, as factories were demolished, some were re-used, or had elaborate plans built around them (above all the Bicocca University/housing project at the ex-Pirelli area and the Bovisa plans). Others were left to crumble, becoming the only available shelter for thousands of immigrants.

At the same time, Milan's populations began to change. Since 1969 the resident, 'sleeping' population has been in decline – and ageing. Milan now has a negative birth rate (in 1990, for example, 9,529 babies were born in the city and there were over 15,000 deaths) and three grandparents for every child. By 1997 25 per cent of this population was over 65 and the average age of Milan's residents was forty-five. One third of these pensioners live alone, as do 42 per cent of all residents (Cirillo 1997; *La Repubblica*, 15 November 1997; 26 January 1993; 9 December 1993). There are far more resident Milanese over eighty than there are under five (Lanzetti 1995). At the same time, this resident population has been shifting away from the centre of the city (a long-term process). Meanwhile, the other 'populations' have been stable (commuters – with far fewer workers and far more service employees) or on the increase (city users and especially business users). This pattern

---

19. Foti describes the big factory in essentially positive terms: as a 'place of solidaristic tissue for the working class, seat of democratic anima and conflict, territory of socialisation and political and cultural education, important social stabiliser' (Foti 1993: 11). For a brilliant analysis of the nostalgia industry and heritage in Britain see Samuel (1994).

of change creates its own problems and patterns – with, at night, the city resembling a form of urban drive-in theme park with its own, semi-forbidden, attractions.

In addition to these changes, which are cited time and again as evidence of the generalized crisis of Milan, the national mix of the urban population has also been changing dramatically. The 1980s and 1990s saw the arrival of large numbers of immigrants from outside Europe. This 'fifth population', a combination of city users, commuters and residents (often without legal status) has probably found more of a welcome in Milan than elsewhere in Italy, not least because of the need for cheap, 'dirty' labour in Milan's enormous service sector – domestic help, restaurants, small commerce, building work. The history of recent immigration to Milan is discussed in Chapter 3. The immigrant presence despite a static housing market is also evidence of the dynamism of the resident population (the *actual* sleeping population) despite evidence to the contrary from most official sources. Between 1985 and 1990, 10 per cent of the new children in Milan's schools were of non-EU origin (Comune di Milano 1997, see Chapter 3 above).

A graphic example of these changes comes from a snapshot of a single housing block on the old Milanese ex-working class periphery. This block, built in the 1890s, has always had a series of small flats available at (low) rents to immigrants to the city. For years, most of the residents were either Milanese single women or southern Italian administrative workers. Dialect could often be heard in the courtyard. By the mid-1990s the population mix of the housing block had been transformed. In fact, the 'population' of the block was made up of an Egyptian family with two children (born in Milan); a Kurdish family, a Cuban woman-Italian man couple; a single Israeli woman; a Sri Lankan family; an Anglo-Italian couple with child; a gay couple; a group of students; a single Argentinian woman; a musician and an artist. Apart from reflecting the economic changes in the city, the mix in the block also highlights the extraordinary (and bohemian) mosaic of the resident/commuter urban populations. This reality is simply ignored in the debates on the future of Milan, which paint a picture of an ageing, static and 'single' city, an image that is both false and ethnocentric, and that disregards both the flexibility of Martinotti's four populations and the permanence of many of the new immigrants. Many similar housing blocks have seen their populations completely transformed three or even four times over the twentieth century. It is in these often dark and crumbling flats that the history of Milan has been written over a hundred years of continual economic and social change.

If the future of our cities, as Castells has recently argued, is to be judged by the treatment of children, then Milan's crisis is truly a deep one. One the one hand, the streets, courtyards and squares of Milan, once in continual use as play areas, are deserted, or used as car parks. Fear, of traffic, of crime, of the city itself keeps Milanese children in the home far more than their parents and grandparents ever were. A graphic illustration of this trend in the use of the city comes from a survey carried out in one school in the city. The survey discovered that 30 per cent of children play alone and in a 'static' way. In the 1950s, 'play', according to 62 per cent of parents, took place mainly in courtyards, today only two per cent can use the courtyard. More striking perhaps was the fact that only three per cent of parents play with their own children (Foti 1993: 86). In the Isola neighbourhood in 1994, 'the courtyard, working-class up to twenty years ago, was presumably animated by voices, shouts, arguments, children . . . now there is absolute silence' (Fantini 1994: 159).

5. The Crisis of Image

A city where there is a conspiracy of silence, a marshland, an impenetrable place. (Dalla Chiesa, cited in Calderoni 1993: 80)

Milano da bere was an attempt to make a virtue of these economic and social changes. The image of the mid-1980s exalted the post-industrial landscape and looked to build a new city based on technology, flexibility, style and consumption. Yet, the 1980s and 1990s were marked by a series of crises that have dominated public debates. In chronological order, these 'crises' can be summarized around certain themes: drugs (particularly heroin); crime; immigration; pollution; traffic; corruption; rubbish; population loss; 'the periphery'.[20] In the late 1980s, as the boom linked to *Milano da bere* came to a halt in the face of the near-bankruptcy of the state (*before* the *Tangentopoli* scandals) these short-lived crises all expressed, in one form or another, the search for a new identity or identities in a post-industrial city. Most visible of all was the cultural crisis that hit the city, as cinemas became porn houses (in 1970 there were 161 cinemas in the city, in 1997 only sixty-eight of which fifteen were dedicated to pornography alone (*La Repubblica*, 11 December 1997), and the much-heralded Nuovo Piccolo Teatro remained a building site. Imperceptibly, and without the action of the judges, the *Milano da bere* image began to take on negative connotations. Milan's image became a succession of horror stories – the daily death-count of heroin overdoses in 1989, or the danger levels reached by pollution in 1990, or the discovery of a no-go neighbourhood ('the illegal city . . . a neighbourhood where the state is absent', *Corriere della Sera*, 9 June 1991) on the urban periphery in 1991 or the bottom place in the crime table 'achieved' by Milan in 1997, or the seven murders in the city in the first week of 1998, or the Mafia murders of 1996 (Barbacetto 1997), or the transportation of the city's rubbish to Apulia for dumping, and finally the politicians

20. Heroin-related deaths rose by 143 per cent from 1986–8, and became a daily feature of the local news (IRER 1992: 6). In 1990, 11 per cent of all deaths of those under 34 in the city were due to overdoses.

in handcuffs confessing to having stolen money from a municipal old-people's home.

All of these 'crises' led to much soul-searching in the press and amongst (mainly Milanese) intellectuals. A new image of Milan began to emerge, in dramatic contrast to that of *Milano da bere*. Milan was an empty city, a city where large parts of the territory were controlled by the Mafia, a dangerous place, a cultural wasteland – a city, to quote Arbasino, 'non da bere' (1997). Milan was also in deep ecological crisis, despite its falling (resident) population and the closure of its polluting industries. Massive car ownership and the failure of successive administrations to decentralize essential services only exacerbated the problem. Milan, in this sense, is nothing like the classic post-industrial 'wasteland' city – Detroit – with its empty roads and unused car parks. Milan is full of cars – always – on its pavements, in its courtyards, on its roads. The city-users and commuters more than compensate for the declining residents.

In the 1990s a series of short-term and short-lived attempts were made to 'solve' the traffic/pollution crisis – the closure of the centre to private cars, the division of the centre into 'slices', the imposition of tight controls on exhaust emissions. Emergency measures were adopted to control pollution, such as the *targa alterna* where half the cars in the city were banned from the roads. Occasionally, even the schools were closed to protect children from the smog. In the late 1990s a series of Sundays saw the banning of private cars, and the city was briefly transformed, quiet and clean. None of these 'solutions' has come close to dealing with the problem – and many have been reversed in the 1990s. The recognition of the traffic issue as a cultural problem linked to modernity and *benessere* (and also to the ideology of *Milano da bere*) – and therefore not easily resolved by legislation – is crucial here. Meanwhile, short-sighted planning decisions only exacerbate the situation – such as the location of the new Fiera near to the town centre (1997) – leading to anti-traffic protests from mothers and children at local schools. The parking problem is even more serious and appears to have no solution. Milan has more cars per head of the population that any similar city in the world, and may be the first city to reach the magical figure of a car for every resident (including children).[21] This is a city with thirty-five car accidents a day which cause 350 injuries a week and a death every four days. In 1996, a quarter of all the car accidents in Italy took place in Milan (*La Repubblica*, 1 October 1997). Taking the wider area of the Province of Milan, there were five and a half million cars with 'MI' on their number plates in 1990. In 1965 there had been one million and in 1947 only 10,000 (Fantini 1994: 70). Milan is also the city in Italy with the

21. In 1997 the number of cars registered in the city was up to 864,000 from 772,000 in 1996, (Bocca 1997b). Northern Italy has become, according to Rota, the most motorized area in the world with one car for every 1.3 people (Rota, 1997: 21–2; see also Viale, 1996).

fastest and most modern transport links in Italy (three underground lines with seventy km of track, integrated tram, bus and trolley-bus services and a light railway – the *Passante*) and the highest use of public transport of all the peninsula.

Yet even this 'issue' has drifted off the agenda – the green movement in the city is very weak (with only one councillor in the late 1990s). Milan has a tiny number of parks (it has far more car parking space than green space) and the motorist always wins out over the resident (of course, these are difficult groups to distinguish). One example will suffice here, in 1996 the residents who live opposite the *cavalcavia Bacula* (part of the second ring road) to the north of the city finally succeeded, after years of campaigning, in having gates put in front of the entrance to the overpass, which were to be closed at night. These houses were compared to gas chambers by their inhabitants, who were forced to keep their windows closed in the summer to keep out the noise and smoke. Signs were put up warning motorists of the impending closure of the bridge. Yet, the gates were only used once. The traffic chaos they created on that unique occasion forced the administration into a u-turn. The gates remained as symbols of yet another failed traffic control measure, just as the Garibaldi-Varesina wasteland near the centre of the city, still abandoned from wartime damage and awaiting a serious project, symbolizes the planning failures of the post-war period.

The traffic/pollution crisis in the city hangs over the urban area like the sword of Damocles – isolated in the public mind and in public debates from the other crises I have mentioned. In fact, all of these mini-crises have been separated from the others – apart perhaps from 'immigration' which has been used as a catch-all crisis for drugs, crime, urban decay and general urban decline. This fragmentation is symptomatic of the failure of the city's governments to plan the future of its urban space, and to move beyond short-term, politically contingent responses. But there is also a more serious, near-insurmountable problem; Milan's four populations all have different needs. Not everyone can be satisfied. A pensioner living alone on the Milanese periphery needs good, cheap transport links. A business-man attending a trade fair wants parking space and empty roads. A child in a tower block needs green space and pollution-free air. The daily commuter cares little about pollution – he can return to the countryside every evening – but wants to be able to get in and out of the city as fast as possible. No administration can meet all these needs, and the economic pressure to help commuters, city users and business users must be weighed up against the social and political pressure to satisfy residents who are also voters and ratepayers.

Conclusion: Whose City? Which City?

1. Shop-window City? Milan and its Others

Milan today is a dynamic, glittering fashion capital which hides the dark side of the urban dream. The billions of lire that circulate around fashion shows, design weeks, advertising companies and private television are underpinned by immigrants working in the 'dirty' jobs which feed this economy. These immigrants are often 'non-people', ignored by the political system (except for short-term propagandist campaigns), marginalized within the urban fabric, lacking in economic and political rights (Dal Lago 1999). In the kitchens, sweatshops, bars and building-sites of Milan, these immigrants provide the labour that maintains Milan's extraordinary post-industrial economy. In the private kitchens and nurseries of the city, thousands of domestic servants and cleaners carry out the menial household tasks that free the Milanese to fulfil their hard-working reputation. Beyond the stunning veneer of the 'block of gold' or the magnificent *Piazza del Duomo* and *Galleria*, Milan's peripheries stretch across the Lombard plain, with their bleak housing estates and ageing 'local' populations. Milan is a *shop-window city*, where the gloss and sparkle are only, and necessarily, skin-deep. This was also true of the first economic miracle, which brought hundreds of thousands of Italian immigrants to the city and its hinterland. Then, the veneer of that city was far less glamorous – Pirelli, Breda, Alfa-Romeo – but the raw material was similar, builders and workers from Apulia and Sicily, the Veneto and the Lombard mountains. Milan has always been a city of population movement and immigration, and the histories of these various movements are at the heart of any understanding of the development of the modern metropolis and its links with the countryside, the nation, Europe and the rest of the world. The region's particular model of industrial development allowed this movement to co-exist with small rural-based industries, industrial districts and seasonal migration, as well as long-term and historic systems of commuting (Consonni 1984, 1993).

2. An Ecological Crisis? The Necessity of Movement

No longer bribesville, no longer boomtown, Milan's identity in the late 1990s was difficult to pin down, as it always had been. The city was faced with a key series of choices concerning the problems that had dominated the administration and organization of Milan since the war. One the one hand, politicians and opinion leaders were still stuck in the mind-warp of the old city boundaries, the canals and the residents of the old, restricted urban area. This vision precluded a realistic vision of the extent of urban change over the last twenty of so years – the transformation to the *peri-urban* – and therefore blocked the adoption of flexible policies able to deal with the myriad problems of 'Milan' and its vast hinterland. The shifting populations who use, work in, or pass through the extended urban areas in and around the city all have different needs and many of these requirements were in contradiction with those of other, more permanent populations. Milan's gleaming international image was combined with a suffocating provincialism amongst its ruling political élites.

The central questions of decentralization, of traffic, of transport and pollution, of green space and industrial space, of education, safety and crime remain unsolved. In fact they were getting worse. *All these questions are bound up with different ideas of what the city is and who is it for.* And these problems are neither simple nor simply linked to the activities of particular populations. Most residents call for a solution to the traffic problem, yet most have cars that they use frequently (and often unnecessarily, and often alone). Most people think decentralization of the trade fair area, for example, was a good idea, but none of these lobbies or interest groups were able to prevent the ecologically disastrous re-centralization of the new *Fiera* development in the mid-1990s. Many Milanese and visitors lament the lack of green space in the city, yet nothing is done against the constant flouting of building regulations or the expansion of motorways across the region. The whole culture of the city is based upon motorization and the primacy of short-term economic gain, to the detriment of long-term and wide-ranging planning. To change this culture requires a revolution of ideas about the city itself, its users and its administrators. It is not enough to say the city should belong to group X or class Y – *everyone* is implicated in the problems of the metropolis. The crisis of the city is not just structural but anthropological. This revolution is not imminent. Milan has never produced a militant green movement or even an organization able to campaign effectively for the rights of any citizen, or any urban child, to walk down a street to their local park without being poisoned, run over, pushed aside or simply scared. The rampant individualism of the modern metropolis has crushed any kind of collective civic culture able to organize society in a rational fashion. A new kind of 'northern familism' was born in Milan during the boom, without any significant relationship with positive forms of communitarianism or civicness, either at a local or a government level. This culture triumphed in the 1980s, creating the Bribesville of *Milano da bere.*[1]

1. This conclusion contradicts that of the influential research of Putnam, Leonardi and Nanetti (1993). For the birth of this familism in Milan see Foot (1995).

The economics and mechanics of the modern metropolis militate against possible radical change. Milan's extreme post-industrial economy requires constant movement, constant servicing, constant updating and technical change. The city is always on the move, and must be so to survive. Yet, this situation creates a blocked city, as no groups have priority in the (failed) rush to make the next appointment on time. Gridlock reigns, but cars are taken out regardless. Often, you can walk to an appointment in less time than it takes you to 'drive'. Small crises (strikes, rain, road-works) lead to a total breakdown in the traffic system. Money, huge amounts of money, circulates – and then moves on, out and through the city without stopping to invest, plan or think ahead. The short term, inevitably, takes precedence over the long term. If Milan ever had a civic culture, it has one no longer.

3. Milan and Italy

Milan has always played a key role in Italian history. It invented fascism and urban reformist socialism. It was host to the end of Mussolini's regime and the birth of a new democracy. The city's economy pulled Italy into the world economy in the 1960s and again dominated key sectors in the 1980s and 1990s. The left first experimented with post-socialist ideas in Milan, and northern regionalism first took power in this city. Finally, Milan produced the first post-political movement to take power in Europe, *Forza Italia!* Berlusconi's movement, just like that of Craxi before him, was a perfect fit for the shop-window city. A political organization that used the most sophisticated modern techniques of marketing and advertising to transmit its messages. Berlusconi's post-modern populism found a rich terrain in the individualist and consumerist cultures that dominated the Milan of the 1990s (Biorcio 2001). This outcome was not inevitable, and many other futures were still possible, but the days of collective mass politics in a city like Milan were gone, forever. Movements cannot be created outside the society in which they work, and Milanese society could not produce any opposition to the prevailing cultures of the city from within its ranks. Too many were integrated into the system and its logical anthropological outcomes for such resistance to be possible. Only from the outside could change come about, perhaps through the influence of the immigrants who were constructing alternative cultures in the city from the 1980s onwards.

4. Post-Industrial Realities: Portrait of a Business

There is a company, near the centre of Milan, which employs about one hundred people in two premises. Most are women, many are without contracts, and therefore without pension rights, sickness benefit or maternity rights. Working conditions are cramped and unhygienic. Many employees become ill through overwork and syndromes of various kinds. Overtime is often essential and usually unpaid. Many employees work late nights, weekends and holidays. The employers in this family firm are usually present and exercise personal surveillance over their employees. There are no union representatives within the firm. This is not a textile sweatshop employing poorly paid immigrants but a publishing firm using the highest forms of technology and highly qualified journalists and graphic designers. Some post-industrial realities in Milan bear a superficial relationship to the conditions of early industrialization. The ideals of flexibility, of the end of the workplace, of the liberation represented by technology are, in this case at least, fully confirmed as myths.

Appendix 1: Films Cited

Banditi a Milano, C. Lizzani, 1968.
Colpire al cuore, G. Amelio, 1982.
Cronaca di un amore, M. Antonioni, 1950.
Edipo Re, P. P. Pasolini, 1967.
Fuori dal mondo, G. Piccioni, 1998.
Hotel Paura, R. De Maria, 1996.
Il Mafioso, A. Lattuada, 1962.
Il Portaborse, D. Lucchetti, 1991
Il Posto, E. Olmi, 1961.
Il tempo dei gitani, E. Kusturica, 1989.
Kamikazen, G. Salvatores, 1988.
L'aria serena dell'ovest, S. Soldini, 1990.
La classe operaia va in paradiso, E. Petri, 1972.
La Notte, M. Antonioni, 1961.
La Rimpatriata, D. Damiani, 1963.
La vita agra, C. Lizzani, 1963.
Marrakech Express, G. Salvatores, 1989.
Milano '83, E. Olmi, 1983.
Milano nera, G. Rocco e P. Serpi, 1964.
Miracolo a Milano, V. De Sica, 1951.
Napoletani a Milano, E. De Filippo, 1953.
Nirvana, G. Salvatores, 1997.
Oggetti Smarriti, G. Bertolucci, 1981.
Renzo e Luciana, M. Monicelli, and *Il Lavoro*, Luchino Visconti – episodes in
    Boccaccio '70, 1962.
Rocco e i suoi fratelli, Luchino Visconti, 1960.
Romanzo popolare, M. Monicelli, 1974.
Sbatti il mostro in prima pagina, M. Bellocchio, 1972.
Sotto il vestito, niente, C. Vanzina, 1985.
Strane storie, S. Baldoni, 1994.
Teorema, P. P. Pasolini, 1968.
Tutto a posto, niente in ordine, L. Wertmüller, 1974.
Un'anima divisa in due, S. Soldini, 1993.
Una storia milanese, Eriprando Visconti, 1962.
Via Montenapoleone, C. Vanzina, 1986.

Appendix 2: The History of Milan since 1945 – Society, Culture and Politics, A Personal Chronology[1]

1945

24–25 April: Insurrection in Milan against the German Nazi Army and the Italian Fascists. Milan is liberated before the Allies arrive. A number of scores are settled with collaborators and Fascists. Bodies turn up outside the Musocco cemetery in Milan. Riccardo Lombardi, of the *Partito d'Azione*, is Prefect of Milan.

27 April: The Mayor of Milan is Socialist Antonio Greppi, at the head of an administration comprising equal numbers of Socialists, Communists and Christian Democrats. This position is confirmed by the elections of April 1946 and remains in place, with small changes, until 1949.

28 April: Mussolini's body, along with those of a number of fascist leaders, are taken to Milan to Piazzale Loreto. The huge crowds force the authorities to hang up the bodies from a petrol station.

Vittorini publishes the first edition of *Il Politecnico*.

1946

7 April: Local council elections. Christian Democrats (DC) 27 per cent; Communist Party (PCI) 24 per cent; Socialist Party (PSIUP) 36 per cent; Liberal Party (PLI) 7 per cent; Republican Party (PRI) 3 per cent.

21–24 April: The 'Revolt of San Vittore'. A massive riot in Milan's main prison leaves four people dead and paralyses the city for four days.

22–23 April: Mussolini's body is 'stolen' from the Musocco cemetery. It is only recovered in August.

11 May: La Scala reopens, after repairs for bomb damage, with a concert directed by Toscanini.

---

1. This chronology is not intended to be comprehensive but to fill some gaps in areas not covered in this book in any detail (for example the local political and electoral situation). Figures have been rounded up or down where appropriate.

1947

January: The split in the Socialist Party in Rome decimates the Milan party. A majority of councillors leave to join the new Social-Democratic Party, including Mayor Greppi, yet the 'Resistance' alliance remains intact in Milan, whilst the left is thrown out of national government.

28 November: workers and ex-partisans occupy the Prefecture in the city centre in protest against the sacking of ex-partisan prefect Troilo. 60 provincial Mayors also resign in protest, after Greppi himself resigns. The sacking is confirmed.

The *Piccolo Teatro* opens in the city under Giorgio Strehler and Paolo Grassi in Via Broletto.

The first work begins on the QT8 experimental neighbourhood on the northern periphery of the city.

Production of the Lambretta scooter begins at the Innocenti factory.

The eighth *Triennale* architectural exhibition is held in Milan under the slogan 'A house for everyone'.

Lucio Fontana, artist, publishes his spatialist manifesto.

1948

January: the Communist Party's Fourth Congress approves a pact with the Socialist Party. In the national elections in April the DC wins a crushing victory.

14 July: After an attempt on Togliatti's life in Rome, massive strikes and demonstrations sweep across Milan and Lombardy.

1949

The Feltrinelli Library opens in Milan.

The city administration changes. The Communists and Socialists go into the opposition, and the Liberals enter the administration. Greppi remains Mayor.

1951

Miracolo a Milano (De Sica) is released. It wins best film award at the Cannes film festival.

Mass internal migration to Milan begins to take off after the floods in the Polesine region (Veneto). Over the next ten years the number of jobs in the city will increase by 54 per cent, with even greater increases in certain sectors (in construction, for example, the increase will be over 180 per cent, 70 per cent of whom will be immigrants).

The first *Coree* (self-constructed urban villages built by immigrants, see Chapter 3) begin to appear in the Milanese hinterland.

27 May: Local elections. DC 30 per cent (30 seats); PCI 22 per cent (13 seats); PSI 14 per cent (8), Social Democrats (PSULI) 14 per cent (15). PLI 6 per cent; Monarchists 3 per cent; MSI (neo-fascists) 6 per cent.

Virgilio Ferrari (PSDI) is appointed Mayor of Milan, at the head of a 'centrist' coalition (Christian Democrats and Social Democrats). He remains Mayor throughout the 1950s.

The first elected provincial government of Milan is set up. In the provincial elections in May the DC wins 42 per cent of the vote, whereas the (united) left only gains 33 per cent. The DC governed the Province in centrist coalitions until 1961, when the centre left took over until 1975. Left-wing administrations were then in control until 1990.

1953

Milan's first General Plan (Piano Regolatore Generale) is ratified by government decree.

The national electricity company (ENI) begins work on the Metanopoli office, residential and industrial complex to the south of the city at San Donato.

1954

3 January: state television in Italy begins transmissions from its studios in Milan.

Alfa Romeo begins production of the Giulietta 1300.

The Feltrinelli publishing house is founded in Milan.

Luchino Visconti begins a series of historic opera productions with Maria Callas at La Scala.

Work begins on the Comasina neighbourhood on the edge of Milan. On completion it is the biggest public housing project in Italy.

Internazionale wins its third Italian Soccer championship in four years.

1955

19 November: Transmission begins of the programme, *Lascia o raddoppia?* hosted by Mike Bongiorno. It is an immediate success.

L'Espresso begins publication.

Giovanni Montini, future Pope, is made Archbishop of Milan

1956

21 April: The newspaper *Il Giorno* begins publication in the city.

27 May: Local elections. DC 30 per cent (25 seats); PCI 18 per cent (15); PSI 20 per cent (16); Social democrats (PSDI) 12 per cent (10); PLI 6 per cent; Monarchists 5 per cent; MSI 6 per cent.

Ferrari is reconfirmed Mayor of Milan.

Provincial elections: The DC wins 40 per cent of the vote; the united left 36 per cent and the PSDI 5 per cent.

1957

The first supermarkets open in Milan.

1958

Most historians argue that the 'economic miracle' or boom began in earnest in 1958 (and lasted until 1963).

The first part of the *Autostrada del Sole* is opened (Milan–Parma).

The Torre Velasca (BBPR) is finished.

1959

A government decree ratifies the formation of an plan for development taking in the city of Milan and a number of zones in the areas surrounding the city, the Pim. In 1965 this planned coordination is widened to take in 136 *comuni* surrounding Milan.

1960

The Pirelli Skyscraper is completed. Work had begun in 1956.

Luchino Visconti's *Rocco e i suoi fratelli* opens in November in Milan. Huge debate and censorship follows.

Peak of migration from the south to the north, and to Milan.

Piero Manzoni shows his provocative 'Merda d'artista' in Milan.

Visconti's production of Testori's *L'Arialda* is banned after the opening night in the city.

Bettino Craxi is elected councillor in the local elections. He becomes an Assessor the following year.

6 November. Local elections 1960: DC 30 per cent; PSI 20 per cent; PCI 20 per cent; PSDI 10 per cent; PLI 8 per cent; MSI 6 per cent.

Provincial elections: DC 39 per cent; PLI 5 per cent; PCI 22 per cent; PSI 19 per cent; PSDI 7 per cent.

Important strikes and demonstrations involving thousands of electro-mechanical workers take place in Milan.

1961

After long negotiations a centre-left (Socialist and Christian Democrat) administration is voted in in Milan, the first such alliance in Italy. The Mayor is Gino Cassinis (PSDI).

In February the Fascist 'anti-urbanization' laws are abolished, allowing immigrants to Milan from within Italy equal rights and access to services. For the first time, accurate immigration figures can be collected by the statistical services.

Ermanno Olmi's *Il Posto*, set in Milan, is released.

Michelangelo Antonioni releases *La Notte*, also set in Milan.

1962

Demonstration against the US blockade of Cuba in Milan. A demonstrator (Communist student Giovanni Ardizzone) dies in clashes with the police.

October: Enrico Mattei, President of ENI, dies after his plane crashes in mysterious circumstances near to Pavia.

Luciano Bianciardi's acidic attack on the Milan of the boom, *La vita agra* is published.

Over four million people visit the annual trade fair in the city.

AC Milan wins its fourth Italian soccer championship since 1955, Internazionale triumphs in 1965 and Milan again in 1966 and 1968, before Internazionale win again in 1971.

1963

A new Alfa Romeo factory is opened outside Milan at Arese. Production begins to wind down at the historic Portello plant in the city.

Milan's Archbishop, Montini, is made Pope (Pope Paul VI, 1963–78).

AC Milan wins the European Cup for the first time, beating Benfica in the final 2–1.

1964

End of the 'economic miracle'.

February: Pietro Bucalossi (PSDI) is appointed Mayor of Milan after the death in office of Cassinis in January.

November: the first line of the Milanese Metro (MM1) is opened. Work begins on the second line MM2.

November: Local elections. DC 24 per cent; PSI 16 per cent; PSU 8 per cent; PLI 21 per cent; PCI 22 per cent; PSDI 8 per cent; PSIUP 2 per cent; MSI 5 per cent. Bucalossi is confirmed Mayor of a centre-left coalition in January 1965, despite the unexpectedly high vote for the Liberal Party.

Provincial elections: DC 33 per cent; PLI 14 per cent; PCI 24 per cent; PSI 15 per cent; PSDI 6 per cent; MSI 4 per cent.

Internazionale win the European cup, beating Real Madrid 3-1 in the final.

1965

Internazionale wins its second European Cup, and the third in a row for the city.

Work on the Tangenziale Ovest (running from the lakes motorway to the Autostrada del sole) begins. It is completed in 1968.

1966

The Zanzara case. A group of students from the Parini school in Milan are taken to court for having carried out an investigation into the sexual habits of some fellow students. They are later acquitted.

Milan's basketball team, sponsored by the canned-meat company Simmenthal, wins the European Cup. Star of the team is future US senator, Bill Bradley.

1967

17 November: Milan's prestigious Catholic University is occupied by students.

Fiorucci (an elegant and innovative clothes and fashion shop) opens in Milan.

November: Bucalossi resigns as Mayor after a long debate over policies and the budget.

December: Aldo Aniasi (PSI) becomes Mayor of Milan at the head of a centre-left coalition.

1968

25 March: clashes between students and police in front of the Catholic University. Sixty-six people are injured.

The first Cubs (local action committees based in factories) are formed at Pirelli and in other Milanese factories.

Huge strike waves hit all Milanese factories.

Students protest at the opening night of La Scala, throwing eggs and chanting 'fascists, ruling classes, your time has come'.

The Liceo Parini in Milan is the first *scuola media* in Italy to be occupied by students.

Bettino Craxi is elected to Parliament with 24,000 preference votes.

1969

November: an agreement is reached with Pirelli workers, including the absolute right to assembly and to elect shop floor delegates.

During clashes with demonstrators following a general strike over housing a policeman dies in the centre of Milan.

12 December: The massacre of Piazza Fontana (see introduction). An innocent anarchist, Pietro Valpreda is arrested on 15 December, the day of the funerals of the victims; he spends three years in prison awaiting trial. Another innocent anarchist, Giuseppe Pinelli, dies the same night after 'falling' from a police station window.

Work begins on the Tangenziale Est (completed in 1975) connecting the Bergamo motorway with the Autostrada del sole.

AC Milan wins the European Cup. From 1963 to 1969 the city's two teams win four European cups and appears in five out of seven finals.

1970

Construction begins on Belusconi's *Milano 2* housing estate, to the east of the city.

June: first Regional elections in Lombardy. The turn-out is over 95 per cent: DC 41 per cent; PCI 23 per cent; PSI 12 per cent; PSU 7 per cent; MSI 4 per cent; PLI 6 per cent; PSIUP 4 per cent. A centre-left administration is set up.

Local elections: DC 26 per cent; PCI 23 per cent; PSI 14 per cent; PSDI 10 per cent; PRI 5 per cent; PLI 11 per cent; MSI 6 per cent.

Provincial elections: DC 34 per cent; PCI 30 per cent; PSI 13 per cent; PSDI 8 per cent; PRI 3 per cent; PLI 7 per cent; MSI 5 per cent.

December: during demonstrations to mark the anniversary of the Piazza Fontana massacre a student, Saverio Saltarelli, is killed by tear gas cannister. Dario Fo stages the first production of *Accidental Death of an Anarchist* in Milan.

1971

January: First act of terrorism by the Red Brigades, a fire at the Pirelli factory at Lainate (MI).

Walter Albini begins his fashion shows in Milan, the first step towards Milan's development as a fashion capital (see Chapter 6).

1972

March: publisher and radical Giangiacomo Feltrinelli is found dead near to a power line outside the city, probably blown up by bombs he was trying to plant.

May: Police chief Luigi Calabresi is shot dead outside his house. Calabresi had been blamed by the left for the death of Giuseppe Pinelli in 1969.

October: the Piazza Fontana trial is moved to Catanzaro thanks to a decision by a judge that such a trial would be too dangerous for Milan.

1973

May: During the commemoration of the death of Calabresi, a man pretending to be an anarchist throws a bomb at the Prime Minister, killing four by-standers.

1974

Economic slowdown. Growth in Lombardy stops until 1981.

Berlusconi's first television channel, *Telemilano*, begins local transmissions.

1975

April: Violence between left activists, the police and fascists. One student is shot by fascists, another is run over by a police car. A young fascist dies after a beating by a group of left wing students.

June: Local elections: PCI 30 per cent; DC 27 per cent; PSI 15 per cent; PSDI 6 per cent; PRI 6 per cent; PLI 5 per cent; MSI 8 per cent; PDUP 3 per cent.

Regional elections: DC 37 per cent; PCI 30 per cent; PSI 14 per cent; MSI 4 per cent; PRI 3 per cent; PLI 3 per cent; PDUP-DP 2 per cent.

Provincial elections: PCI 34 per cent; DC 31 per cent; PSI 14 per cent; PSDI 5 per cent; PRI 4 per cent; PLI 3 per cent; MSI 5 per cent; PDUP 3 per cent.

July: First left-wing administration in Milan, the Mayor is still Aldo Aniasi. The DC are in opposition for the first time since the war.

1976

July: A dioxin cloud is released by a chemical factory in Seveso, just outside Milan, causing massive environmental damage to the surrounding zone.

Milan draws up its second PRG since the war.

May: Carlo Tognoli (PSI) becomes Mayor of Milan as Aniasi is promoted to a ministry in central government in Rome.

Craxi becomes National Secretary of the Socialist Party.

1978

Telemilano begins real television transmission.

1980

June: Local elections: DC 26 per cent; PCI 26 per cent; PSI 20 per cent; PRI 4 per cent; PLI 6 per cent; DP 3 per cent; PSDI 5 per cent. Tognoli is confirmed as Mayor.

Regional elections: DC 39 per cent; PCI 28 per cent; PSI 14 per cent; MSI 4 per cent; PSDI 4 per cent; PRI 3 per cent; PLI 3 per cent; PDUP 1 per cent; DP 2 per cent.

Provincial elections: DC 32 per cent; PCI 31 per cent; PSI 16 per cent; PSDI 4 per cent; PRI 4 per cent; PLI 4 per cent; MSI 5 per cent; PDUP 1 per cent; DP 2 per cent.

Canale 5 begins transmission. (One of Silvio Berlusconi's national channels.)

1981

March: all those accused of organizing the massacre of Piazza Fontana are absolved.

Giorgio Armani opens his first Emporio Armani store in Milan.

AC Milan are in serie B.

1982

Berlusconi buys another national television channel from Rusconi, *Italia 1*.

1983

Bettino Craxi becomes President of the Council (Prime Minister). He remains in power for four years.

1985

Local elections: DC 24 per cent; PCI 25 per cent; PSI 20 per cent; MSI 8 per cent; PRI 10 per cent; PLI 4 per cent; PSDI 3 per cent; Verdi 3 per cent; DP 3 per cent. Tognoli is elected Mayor for the third time, but his administration excludes the PCI, thus ending ten years of left-wing local government administrations. The DC are back in Palazzo Marino.

Regional elections: DC 36 per cent; PCI 27 per cent; PSI 15 per cent; MSI 6 per cent; PRI 5 per cent; PSDI 3 per cent; PLI 2 per cent; Verdi 2 per cent; DP 2 per cent; *Liga* 0.5 per cent.

September: the Bicocca plan for the redevelopment of the Pirelli zone is officially presented.

1986

November: the Mayor of Milan, Carlo Tognoli, resigns to become a government minister. Paolo Pillitteri, brother-in-law of Bettino Craxi, takes over in December.

Berlusconi becomes president of AC Milan.

1988

AC Milan wins its first Italian soccer championship in nine years, with the Dutch trio of Gullit, Rijkaard and Van Basten.

1989

December: Berlusconi gains control of Mondadori, further consolidating his media power. Inter Milan wins the Italian championship.

AC Milan wins the European Cup, beating Steaua Bucherest 4-0 in the final. Inter wins the Italian championship.

1990

May: Local elections: DC 21 per cent; PCI 20 per cent; PSI 19 per cent; MSI 4 per cent; PRI 6 per cent; PLI 3 per cent; PSDI 2 per cent; Verdi 6 per cent; DP 2 per cent; Lega 13 per cent; Pensionati 3 per cent.

Regional elections: DC 29 per cent; PCI 19 per cent; PSI 14 per cent; Lega Lombardia 19 per cent; Verdi 5 per cent; MSI 2 per cent; PRI 3 per cent; PSDI 2 per cent; PLI 1 per cent.

Provincial elections: DC 24 per cent; PCI 22 per cent; PSI 16 per cent; MSI 3 per cent; Greens 4 per cent; Lega 15 per cent; PRI 4 per cent.

The regionalist *Lega Lombarda* begins to eat into the vote of the main parties. Political fragmentation begins to dominate the system.

Film director Silvio Soldini makes *L'aria serena dell'ovest*.

AC Milan wins the European cup again, beating Benfica 1-0 in the final.

8 June: Italia '90, the World Cup, begins. The opening match is at the re-built San Siro stadium in Milan.

Temporary housing centres are opened across the city for foreign immigrants. The biggest is in Via Corelli.

1992

February: A minor Socialist official, Mario Chiesa, is arrested for corruption – the first act of the massive *Tangentopoli* scandal (see Chapter 8). In May two former Mayors are placed under investigation, Pillitteri and Tognoli. Later, Craxi himself will be investigated and convicted.

Gian Piero Borghini (ex-PCI) becomes Mayor of Milan after the resignation of Pillitteri.

1993

June: Marco Formentini (Lega Nord) is elected Mayor of Milan under the new direct electoral system, beating anti-corruption candidate Nando Dalla Chiesa in the second round (by 57 per cent to 43 per cent). All the major parties involved in the corruption scandals take heavy losses, from the Socialists who fall to less than 2 per cent to the ex-communists, the PdS, who lose to the far-left party *Rifondazione comunista*. The Social-Democrats all but disappear.

The *Lega* list wins 41 per cent of the vote. PdS 9 per cent; *Rifondazione* 11 per cent; Patto per Milano 7 per cent; DC 9 per cent; PSI 1.6 per cent; PSDI 0.4 per cent.

A bomb designed to destabilize Italy explodes in Via Palestro in Milan, killing five people.

1994

April: Silvio Berlusconi is elected President of the Council (Prime Minister) in national general elections. He forms a government with the Northern leagues, but it lasts only nine months before the Leagues withdraw their support.

AC Milan wins its third European Cup in 4 years, beating Barcelona 4-0 in the final. At home the team wins its third championship in a row.

1995

Regional elections. Victory of the centre-right coaliton with a new (incredibly complicated) electoral law. Roberto Formigoni, ex-DC, is elected President. Forza Italia!/Alleanza Nazionale/CCD/Pensionati 41 per cent; centre-left candidate 27 per cent; *Rifondazione* 8 per cent; Lega 19 per cent.

1996

The last Falck factory closes at Sesto San Giovanni, after ninety years of production.

1997

Industrialist Gabriele Albertini is elected Mayor of Milan at the head of a coalition that includes Berlusconi's *Forza Italia!*, the ex-fascists in the guise of *Alleanza Nazionale* but not the *Lega Nord*. He beats moderate centre-left candidate Aldo Fumagalli in the second ballot with 53 per cent of the vote (against 47 per cent).

Results: *Forza Italia!* 30 per cent; PdS 19 per cent; *Lega Nord* 16 per cent; *Alleanza Nazionale* 12 per cent; *Rifondazione* 9 per cent; PPI 3 per cent; Verdi 3 per cent.

1999

A new immigrant detention centre opens in Via Corelli.

A new trial begins with relation to the Piazza Fontana massacre, this time in Milan.

AC Milan wins its fifth Italian soccer championship of the 1990s.

2000

A new international airport opens at Malpensa, 46 km to the north of Milan.

Regional elections: Formentini is re-elected under the new direct electoral system as President of the Region, with over 60 per cent of the vote at the head of a centre-right coalition including the Northern Leagues. Berlusconi's *Forza Italia!* wins 34 per cent of the vote in the region, the centre-left parties only 20 per cent, the Lega 15 per cent, Alleanza Nazionale 10 per cent and Rifondazione comunista 6 per cent.

Provincial elections: *Forza Italia!* candidate Ombretta Colli is elected President of the Province with just over 50 per cent of the vote.

2001

13 May: National and local elections. Albertini is re-elected with 57 per cent of the vote in the first round. Berlusconi triumphs in national elections.

June: Berlusconi is appointed President of the Council (Prime Minister) at the head of a centre-right coalition

Bibliography

(All places of publication are Milan unless otherwise stated.)

ADI (1979), *Design and Design*, Comune di Milano.

Adorno, T. and Horkheimer, M. (1986), *Dialectic of Enlightenment,* London: Verso.

Alasia, F. and Montaldi, D. (1960), *Milano, Corea. Inchiesta sugli immigrati*, Feltrinelli.

Alberoni, F. (1960), *Contributo allo studio dell'integrazione sociale dell'immigrato*, Vita e Pensiero.

—— and Baglioni, G. (1965), *L'integrazione dell'immigrato nella società industriale*, Bologna: Il Mulino.

Alberoni, G. (1999), 'Via Sant'Andrea' in Vergani (ed.): 690–1.

Albertelli, G. and Ziliani, G. (1970), 'Le condizioni alloggiative della popolazione immigrata' in Pellicciari (ed.): 283–303.

Allievi, S. (ed.), (1993), *Milano plurale. L'immigrazione fra passato presente futuro*, Tiemme.

Amatori, F. and Sillano, M. T. (1996), 'L'attività commerciale' in *Storia di Milano*, vol. XVIII, *Il Novecento*, Rome: Treccani: 182–236.

Ambasz, E. (ed.), (1972), *Italy: the New Domestic Landscape*, New York: Museum of Modern Art.

Ambrosini, M. (1993), 'Cittadinanza economica e cittadinanza sociale: Il caso lombardo' in M. Delle Donne, U. Melotti, and S. Petrilli, (eds), *Immigrazione in Europa. Solidarietà e conflitto*, Rome: CEDISS: 347–64.

—— (1997), 'Alla scoperta della diversità: un panorama dell'immigrazione in Italia', in Caritas Ambrosiana, *Il valore della differenza. Tendenza, problemi, interventi sull'immigrazione straniera*, Paoline: 12–66.

—— (1999), *Utili invasori. L'inserimento degli immigrati nel mercato del lavoro italiano*, Franco Angeli.

Amendola, G. (1995), 'Le forme urbane della paura', *Urbanistica*, 104: 16–19.

Anania, F. (1994), 'Fabbrica dei sogni o specchio della realtà. Le indagini della Rai e le grandi inchieste degli Istituti di ricerca negli anni Cinquanta e Sessanta', *XX secolo*, 10: 141–72.

—— (1997), *Davanti allo schermo. Storia del pubblico televisivo*, Rome: Nuova Italia Scientifica.

Andreoli, M. 'Garofano City', *Panorama*, 25 June 1989.

Angeleri, G. and Columba, C. (1985), *Milano Centrale: storia di una stazione*, Rome: Edizioni Abete.

Antonioli, M., Bergamaschi, M., Ganapini, L., (eds), (1993), *Milano operaia dall'800 a oggi*, Vols. I and II, Cariplo/Laterza.

Arbasino, A. 'Una Milano da non bere', *La Repubblica*, 19 December 1997.

Ascoli, U. (1979), *Movimenti migratori in Italia*, Bologna: Il Mulino.

Asnaghi, L. (1999), 'Dolce & Gabbana' in Vergani (ed.): 219–20.

Associazione Famiglia Agirina di Milano (1997), *Avvocato Angelo Valenti. XX Anniversario.*

Augé, M. (1995), *Non-Places. Introduction to an Anthropology of Supermodernity*, London: Verso.

Avanti!, 'Rocco e i suoi fratelli', 14 October 1960.

Baglioni, G. (1962), *Una ricerca sull'integrazione degli immigrati nella città di Milano*, Liberty.

Baglivo, A. and Pellicciari, G. (1970), *Sud Amaro: esodo come sopravvivenza. Libro bianco sull'Italia depressa*, Sapere.

Bagnasco, A. (1986), *Torino. Un profilo sociologico*, Turin: Einaudi.

—— (ed.), (1990), *La città dopo Ford: il caso di Torino,* Turin: Bollati Boringhieri.

Bai, G. (1984), *Istituto Autonomo Case Popolari Milano 1908–1983: dal lavatoio al 'solare'*, Rizzoli.

Balbo, L. (1962), *Condizioni di primo insediamento degli immigrati – Pensioni e camere ammobiliate*, ILSES.

—— (1976), *Stato di famiglia. Bisogni. Privato. Collettivo*, Etas libri.

—— and Manconi, L. (1992), *I razzismi reali*, Feltrinelli.

—— and Manconi, L. (1993), *Razzismi. Un vocabolario*, Feltrinelli.

Balestrini, N. and Moroni, P. (1997), *L'orda d'oro. 1968–1977. La grande ondata rivoluzionaria e creativa, politica ed esistenziale,* Feltrinelli.

Barbacetto, G. (1996), 'Mani pulite. La rivoluzione è stanca', *Diario della settimana*, 18–23 December.

—— (1997), 'La donna nel bagagliaio', *Diario della settimana*, 15–21 January.

—— and Veltri, E. (1991), *Milano degli scandali*, Bari: Laterza.

Barbagli, M. (1998), *Immigrazione e criminalità in Italia*, Bologna, Il Mulino.

Barber, S. (1995), *Fragments of the European City*, London: Reaktion Books.

Barbieri, F. (1993), 'Il voto a Milano', *La Repubblica*, 6 May.

Barile, G., Dal Lago, A., Marchetti, A., Galeazzo, P., (1994), *Tra due rive. La nuova immigrazione a Milano*, IRER, Franco Angeli.

Barthes, R. (1994), *Miti d'oggi*, Turin: Einaudi.

Barzini, L. (1954), 'Occhio al vetro. La "prima" della televisione', *La Stampa*, 5 Jan.

Basilico, G. (1999), *Interrupted City*, Barcelona: ACTAR.

Bass, D. (1995–6), 'Window/Glass: Reflections on Antonioni', *Scroope*, 7.

—— (1997), 'Insiders and Outsiders. Latent Urban Thinking in Movies of Modern Rome' in F. Penz, and M. Thomas, (eds), *Cinema and Architecture. Méliès, Mallet-Stevens, Multimedia*, London: British Film Institute: 84–99.

Battacchi, M. W. (1972), *Meridionali e settentrionali nella struttura del pregiudizio etnico in Italia*, Bologna: Il Mulino.

Bechelloni, G. (1984), *L'immaginario quotidiano. Televisione e cultura di massa in Italia*, Turin: RAI.

Bellotto, A. (1962), *La televisione inutile*, Comunità.

—— (1963a), 'Gli italiani al video: uno nessuno tre milioni', *Avanti!*, 9 Feb.

—— (1963b), 'L'avvento televisivo spiegato all'italiana', *Avanti!*, 17 Feb.

Benjamin, W. (1971), *Immagine di città*, Turin: Einaudi.

—— (1999), *The Arcades Project*, Cambridge and London: Harvard University Press.

Berman, M. (1993), *All That is Solid Melts into Air*, London: Verso.

Bermani, C. and Coggiola, F. (eds), (1986), *Memoria operaia e nuova composizione di classe. Problemi e metodi della storiografia sul proletariato*, Istituto Ernesto de Martino, Maggioli Editore.

Bernardi, M. (1997), 'La città è bella ma avvelena i bambini', *La Repubblica*, 11 November.

Bertoli, G. (ed.), (1980), *Ripresa operaia e unità sindacale. Il movimento dei metalmeccanici milanesi dal 1959 al 1963*, Archivi di classe, La Pietra.

Bettetini, G. (1990), 'Un "fare" italiano nella televisione', in *Televisione: la provvisoria identità italiana*, Fondazione Giovanni Agnelli, Turin: 17–19.

Bezza, B., Datola, S. Gallessi, R., (eds), (1981), *Le lotte degli elettromeccanici*, Franco Angeli.

Biagi, E. (1989), 'La piramide di Panseca e il culto del Dio Sole', *Corriere della Sera*, 18 May.

Bianchi, E. (1990), 'Il vissuto della periferia con riferimento all'esperienza italiana', *Rivista Geografica Italiana*, 97: 591–8.

—— and Perussia, F. (1988), 'Lo spazio vissuto della periferia: una ricerca pilota', *Ikon*, 17: 175–212.

Bianciardi, L. (1960), 'La folla del mattino a Milano' in *Le Vie d'Italia*, Dec. 1960 now in *Chiese escatollo e nessuno raddoppiò. Diario in pubblico 1952–1971*, Baldini & Castoldi, 1995: 127–33.

—— (1995), *La vita agra*, Bompiani.

Bigatti, G. (2000), *La città operosa. Milano nell'Ottocento*, Franco Angeli.

Bigazzi, D. (1988), *Il Portello. Operai, tecnici e imprenditori all'Alfa Romeo 1906–1926*, Franco Angeli.

—— (1996), 'Un inventario del progetto del saper fare' in Pansera (ed.): 11–14.

Biorcio, R. (1994), 'Le ragioni della sinistra. Le risorse della destra', I. Diamanti and R. Mannheimer (eds), *Milano a Roma. Guida all'Italia elettorale del 1994*, Rome: Donzelli: 159–68.

—— (1997), *La Padania promessa. La storia, le idee e la logica d'azione della Lega nord*, Il saggiatore.

—— (2000), 'La società civile lombarda e la politica: dagli anni del boom a fine millennio'in D. Bigazzi and M. Meriggi (eds), *Storia d'Italia. Le regioni. La Lombardia*, Turin: Einaudi: 1025–64.

Bocca, G. (1980), *Miracolo all'italiana*, Feltrinelli.

—— (1998), 'Milano invasa per la terza volta', *La Repubblica*, 6 June.

—— (1991), 'Viaggio nei Bronx', *La Repubblica*, 6 July.

—— (1993), *Metropolis. Milano nella tempesta italiana*, Mondadori.

—— (1997a), 'Milano fine secolo metropoli usa e consuma', *La Repubblica*, 1, 14 October.

—— (1997b), 'Milano, la città-auto prigioniera dell'ingorgo . . .', *La Repubblica*, 16 October.

Boeri, S. (1997), 'I detective dello spazio', *Il Sole–24 Ore,* 16 March.

—— (1997), 'Per un "Atlante eclettico" del territorio italiano' in G. Basilico, S. Boeri, *Sezioni del paesaggio italiano*, Udine: Arte e editore: 9–24.

—— (1997), 'Eclectic atlases' in *Documenta X. Documents 3,* Senefelderstr: Cantz Verlag: 4–10.

—— and Lanzani, A. (1992), 'Gli orizzonti della città diffusa', *Casabella*, 588: 44–58.

—— and Lanzani, A., Marini, E. (1993), *Il territorio che cambia. Ambienti, paesaggi e immagini della regione milanese,* Abitare Segesta.

—— and Marinoni, G. Zardini, M. Zucchi, C., (1995), 'Pioltello-Rodano' in *Il Centro altrove. Periferie e nuove centralità nelle aree metropolitane*: 161–2.

—— and Martinotti, G. (1997), 'Oltre i navigli', presented at the conference *Milano: dritto e rovescio*, 16–18 Oct. 1997, Triennale, Milan.

Boffi, M., Cofini, S., Giasanti, A., and Mingione, E., (1972), *Città e conflitto sociale. Inchiesta al Garibaldi-Isola e in altri quartieri periferici di Milano,* Feltrinelli.

Bolaffi, G., Gindro, S., Tentori, T. (eds), (1998), *Dizionario della diversità: le parole dell'immigrazione, del razzismo e della xenofobia*, Florence: Libri Liberal.

Bonasia, A. (1978), *Vivere a Milano*, CSAPP.

Bongiorno, M. (2000), 'Mike Bongiorno' in Ferrari and Giusto (eds): 107–18.

Bongiovanni, B. and Tranfaglia, N. (1996), *Dizionario storico dell'Italia unita*, Bari: Laterza.

Bonomi, A. (1997), *Il Capitalismo molecolare. La società al lavoro nel Nord Italia*, Turin: Einaudi.

Bontempi, P. C. (1991), 'L'informazione sul design. Il ruolo storico delle riviste di architettura e design in Italia' in Casciani and Di Pietrantonio (eds): 155–9.

Booth, C. (1902), *Life and Labour of the People in London*, London: Macmillan, 17 volumes.

Borioli, G. (1999), 'Nicola Trussardi' in Vergani (ed.): 774–5.

Bosio, G. (1975), *L'intellettuale rovesciato*, Edizioni Bella Ciao.

Bosoni, G. and Confalonieri, F. (1988), *Paesaggio del design italiano, 1972–1988*, Edizioni comunità.

Bottiglieri B. and Ceri P. (eds), (1987), *Le culture del lavoro: l'esperienza di Torino nel quadro europeo*, Bologna, Il Mulino.

Bottoni, P. (1945), *La casa a chi lavora*, Gorlich.

—— and Bombelli Tiravanti, L. (1947), *Ottava Triennale di Milano, Catalogue-guida*.

Bovone L. (ed.), (1997), *Mode*, Franco Angeli.

—— (ed.), (1999), *Un quartiere alla moda. Immagini e racconti del Ticinese a Milano*, Franco Angeli.

Branzi, A. (*Interview*), http://www.educational.rai.it/lezionidisign/designers/BRANZIA.htm.

Branzi, A. (1984), *Esperienze del Nuovo Design Italiano*, Idea Books Edizioni.

—— (1984), *The Hot House. Italian New-Wave Design*, London: Thames & Hudson.

—— (1985), 'Introduzione', *Centrokappa*: 17–24.

—— (1988), *Learning from Milan. Design and the Second Modernity*, Cambridge (Mass.), MIT Press.

—— (1994), 'Italian Design and the Complexity of Modernity', in Celant (ed.): 597–606.

—— (1995), 'Tutto è metropoli', *Lotus*, 84: 116–9.

—— (1996), *Il design italiano, 1964–1990*, Electa.

—— (1999), *Introduzione al design italiano: una modernità incompleta*, Baldini & Castoldi.

Breward, C. (1995), *The Culture of Fashion*, Manchester, MUP.

Brunetta, G. P. (1993), *Storia del cinema italiano, 1960–1993*, Rome: Riuniti.

—— (1995), 'Il cinema legge la società italiana', in *Storia dell'Italia Repubblicana*, Vol. 2, Turin: 781–844.

Brunetti, F. (1996), *BBPR, La Torre Velasca*, Alinea.

Bull, A. (1996), 'An end to collective identities. Political culture and voting behaviour in Sesto San Giovanni and Erba', *Modern Italy*, 1, 2: 23–43.

—— and Corner, P. (1993), *From Peasant to Entrepreneur. The Survival of the Family Economy in Italy*, Oxford: Berg.

Butazzi, G. and Molfino, A.M. (eds), (1987), *La Moda italiana: Dall'antimoda allo stilismo*, Electa.

Buttafava, G. (1980), 'Un sogno americano. Quiz e riviste TV negli anni Cinquanta', in G. Bettetini, *American way of television. Le origini della TV in Italia*, Florence: Sansoni editore: 60–81.

Calderoni, P. (ed.), (1993), *Nando dalla Chiesa, Milano-Palermo. La nuova resistenza*, Baldini & Castoldi.

Calvarese, E. and Breda, U. (1998), 'La delittuosità degli immigrati nel Comune di Milano (1991–1996): è vero aumento?', *Rassegna italiana di criminologia*, IX, 3–4, July–December: 517–28.

Camagni, R. (1994), *Milano città d'Europa. Progetti possibili, risorse attivabili*, Abitare Segesta, MeglioMilano.

Campbell., B. (1984), *Wigan Pier Revisited: Politics and Poverty in the 1980s*, London: Methuen.

—— (1993), *Goliath: Britain's Dangerous Places*, London: Methuen

Canova, G. (1996), *Nirvana. Sulle tracce del cinema di Gabriele Salvatores*, Zelig.

Caputo, P. (ed.), (1993), *Milano: percorsi del progetto*, Guerini e associati.

Caritas Diocesana di Roma (1997), *Immigrazione. Dossier Statistico 1997*, Mondadori.

Carloni, M. V. (1999a), 'Gianni Versace' in Vergani (ed.): 798–801.

—— (1999b), 'Prada' in Vergani (ed.): 625–7.

Carlucci, A. (1992), *Tangentomani*, Baldini & Castoldi.

Carrieri, M. (1959), *Milano, Italia*, Lerici editore.

Casciani, S. and Di Pietrantonio, G. (eds), (1991), *Design in Italia, 1950–1990*, Giancarlo Politi Editore.

Castells, M. (1996), *The Rise of the Network Society*, vol. 1, Oxford: Blackwells.

Castronovo, V. (1974), 'L'IACP di Milano dal 1908 al 1970 nel quadro della politica edilizia nazionale' in A. Predetti, (ed.), *Case popolari: urbanistica e legislazione, Milano, 1900–1970*, Edilizia Popolare: 13–96.

—— (1977), *Il Piemonte*, Turin: Einaudi.

Cavallazzi, G. and Falchi, G. (1989), *La storia di Milano*, Bologna: Zanichelli.

Cavalli, L. (1964), *Gli immigrati meridionali e la società ligure*, Feltrinelli.

—— (1978), *La città divisa: sociologia del consenso e del conflitto in ambiente urbano*, Giuffré.

Cella, G. P. and Reyneri, E. (eds), (1974), 'Il contributo della ricerca all'analisi della composizione della classe operaia italiana', *Classe*, 10: 33–58.

Centrokappa (1985), *Il design italiano degli anni '50*, Ricerche design editrice.

Cenzatti, M. and Crawford, M. (1993), 'Spazi pubblici e mondi paralleli', *Casabella*, 597–598: 34–8.

Cerasi, M. (1974), *La residenza operaia a Milano*, Rome: Officina.

Cerati, C. (1997), *Milano (1960–1970)*, Barbieri.

Cerutti, S. (n.d.), 'Il linguistic turn in Inghilterra: note su un dibattito e le sue censure', (unpublished paper).

Bibliography

Cevini, P. (1996), *Grattacielo Pirelli*, Rome: NIS.

Chiaramonte, G. (1995), 'L'occhio sull'infinito', in *Il Centro altrove. Periferie e nuove centralità nella aree metropolitane*, Electa: 37–49.

Chiaromonte, N. (1992), *Il tarlo della coscienza*, Bologna, Il Mulino.

Cirillo, A. (1997),'La città dai capelli grigi', *La Repubblica*, 17 October.

—— (2000), 'La città è del design', *La Repubblica*, 10 April.

Civile, G. (ed.), (1987), 'Piccolo è utile', *I viaggi di Erodoto*, 4, 1/2: 60–9.

Codeluppi, V. (1996), *Sociologia della moda*, Cooperativa Libraria IULM.

Colaprico, P. (1996), *Capire Tangentopoli*, Il Saggiatore.

Cologna, D., Breveglieri, L., Granata, E., Novak, C., (eds), (1999), *Africa a Milano. Famiglie, ambienti e lavori delle popolazioni africane a Milano*, Abitare Segesta.

Colombo, A. (1998), *Etnografia di un'economia clandestina. Immigrati algerini a Milano*, Bologna: Il Mulino.

Colombo, E. and Navarini, G. (1999), *Confini dentro la città. Antropologia della Stazione Centrale di Milano*, Guerini.

Colombo, F. (1990), 'Le tre stagioni', *Problemi dell'informazione*, 4: 593–7.

—— (ed.), (1998), *Libri, giornali e riviste a Milano. Storia delle innovazioni nell'editoria milanese dall'Ottocento ad oggi*, Abitare Segesta.

Coluccia, A. and Ferretti, F. (1996), 'Immigrazione tra disagio sociale e devianza: considerazioni in margine al dibatitto', *Rassegna italiana di criminologia*, 1: 75–120.

Commissione per il coordinamento dei servizi e lavori pubblici in periferia (1962), *Il rapporto al consiglio comunale (52 zone). Bozze di stampa e allegati*, Comune di Milano.

Comune di Milano (1963), *Guida del lavoratore*, Comune di Milano.

—— (1993), *Via Palestro, martedi 27 Luglio 1993*, Comune di Milano.

—— (1997), *Milano in Comune*, III, 2, June.

—— (1999), *L'occhio dell'architetto. Piccoli film su Milano*, Comune di Milano.

Consonni, G. (1993), 'Dalla città alla metropoli. La classe invisibile' in Antonioli *et al.* (eds): 19–36.

—— and Tonon, G. (1984), 'Alle origini della metropoli contemporanea in C. Pirovano, *Lombardia: il territorio, l'ambiente, il paesaggio*, vol. 4, *L'età delle manifatture e della rivoluzione industriale*, Electa: 89–164.

Contessi, G. (1995), ' "Una promenade architecturale et métallurgique". Luciano Baldessari: i padaglioni Breda alla Fiera Campionaria di Milano' in A. Giorgi and R. Poletti (eds), *Accoppiamenti giudiziosi. Storie di progettisti e costruttori*, Skira: 66–99.

Corriere della Sera, Il (1960), 'Nella XXXVIII Fiera di Milano la trionfale documentazione delle pacifiche conquiste del lavoro, della tecnica, della collaborazione fra i popoli', 13 April.

—— (1962), 'Per comprarsi il televisore il primo debito degli immigrati', 18 April.

—— (1991), 'A Milano c'è un quartiere senza stato', 9 June.

—— (1995), 'Nei container, vittime del gelo', 7 January

—— (1995), 'Ruspe in Via Corelli. Raso al suolo il centro accoglienza', 15 October.

—— (1998), 'MM in attivo, grazie a Tangentopoli', 19 February.

—— (1998), 'Quartiere Spaventa, sorveglianza speciale', 6 June.

Corriere Lombardo, (1955), 'Il paralitico sogna un televisore', 12–13 November.

—— (1956), 'Felice il paralitico accanto al televisore', 2–3 January.

—— (1956), 'Anche i bambini alla Biblioteca del Parco', 19–20 January.

—— (1956), 'Tele-bar', 21–22 February.

—— (1956), '"Lascia o raddoppia" ad uso degli scolari', 6–7 March.

Crainz, G. (1996), *Storia del miracolo italiano. Culture, identità, trasformazioni*, Rome: Donzelli.

Craxi, B. (1985), *Il progresso italiano*, Sugarco Edizioni.

CRIS, (1962), *Immigrazione e industria,* Comunità.

Cross, G. (1993), *Time and Money. The Making of Consumer Culture*, London: Routledge.

Crus (1974), 'Per un nuovo ruolo della zona Bovisa-Dergano nell'ambito metropolitano milanese', (unpublished manuscript).

Curcio, A. M. (1995), *La moda: identità negata*, Franco Angeli.

Dagrada, E. (1996), 'Television and its critics: A parallel history', in Forgacs and Lumley (eds): 233–47.

Dal Lago, A. (1994), 'La nuova immigrazione a Milano. Il caso del Marocco', in Barile *et al.* (eds): 135–240.

—— (1997), 'Il frame oscuro: La notte come categoria sociale' in Bovone (ed.): 125–34.

—— (1999), *Non-persone. L'esclusione dei migranti in una società globale*, Feltrinelli.

Dalla Chiesa, N. (1995), *I trasformisti*, Baldini & Castoldi.

Dallamano, P. (1955), 'Il televisore', *Il Contemporaneo*, II, 36: 8.

Dalmasso, E. (1972), *Milano capitale economica d'Italia*, Franco Angeli.

Datola, S. Fajertag, G. Lissa, F. (1977), 'L'industria metalmeccanica milanese: 1945–1975' in Isrmo (eds), *Un minuto più del padrone. I metalmeccanici milanesi dal dopoguerra agl'anni Settanta*, Vangelista: 113–27.

Davis, M. (1990), *City of Quartz. Excavating the Future in Los Angeles*, London: Vintage.

De Bernardi, A. and Ganapini, L. (1996), *Storia d'Italia, 1860–1995*, Bruno Mondadori.

De Berti, R. (1996), 'Milano nel cinema. L'immagine della città sullo schermo', in ibid. (ed.), *Un secolo di cinema a Milano*, Il Castoro: 431–46.

—— (1997), 'I cangianti orizzonti della Lombardia' in G. Martini, and G. Morelli (eds), *Patchwork due. Geografia del nuovo cinema italiano*, Il Castoro: 34–45.

De Carlo, G. (1998), 'Cronaca di un'occupazione annunciata' (Interview edited by S. Boeri), in G. Calvenzi (ed.), *Il '68 e Milano*, Leonardo: 66–9.

De Felice, F. (1995), 'Nazione e sviluppo: un nodo non sciolto', in *Storia dell'Italia repubblicana*, vol. 2, 1, Turin: 783–832.

De Giorgi, M. (1995), 'Cemento armato a +125,60 metri. Il cantiere della Torre Pirelli' in Giorgi and Poletti (eds): 101–34.

—— (1996), 'Il disegno industriale', in *Storia di Milano*, vol. XVIII, *Il Novecento*, Rome: Treccani: 564–604.

De Grazia, V. (1981), *Consenso e cultura di massa nell'Italia fascista. L'organizzazione del dopolavoro*, Bari: Laterza.

De Martino, E. (1977), 'Intorno a una storia del mondo popolare subalterno', in P. Angelini, (ed.), *Dibattito sulla cultura delle classi subalterne (1949–1950)*, Rome: Savelli: 49–72.

De Mauro, T. (1973), 'Il linguaggio televisivo e la sua influenza' in G. L. Beccaria (ed.), *I linguaggi settoriali in Italia*, Bompiani: 107–17.

—— (1979), 'La cultura' in A. Gambino, G. Galli and L. Colletti, *Dal '68 a oggi. Come siamo e come eravamo*, Bari: Laterza: 167–76.

—— (1992), *L'Italia delle italie*, Rome: Riuniti.

De Rita, G. (1990), 'L'enigma della non-città' in A. Clementi e F. Perego (eds), *EUPOLIS. La riqualificazione delle città in Europa. I. Periferie oggi,* Bari: Laterza, I: 55–62.

De Rita, L. (1964), *I contadini e la televisione. Studio sull'influenza degli spettacoli televisivi in un gruppo di contadini lucani*, Bologna: Il Mulino.

de Solà-Morales, M. (1994), 'Città tagliate. Appunti su identità e differenze', *Il racconto dell'abitare. Un seminario. Una mostra*, Abitare-Segesta: 184–9.

Decleva, E. (1980), 'L'Esposizione del 1881 e le origini del mito di Milano', in S. Pizzetti (ed.), *Dallo stato di Milano alla Lombardia contemporanea*, I, Cisalpino-La Goliardica: 181–211.

Della Peruta, F. (1985), 'Alle origini della Brianza mobiliera' in *Le affinità elettive*: 15–30.

—— (1993), 'La fisionomia della classe operaia' in Antonioli *et al.* (eds): 3–18.

Della Porta, D. (1993), 'Milan: Immoral Capital', in *Italian Politics, 1992*, London: Pinter: 98–115.

—— (1995), 'Political Parties and Corruption: Reflections on the Italian case', *Modern Italy*, 1: 97–114.

—— (1996), *Movimenti collettivi e sistemi politici in Italia, 1960–1995*, Laterza: Bari.

Della Valentina, G. (1986), 'La 'Berloca' e la sveglia. Classi sociali rurali tra rendita, protezionismo e liberismo', in Petrillo and Scalpelli (eds): 222–50.

Dematteis, G. (1990), 'Dai cerchi concentrici al labirinto', in Clementi (ed.): 127–36.

Dente, B. and Fareri, P. (eds), (1997), *Innovazione amministrativa a Milano*, AIM, Quaderno 34.

Di Bella, F. (1965), 'Il televisore in soffitta' in A. Perroni (ed.), *Cronache della immigrazione siciliana a Milano*, COI: 48–9.

Di Biase, C. (1985), 'Due quartieri milanesi', in F. Della Peruta, R. Leydi and A. Stella (eds), *Milano e il suo territorio*, Silvana editoriale, Provincia di Milano: 87–164.

Dickens, C. (1987), *Little Dorrit*, Oxford: OUP.

Dickie, J. (1994a), 'La macchina da scrivere. The Victor Emmanuel Monument in Rome and Italian Nationalism', *The Italianist*, 14: 261–85.

—— (1994b), 'The South as Other: From Liberal Italy to the Lega Nord', *The Italianist*, 14: 124–40.

—— (1999), *Darkest Italy. The Nation and Stereotypes of the Mezzogiorno, 1860–1900*, New York: St. Martins Press.

Diena, L. (1960), *Gli uomini e le masse. Saggio di ricerca su atteggiamenti di vita e di lavoro in una grande città industriale*, Turin: Einaudi.

—— (1963), *Borgata milanese*, Franco Angeli.

Documenta X – the Book. Politics-Poetics (1997), Cantz Verlag, Ostifildern-Ruit.

Dorfles, G. (*Interview*), http://www.educational.rai.it/lezionidididesign/designers/DORFLESG.htm

Dragone, F. B. (1998), 'Via Spiga, il Quadrilatero e la moda' in *Milano: venticinque secoli di storia attraverso i suoi protagonisti,* CELIP: 390.

Ecco la grande Milano (1970), Nuova Mercurio.

Eco, U. (1963), 'Fenomenologia di Mike Bongiorno', in *Diario Minimo*, Bompiani: 30–35 (in English (1993), 'The Phenomenology of Mike Bongiorno' in *Misreadings*, New York: Harcourt Brace: 156–65).

—— (1973), 'Il pubblico fa male alla televisione?' in *Le emittenti radiotelevisive e il loro pubblico*, Turin: Premio Italia.

—— (1993), *Apocalittici e integrati. Comunicazioni di massa e teorie della cultura di massa*, Bompiani.

Eiserman, G. and Acquaviva, S. (1971), *La montagna del sole. Il Gargano: rottura dell'isolamento e influenza dei mezzi di comunicazione di massa in una società in transizione*, Edizioni di Comunità.

Eri, (1958), *1956–1957. Due anni di Lascia o raddoppia?,* Turin.

—— (1968), *Televisione e vita italiana*, Turin.

Escobar, R. (1993), 'La metropoli assente. Immagini milanesi nel cinema italiano', in Caputo (ed.): 329–60.

Fantini, L. (1994), *Milano 1994. Percorsi nel presente metropolitano*, Feltrinelli.

Farè, I. (ed.), (1992), *Il discorso dei luoghi: genesi e avventure dell'ordine moderno*, Naples: Liguori.

Bibliography

Fareri, P. (1991), 'Milano: progettualità diffusa e difficoltà realizzativa' in Cresme Ricerche, *La costruzione della città europea negli anni '80*, vol. II, Rome: Credito Fondiario SPA.

Farina, P., Cologna, D., Granata, E., Costa, M. (1997), *Cina a Milano: famiglie, ambienti e lavoro della popolazione cinese a Milano*, Abitare Segesta.

Farinotti, P. (1985), *I maghi del canale*, Rizzoli.

Fazio, F. (1994), *Una volta qui era tutta campagna*, Zelig.

Fazio, L. (1999), 'Corelli story', *il manifesto*, 25 Nov.

Ferrante, P. (1982), 'Bollate: un territorio non pianificato', *Casabella*, 476–7: 36–40.

Ferrari, A. and Giusto, G. (eds), (2000), *Milano città della radiotelevisione, 1945–1958*, Franco Angeli.

Ferrari, G. (1990), *Il padrone del diavolo: storia di Silvio Berlusconi*, Camunia.

Ferretti, C., Broccoli, U., Scaramucci, B. (eds), (1997), *Mamma Rai. Storia e storie del servizio pubblico radiotelevisivo*, Florence: Le Monnier.

Ferzetti, F. (1988), 'Città e cinema. La periferia urbana nella filmografia italiana' in F. Fiorentini (ed.), *Città come . . .*, Rome: Argos: 21–44.

Fiera Milano 1920–1995. Un percorso fra economia e architettura (1995), Electa.

Filippucci, P. (1996), 'Anthropological Perspectives on Culture in Italy', in Forgacs and Lumley (eds): 52–72.

Finetti, U. (1985), *Socialismo milanese. Il confronto politico per il decollo postindustriale*, Franco Angeli.

Fiorese, G. (ed.), (1984), *Milano Zona Sette: Bovisa-Dergano*, Comune di Milano/ Clup.

—— (1987), 'Al gran teatro della condizione metropolitana. John Hedjuk a Bovisa', *Lotus International*, 54.

—— (1990), 'Immagine di Bovisa', *Quaderni del dipartimento di progettazione dell'architettura*, 11: 27–43.

—— (1999), 'Identità di Bovisa' in ibid. and P. Caputo (eds), *Politecnico Bovisa: progetti per l'area dei gasometri*, Abitare-Segesta: 16–31.

Fiori, G. (1996), *Il venditore. Storia di Silvio Berlusconi e della Fininvest*, Garzanti.

Foa, V. and Ginsborg, P. (eds), (1994), *Le virtù della Repubblica*, Il Saggiatore.

Fofi, G. (1964), *L'immigrazione meridionale a Torino*, Feltrinelli (revised edition, 1975).

Folin, M. (1997), 'Postfazione' in Basilico and Boeri: 146–7.

Foot, J. (1991), *Alliances and Socialist Theory. Milan and Lombardy, 1914–1921* (Unpublished PhD thesis, Cambridge, 1991).

—— (1995), 'The Family and the 'Economic Miracle': Social Transformation, Work, Leisure and Development at Bovisa and Comasina (Milan), 1950–1970', *Contemporary European History*, 4, 3: 315–38

—— (1997), 'Migration and the 'Miracle' at Milan. The Neighbourhoods of Baggio, Barona, Bovisa and Comasina in the 1950s and 1960s', *Journal of Historical Sociology*, 10, 2: 184–212.

—— (1998a), 'Words. Songs and Books. Oral History in Italy. A Review and a Discussion', *Journal of Modern Italian Studies*, 3, 2: 164–74.

—— (1998b), 'The Tale of San Vittore. Prisons, Politics, Crime and Fascism in Milan, 1943–1946', *Modern Italy,* 3, 1: 25–48.

—— (1999a), 'Cinema and the City. Milan and Luchino Visconti's *Rocco and his Brothers*, (1960)', *Journal of Modern Italian Studies*, 4, 2: 209–35.

—— (1999b), 'From Boomtown to Bribesville: the Images of the City, 1980–1997', *Urban History*, 26, 3: 419–39.

—— (1999c), 'Immigration and the City. Milan and Mass Migration, 1950–1998', *Modern Italy*, 4, 2: 159–72.

—— (1999d), 'Mass Cultures, Popular Cultures and the Working Class in Milan, 1950–1970', *Social History*, 24, 2: 134–57.

—— (1999e), 'Television and the city. The impact of television in Milan, 1954–1960', *Contemporary European History*, 9, 3: 379–94.

—— (2000), 'The Creation of a "Dangerous Place". San Salvario, Turin, 1990–1999' in R. King (ed.), *The Mediterranean Passage. Migration and New Cultural Encounters in Southern Europe*, Liverpool: Liverpool University Press: 206–30.

—— (2001), 'The Urban Periphery. Myth and Reality. Milan, 1950–1998', *City*, n.s., 4, 1: 7–26.

Forgacs, D. (1992), *L'industrializzazione della cultura italiana, 1880–1980*, Il Mulino: Bologna.

—— (1996), 'Cultural Consumption, 1940s to 1990s', in Forgacs and Lumley (eds): 273–90.

—— (1998), 'Spettacolo: teatro e cinema' in M. Firpo, N. Tranfaglia and P. G. Zunino (eds), *Guida all'Italia contemporanea, 1861–1997*, IV. *Comportamenti sociali e culturali*, Garzanti: 203–94

—— and Lumley, R. (1996), 'Approaches to Culture in Italy' in ibid. (eds): 1–12.

—— and Lumley, R. (eds), (1996), *Italian Cultural Studies: an Introduction*, Cambridge: CUP.

Formica, L. (1994), *Berlusconi Blob*, Libera Informazione Editrice.

Fortini, F. (1977), 'Il diavolo sa travestirsi da primitivo', in Angelini (ed.): 77–80.

—— (1993), *Attraverso Pasolini*, Turin: Einaudi.

Forty, A. (1995), *Objects of Desire. Design and Society since 1750*, London: Thames & Hudson.

Foti, F. (1993), *Milano: metropoli frammentata*, IRER, Franco Angeli.

Francesconi, R. (1994), *Azienda come cultura. La Rinascente*, Baldini & Castoldi.

Franzosi, R. (1995), *The Puzzle of Strikes. Class and State Strategies in Postwar Italy*, Cambridge: CUP.

Frateili, E. (1995), '"Lo stile nella produzione" di Ponti', in La Pietra: XVIII–XX.

Frye Jacobson, M. (1998), *Whiteness of a Different Colour. European Immigrants and the Alchemy of Race*, Cambridge and London: Harvard University Press.

Fumagalli, A. (1997), *Il programma in sintesi.*

Galbiati, M. (ed.), (1989), *Proiezione urbane*, Tranchida.

Galeotti, G. (1976), 'Evoluzione del comportamento di consumo e diffusione della televisione in Italia', in G. Campa (ed.), *Pubblicità e consumi in Italia. Analisi empirica e problemi teorici*, Franco Angeli: 89–159.

Gallanti, F. (1997), 'Political Architecture in Italy' in *Documenta X*, 66–75: 286–93.

Galli, G. (1999), 'I referendum impropri su Silvio Berlusconi', *Il Mulino*, 5: 853–8.

Gallino, L. (1993), *Dizionario di sociologia*, Turin: UTET.

Gambirasio, G., Guiducci, R., La Pietra, U. Menghi, R. (1990), *Da periferie a città. Studi sulle aree periferizzate dei capoluoghi lombardi,* Ferrovie Nord.

Ganapini, L. (1986), *Una città, la guerra: lotte di ideologie e forze politiche a Milano, 1939–1951*, Franco Angeli.

—— (1993), 'Cultura operaia e composizione di classe: risultati della storiografia e ipotesi di ricerca (1945–1970)', in Antonioli *et al.* (eds), II: 321–33.

Garcia Marquez, G. (1999), 'Quanti bei miracoli a Milano', *La Repubblica*, 25 January.

Garreau, J. (1991), *Edge City. Life on the New Frontier*, New York: Doubleday.

Gasparini, A. (1982), *Crisi della città e sua reimmaginazione. Effetti simbolici e valori di progettazione nel recupero del centro storico e delle aree urbane*, Franco Angeli.

Gastel, M. (1995), *50 anni di moda italiana. Breve storia del pret-a-porter*, Milan: Garzanti.

Gelder, K. and Thornton, S. (eds), (1997), *The Subcultures Reader,* London: Routledge.

Giacomoni, S. (1984), *L'Italia della moda*, Gabriele Mazzotta editore.

Giddens, A. (1989), *Sociologia*, Bologna, Il Mulino.

—— (1991), *Sociologia*, Bologna: Il Mulino.

Gieri M. (1999), 'Landscapes of Oblivion and Historical Memory in the New Italian Cinema', *Annali d'Italianistica*, 17: 39–54.

Ginsborg, P. (1989), *A History of Contemporary Italy. Society and Politics 1943–1988*, London, Penguin.

—— (1998), *L'Italia del tempo presente. Famiglia, Società Civile, Stato, 1980–1996*, Turin: Einaudi.

Ginzburg, C. (1974), *Miti emblemi spie*, Turin: Einaudi.

—— (1980), *The Cheese and the Worms. The Cosmos of a Sixteenth-Century Miller*, London, Routledge.

—— (1998), *Occhiacci di legno. Nove riflessioni sulla distanza,* Feltrinelli.

Giovenzana, G. (1991), in L. Benevolo (ed.), *Periferie: confronto Parigi-Milano*, Ferrovie Nord.

Gismondi, E. (*Interview*), http://www.educational.rai.it/lezionididesign/designers/ GISMONDIE.htm

Giusti, M. (1995), *Il grande libro del Carosello*, Sterling & Kupfer.

Goldthorpe, J. Lockwood, D., Bechhofer, F., Platt, J. (1967), *The Affluent Worker*, Cambridge: CUP.

Graham, S. and Marvin, S. (1996), *Telecommunications and the City: Electronic Spaces, Urban Places*, London: Routledge.

Gramigna, G. (1985), *1950/1980 Repertorio. Immagini e contributi per una storia dell'arredo italiano*, Arnoldo Mondadori Editore.

Granata, E. and Novak, C. (1999), 'Immigrazione africana e territorio' in Cologna *et al* (eds): 125–92.

Grandi M. and Pracchi, A. (1980), *Milano: Guida all'architettura moderna*, Zanichelli: Bologna.

Grassi, A. and Pansera, A. (1980), *Atlante del design italiano, 1940–1980,* Gruppo Editoriale Fabbri.

Grasso, A. (1989), *Linea allo studio. Miti e riti della televisione italiana*, Bompiani.

—— (1992), *Storia della televisione italiana*, Garzanti.

—— (1993), *Al paese dei Berlusconi*, Garzanti.

—— (1996a), 'L'attività radiofonica e telefonica a Milano' in *Storia di Milano*, XVIII, *Il Novecento****, Istituto delle Enciclopedia Italiana, Rome: Treccani: 360–94.

—— (ed.), (1996b), *Enciclopedia della Televisione*, Garzanti.

—— (2000), 'La televisione a Milano' in Ferrari and Giusto (eds): 55–61.

Gravinelli, C. (1990), 'Le trasformazioni dell'architettura milanese del secondo dopoguerra: verso l'epoca post-moderna' in *Guida di architettura. Milano*, Umberto Allemandi & Co.: 244–5.

Grecchi Ruscone, A. (1987), 'L'antimoda, esempi milanesi' in Butazzi and Molfino (eds): 50–3.

Gregotti, V. (*Interview*). http://www.educational.rai.it/lezionididesign/designers/ GREGOTTIV.htm.

Gregotti, V. (1993), 'Gli spazi aperti urbani: fenomenologia di un problema progettuale', *Casabella*, 597–8, LVII: 2–3.

—— (1994a), 'Reconstructing a History' in Celant (ed.): 558–65.

—— (1994b), *Il disegno del prodotto industriale. Italia, 1860–1980*, Electa.

Gribaudi, M. (1981), 'Un gruppo di amici. Strategie individuali e mutamento sociale' in *Relazioni sociali e strategie individuali in ambiente urbano: Torino nel Novecento*, Regione Piemonte: 15–31 (Introduction), and 97–155.

—— (1987), *Mondo operaio e mito operaio. Spazi e percorsi sociali a Torino nel primo Novecento*, Turin: Einaudi.

Grignaffni, G. (1987), 'Una questione di performance' in Butazzi and Molfino (eds): 16–25.

Guidicini, P. and Pieretti, G. (eds), (1990), *I volti della povertà urbana*, Franco Angeli.

Guiducci, R. (1990), 'Male di periferizzazione e da emarginazione' in Gambirasio *et al.* (eds): 37–43.

—— (1991), *Periferie tra degrado e riqualificazione,* Franco Angeli.

—— (1993), 'Il dramma delle periferie milanesi' in ibid (ed.): 9–26.

—— (1993), *Periferie: le voci dei cittadini*, Franco Angeli.

Guiotto, L. (1986), 'L'occupazione e le condizioni di vita e di lavoro' in Petrillo and Scalpelli (eds), Franco Angeli: 25–78.

Gundle, S. (1986), 'L'americanizzazione del quotidiano. Televisione e consumismo nell'Italia degli anni Cinquanta', *Quaderni Storici*, 2: 561–94.

—— (1995), 'Il sorriso di Berlusconi', *Altrochemestre*, 3: 14–17.

—— (1996), 'Fame, Fashion and Style: The Italian Star System', in Forgacs and Lumley (eds): 318–9.

—— and O'Sullivan, N. (1996), 'The Mass Media and the Political Crisis' in Gundle and Parker (eds): 206–21.

—— and Parker, S. (1996), 'Introduction: the New Italian Republic' in ibid. (eds): 1–18.

—— and Parker, S. (eds), (1996), *The New Italian Republic. From the Fall of the Berlin Wall to Berlusconi*, London: Routledge.

Hall, S., Crichter, C., Jefferson, T., Clarke, J. and Roberts, B. (1978), *Policing the Crisis: Mugging, the State and Law and Order*, London: Macmillan.

Harvey, D. (1994), 'Monument and Myth. The Building of the Basilica of the Sacred Heart' in ibid., *The Urban Experience*, Oxford: Blackwells: 200–28.

Hauffe, T. (1998), *Design: A Concise History*, London: Laurence King.

Hedjuk, J. (1987), *Bovisa*, New York: Rizzoli International.

Hudson, M. (1994), *Coming Back Brockens. A year in a mining village*, London: J. Cape.

Huysmans, J. (1995), 'Migrants as a Security Problem: Dangers of "Securitizing" Societal Issues' in Miles and Thrändhardt (eds): 53–72.

IACPM (1958), *Quartiere autosufficiente Comasina. Milano 1955–1958*, IACPM.

Il segno della memoria: 1945–1995. BBPR, Monumento ai caduti nei campi nazisti, (1995), Electa.

ILSES (1964a), *Ricerca sull'integrazione sociale in cinque quartieri di Milano*, ILSES, five volumes.

ILSES (1964c), *L'integrazione sociale in cinque quartieri di Milano*. Vol. III, *Il quartiere Baggio Vecchio*, ILSES.

ILSES (1964d), *L'integrazione sociale in cinque quartieri di Milano,* Vol. IV, *Il quartiere Comasina*, ILSES.

ILSES (1964e), *L'integrazione sociale in cinque quartieri di Milano*. Vol. V, *Strutture di relazione e vita sociale nei quartieri della periferia di Milano. Monografie di quartiere: Barona, Forlanini* , ILSES.

Iosa, A. (1971), *I quartieri di Milano*, Centro Culturale C. Perini.

Irace, F. (1988), *Giò Ponti. La casa all'italiana*, Electa.

—— and Pasca, V. (1999), *Vico Magistretti: architetto e designer*, Electa.

IRER (1992), *Le trasformazioni degli anni Ottanta. Conferenza d'Istituto 1991,* Irer.

Istituto De Agostini (1995), *Il Dizionario della Lingua Italiana,* Novara.

Italia 70. La carta delle Regioni (1971), A. Mondadori Editore.

Kaschuba, K. (1995), 'Popular Culture and Workers' Culture as Symbolic Orders. Comments on the Debate about the History of Culture and Everyday Life' in A. Lüdtke (ed.), *The History of Everyday Life. Reconstructing Historical Experiences and Ways of Life*, Princeton: Princeton University Press: 169–97.

Katznelson, I. (1982), *City Trenches. Urban Politics and the Patterning of Class in the United States*, Chicago and London: The University of Chicago Press.

Kohn, M. L. (1974), *Società, classe, famiglia,* Franco Angeli.

L'Espresso 1955–1980 (1981), L'Espresso.

L'Unità, (1993), 'La sera andavamo al cinema Abanella', 29 July.

—— (1993), 'A Segrate la cerimonia islamica per Driss Moussafir', 30 July.

La Face-Standard nel suo cinquantenario: 1909–1959 (1959), FACE.

La Pietra, U. (1973), 'L'uso della città', *Inpiù*.

—— (1990), 'Quantità e qualità nella periferia' in Gambirasio *et al.* (eds): 27–36.

—— (1995), *Giò Ponti*, Rizzoli.

La Repubblica, 'I nonni di Milano. 360.000 sopra i 60', 26 January 1993.

—— 'Via Calvairate, terra di nessuno', 18 February 1993.

—— 'Viale Fulvio Testi ostaggi a equo canone', 3 April 1993.

—— 'La Milano dai capelli bianchi', 9 December 1993.

—— 'Bovisa, sipario sul gasometro', 12 July 1994.

—— 'Sei domande sulla Milano che verrà, i candidati rispondono', 23 April 1997.

—— 'Strade, Milano città a rischio', 1 October 1997.

—— 'Vendesi ex Alfa con operai', 1 October 1997.

—— 'L'azienda modello vicente', 18 October 1997.

—— 'La città allo specchio', 15 November 1997.

—— 'Da Stalingrado d'Italia a capitale dei bambini', 27 November 1997.

—— 'La sera andavamo al cinema Abanella', 11 December 1997.

—— 'Gli anni di Trussardi e della Milano da bere', 16 April 1999.

—— 'Milano, regno di Bettino', 20 January 2000.

—— 'Una città "prestata" alla moda', 17 February 2000.

La Triennale di Milano e il Palazzo dell'arte (1985), Electa.

Lacoste, Y. (1980), *Geografia del sottosviluppo*, Il Saggiatore.

Lagazzi M., Malfatti, D., Pallestrini, E., Rossoni, N. (1996), 'Immigrazione, comportamento criminale e sanzione penale. Riflessioni sulla figura dell' "immigrato spacciatore" nella città di Genova', *Rassegna italiana di criminologia*, 1: 145–64.

Lanaro, S. (1992), *Storia dell'Italia repubblicana. Dalla fine della guerra agli anni Novanta*, Venice: Marsilio.

Lanzardo, D. (1979), *La rivolta di Piazza Statuto. Torino, Luglio 1962,* Feltrinelli.

Lanzetti, C. (1995), 'I cambiamenti nella struttura della popolazione e nei comportamenti familiari', in E. Zucchetti (ed.), Fondazione Ambrosianeum, *Milano '94. Rapporto sulla città*, Franco Angeli: 29–56.

Le affinità elettive. La Brianza e Lissone. Studi e ricerche nell'area del mobile. Per un "altra" storia del design (1985), Lissone: Edizioni Arti Grafiche Meroni.

Lega 'Bovisa' di Milano, 'Libro sulle condizioni di vita e di lavoro alla FACE' (n.d. but 1955), in L. Ganapini, and V. Rieser, (eds), (1981), *Libri bianchi sulla condizione operaia negli anni Cinquanta. Una ricerca promossa dal Centro ricerche e studi sindacali della Fiom-Cgil di Milano*, Bari: De Donato: 83–91.

Legnani, M. (1984), 'Il mito della "capitale morale" tra politica e letteratura', *Italia contemporanea*, 154: 123–7.

Lemann, N. (1991), *The Promised Land. The Great Black Migration and how it Changed America,* London: Macmillan.

Leonini, L. (ed.), (1998), *Andar di notte. L'altro volto di Milano*, Unicopli.

Lepre, A. (1993), *Storia della prima repubblica. L'Italia dal 1942 al 1992,* Bologna: Il Mulino.

Lequin, Y. (1983), 'Lineamenti per una storia della cultura operaia in Francia' in 'Cultura operaia e disciplina industriale', *Annali della Fondazione Lelio e Lisli Basso*, Isocco, Roma vol. VI, Franco Angeli: 234–51.

Lerner, G. (1988), *Operai. Viaggio all'interno della Fiat. La vita, le case, le fabbriche di una classe che non c'è più,* Feltrinelli.

Levi, G. (1993), 'On Microhistory' in Burke, P. (ed.), *New Perspectives on Historical Writing,* Bari: Laterza: 93–113.

Levi, P. (1995), 'Capire e far capire: dichiarizioni raccolte da Milvia Spadi', *La Terra,* 1.

Leydi, R. (1964a), 'La vita è un video', *L'Europeo*, 4: 42–4.

—— (1964b), 'I prigionieri', *L'Europeo*, 5: 34–5.

Licata, S. (1996), 'Nonluoghi ed eterotopie. Indagine sui luoghi dell'altrove', *Urbanistica*, XLVIII: 199–205.

Lisbona, F. and Brunasti, M. (1998), 'Il paese invisibile nella città dei sordi', in *Milano, Stadera: immigrazione, leggi e norme sociali*, Franco Angeli: 34–77.

Livolsi, M. (1998), *La realtà televisiva. Come la TV ha cambiato gli italiani*, Bari: Laterza.

Lo Zingarelli, (1991, 1995), Bologna: Zanichelli.

Longoni, G. M. (1987), *La Fiera nella storia di Milano*, Federico Motta Editore.

Losito, G. (1986), 'L'offerta di radio e televisione in Italia. Problemi e tendenze', in M. Morcellini, *Lo spettacolo del consumo. Televisione e cultura di massa nella legittimazione sociale*, Franco Angeli.

Lotus (1994), 'Guardando Tangentopoli', 82: 108–31.

Lucas, U. (1977), *Emigranti in Europa*, Turin: Einaudi.

Lumley, R. (1989), *States of Emergency. Cultures of Revolt in Italy from 1968 to 1978,* London: Verso.

Luzzatto-Fegiz, P. (1966), *Il volto sconosciuto dell'Italia. II serie, 1956–1965*, Giuffrè.

Lynch, K. (1960), *The Image of the City*, Cambridge MA., MIT.

Macri, T. (1995), 'Metropolis', in M. Canevacci, R. De Angelis and F. Mazzi (eds), *Culture del conflitto: giovani, metropoli, comunicazione*, Genoa: Costa e Nolan: 227–33.

Madron, P. (1994), *La gesta del Cavaliere*, Sperling & Kupfer.

Mafai, M. (1997), *Il sorpasso. Gli straordinari anni del miracolo economico 1958–1963*, Mondadori.

Maffioletti, S. (1994), *BBPR*, Bologna: Zanichelli.

Magatti, M. (2000), *'Le imprese culturali a Milano e al Ticinese'*, (unpublished conference paper. *Imprese culturali e futuro della città*, Università Cattolica, 7 March).

Maggia, F. and Basilico, G. (eds), (1991), *Gabriele Basilico: Cityscapes*, Baldini & Castoldi.

Magistretti, V. (*Interview*), http://www.educational.rai.it/lezionidididesign/designers/MAGISTRETTIV.htm

Manconi, L. (1995), 'Piú ricchi, piú sani, ma . . .', *La Repubblica*, 3 February.

Mannheimer, R. and Micheli, G. (1974), 'Alcune ipotesi sul concetto di integrazione degli immigrati (in relazione al ciclo di lotte operaie '68–'70)', *Quaderni di Sociologia*, 23: 82–113.

Manzini, G. (1985), 'Dalla bottega ai mercanti del mondo', in *Le affinità elettive*: 33–48.

Marchese, R. and Mancini, B. (eds), (1991), *Dizionario di politica e scienze sociali,* Florence: La Nuova Italia.

Marchetti, A. (1994), 'La nuova immigrazione a Milano. Il caso senegalese' in Barile (ed.): 241–366.

Marcoaldi, F. (1994), 'Le mani nel sacco', *La Repubblica*, 19 January.

Marcuse, H. (1964), *One-dimensional Man. Studies in the Ideology of Advanced Industrial Society*, Boston: Beacon Press.

Marietta, C. A. (1995), 'I media e la politica', in G. Pasquino (ed.), *La politica italiana. Dizionario critico, 1945–1995*, Bari: Laterza: 433–44.

Martinotti, G. (ed.), (1988), *Milano ore sette: come vivono i milanesi*, Comune di Milano.

—— (1993a), *Metropoli. La nuova morfologia sociale della città*, Bologna: Il Mulino.

—— (1993b), 'La disuaglianza dei luoghi. Qualità della vita urbana e nuove popolazioni urbane' in L. Gallino, (ed.), *Disgualianze ed equità in Europa*, Bari: Laterza: 112–85.

—— (1994), 'Martinotti, sociologo della metropoli estesa', *La Repubblica*, 22 March.

—— (1996), 'Ordine e disordine nella città delle cose e nella città dei messaggi', in A. Clementi, G. Dematteis, P. C. Palermo, (eds), *Le forme del territorio italiano. 1. Temi e immagini del mutamento*, Bari: Laterza: 153–72.

—— (1997), 'Dimenticare i Navigli', *La Repubblica*, 17 October.

Masperò, F. (1994), *Roissy Express. A Journey through the Paris suburbs*, London: Verso.

McCarthy, P. (1996), 'Forza Italia: the New Politics and Old Values of a Changing Regime' in Gundle and Parker (eds): 130–46.

—— (1997), *The Crisis of the Italian State: From the Origins of the Cold War to the Fall of Berlusconi*, New York: St. Martin's Press.

Mela, A. (1996), *Sociologia della città* Rome: La Nuova Italia Scientifica.

Meletti, J. (1996), 'Solo la dinamite salverà via Artom', *L'Unità*, 23 December.

Melis, A. and Martinotti, G. (1998), 'Recenti tendenze demografiche negli insediamenti urbani italiani', *Sociologia urbana e rurale*, 56: 11–37.

Melone, A. (1994), 'Il crepuscolo di Milano', *L'Unità*, 27 January.

Melossi, D. (2000), 'The Other in the New Europe: Migrations, Deviance, Social Control', in P. Green and A. Rutherford (eds), *Criminal Policy in Transition*, Oxford: Hart Publishing: 151–66.

Melotti, U. (1996), 'Quelli che l'immigrazione . . . Sciocchezze, contraddizioni ed estremismi sull'immigrazione straniera in Italia', *Mondo 3*, 1–2: 448–88.

Mendini. A. (*Interview*), http://www.educational.rai.it/lezionidididesign/designers/MENDINIA.htm

Menduni, E. (1996), *La più amata dagli italiani. La televisione tra politica e telecomunicazioni*, Bologna: Il Mulino.

Meneghetti, L. (1986), 'Immigrazione e habitat nell'hinterland milanese: I casi di Bollate, Pero, Rho' in Petrillo and Scalpelli (eds), Franco Angeli: 251–359.

Mereghetti, P. (ed.), (1997), *Dizionario dei film 1998*, Baldini & Castoldi.

Meriggi, M. (1996), *Storia dell'Italia Settentrionale*, Rome: Donzelli.

Milano fra guerra e dopoguerra (1979), Bari: De Donato.

Miller, D. (ed.), (1995), *Acknowledging Consumption: A Review of New Studies*, London: Routledge.

Minucci, A. and Vertone, S. (1960), *Il grattacielo nel deserto*, Rome: Riuniti.

Moncalvo, G. (1977), *Milano No*, Elle.

Montaldi, D. (1961), *Autobiografie della leggera. Ricerca sociologica sulla classi sociali nella bassa Lombardia,* Turin: Einaudi.

—— (1994), *Bisogna sognare. Scritti 1952–1975*, Gabriella Montaldi-Seelhorst.

Montanelli, I. and Cervi, M. (1991), *Milano: ventesimo secolo*, Rizzoli.

Monteleone, F. (1992), *Storia della radio e della televisione in Italia. Società, politica, programmi 1922–1992*, Venice: Marsilio.

Mora, E. (1995), 'Stili di vita e consumi a Milano: città da bere?' in Fondazione Ambrosianeum: 164–78.

Morandi, C. (1980), '1954–1960. Sviluppo economico e crescita urbana negli anni del centrismo' in P. Gabellini, C. Morandi and P. Vidulli (eds), *Urbanistica a Milano. 1945–1980*, Rome: Edizioni delle autonomie: 77–102.

Morcellini, M. (1986), *Lo spettacolo del consumo. Televisione e cultura di massa nella legittimazione sociale*, Franco Angeli.

—— (1995), *La televisione in Italia*, Roma: Stampa alternativa.

Moretti, G. (1970), 'Un'analisi statistica del mutamento sociale nella realtà italiana, con specifico riferimento all'influenza dei movimenti migratori', in Pellicciari (ed.): 49–184.

Morini, E. and Bocca, N. (1987), 'Lo stilismo nella moda femminile' in Butazzi and Molfino (eds): 64–179.

Moroni, P. (1992), 'Milano, istruzioni per l'uso' in Farè (ed.): 313–35.

—— (1999), 'Intervista' in L. Bovone (ed.): 262–72.

Morpurgo, G. (1975), 'Milano fino agli anni Sessanta: dalla ricostruzione al boom economico', in U. Dragone, (ed.), *Milano tra passato e futuro*, Italia Nostra: 13–21.

Morris, J. (1993), *The Political Economy of Shopkeeping in Milan, 1885–1922*, Cambridge: CUP.

Motta, G. and Pizzigoni, A. (1981), *I frammenti della città e gli elementi semplici dell'architettura*, Clup.

—— (1991), *La casa e la città. Saggi di analisi urbana e studi applicati alla periferia*, Clup.

Muir, E. and Ruggiero, G. (eds), (1991), *Microhistory and the Lost Peoples of Europe*, London: John Hopkins U.P.

Muirhead, T. (1998), *Milan. A Guide to Recent Architecture*, Köln: Könmann.

Murialdi, P. (1990), 'Cavaliere, quante cose ci ha mostrato', *Problemi dell'informazione*, 4: 487–90.

Musso, S. (1980), *Gli operai di Torino. 1900–1920*, Feltrinelli.

—— (1988), 'La famiglia operaia' in P. Melograni (a cura di), *La famiglia italiana dall'Ottocento a oggi*, Bari: Laterza: 61–105

Nascimbeni, E. and Pamparana, A. (1992), *Le mani pulite. L'inchiesta di Milano sulle tangenti*, Mondadori.

Natale, P. (1988), 'Sport, tifo e violenza' in Martinotti (ed.): 259–74.

Necessario indispensabile. 1952–1991. Oggetti ed eventi che hanno cambiato la nostra vita (1991), Arnoldo Mondadori Arte.

Negri, A. (1979), *Dall'operaio massa all'operaismo sociale*, Multhipla Edizioni.

Noorda, B. (*Interview*), http://www.educational.rai.it/lezionidididesign/designers/ NOORDAB.htm

Nuova Società Civile. Milano-Italia, II, 2, 1995.

O'Hara Callan, G., (1998), *Dictionary of Fashion and Fashion Designers*, London: Thames & Hudson.

Olmi, E. (1999), 'Quella mia Bovisa fatta di orti e civiltà', *La Repubblica*, 27 April.

Ortese, A. M. (1998), *Silenzio a Milano*, Turin: La Tartaruga edizioni.

Ortoleva, P. (1995), *Un ventennio a colori. Televisione privata e società in Italia*, Florence: Giunti.

—— (1996), 'A Geography of the Media since 1945' in Forgacs and Lumley (eds): 185–98.

Ottieri, M. P. (1998), 'L'insostenibile convivenza', *Diario della Settimana*, 17–23 June.

Packard, V. (1957), *The Hidden Persuaders,* New York: David McKay.

Palidda, S. (1994), 'Devianza e criminalità tra gli immigrati. Ipotesi per una ricerca sociologica', *Inchiesta*, 103: 25–39.

—— (1997), 'La conversione poliziesca delle politiche migratorie' in Dal Lago A. (ed.), (1997), *Lo straniero e il nemico*, Costa e Nolan: 209–35.

—— (2000a), *Polizia postmoderna. Etnografia del nuovo controllo sociale*, Feltrinelli.

—— (ed.), (2000b), *Socialità e inserimento degli immigrati a Milano,* Franco Angeli.

Pansera, A. (1978), *Storia e cronaca della Triennale*, Longanesi & C.

—— (1990), *Il design del mobile italiano dal 1946 a oggi*, Bari: Laterza.

—— (ed.), (1996), *L'anima dell'industria: un secolo di disegno industriale nel Milanese*, Skira.

Paolozzi, L. (1992), 'La città senz'anima ma con tante speranze', *L'Unità*, 3 February.

Parker, S. (1996), 'Political Identities' in Forgacs and Lumley (eds): 107–28.

Parola, L. (2000), 'Gli abbonamenti alla televisione nei primi anni di trasmissione' in Ferrari and Giusto: 31–8.

Pasca, V. (1999), 'Vico Magistretti: design e razionalità', in Irace and Pasca (eds): 103–27.

Pasculli, E. (1998), *Milano cinema prodigio. Anticipazioni e primati in un secolo di avventure*, Canal e I nodi.

Pasolini, P. P. (1976), *Lettere luterane*, Turin: Einaudi.

—— (1992), *I Dialoghi*, Rome: Riuniti.

—— (1993), *Scritti corsari*, Garzanti.

—— (1995a), *Interviste corsare sulla politica e sulla vita, 1955–1975*, M. Gulinucci (ed.), Rome: Atlantide editore.

—— (1995b), 'La nebbiosa', E. Bruno (ed.), *Filmcritica*, November–December: 459–60.

Passerini, L. (1980a), 'Partecipazione politica e coscienza di classe nel movimento operaio torinese durante il fascismo' and 'Fonti orali e storia della classe operaia in regime fascista' in A. Agosti and G. M. Bravo (eds), *Storia del movimento operaio, del socialismo e delle lotte sociali in Piemonte*, vol. 3, *Gli anni del fascismo*, Bari: De Donato: 401–52 and 453–99.

—— (1984), *Torino operaia e fascismo: Una storia orale*, Bari: Laterza.

—— (1987), *Fascism in Popular Memory. The Cultural Experience of the Turin Working Class*, Cambridge: CUP.

—— (1988a), *Storia e soggettività. Le fonti orali, la memoria*, Florence: La Nuova Italia.

—— (1988b), *Autoritratto di gruppo*, Florence: Giunti.

Passigli, S. (1969), *Emigrazione e comportamento politico*, Bologna: Il Mulino.

Pavolini, L. (1961), 'Baracche e televisori', *Vie Nuove,* 5 August.

Pavolini, P. (1963), 'I coreani di Milano', *Il Mondo,* 29 January.

Pellicciari, G. (1963), *Condizioni di vita nelle baracche dei cantieri edili: Storia di un cantiere tipo*, ILSES.

—— (1964), *Strutture di relazione e vita sociale nei quartieri della periferia di Milano. Monografie di quartiere: Comasina-Baggio*, ILSES.

—— (1970), 'Introduzione' in ibid., (ed.), *L'immigrazione nel triangolo industriale*, Franco Angeli.

Pes, L. (1998), 'Descrivere il territorio: il punto di vista storico', *I viaggi di Erodoto*, 12, 34, January–April: 48–51.

Petrillo, G. (1992a), 'Immigrati a Milano, 1951–1963' in G. Marcialis and G. Vignati (eds), Istituto milanese per la storia della Resistenza e del movimento operaio. *Annali 1*, Franco Angeli: 631–61.

—— (1992b), *La capitale del miracolo. Sviluppo, lavoro, potere a Milano 1953–1962*, Franco Angeli.

—— (1995), 'Da santificazione a consumo. La domenica della Milano operaia negli anni Cinquanta', in Istituto milanese per la storia della Resistenza e del movimento operaio, *Tempo libero e società di massa nell'Italia del Novecento*, Franco Angeli: 183–205.

—— (1998a), 'Territorio, società e ideologie in Lombardia durante la resistenza', *Storia in Lombardia*, 2–3: 125–71.

—— (1998b), 'La piccola mela: Milano città di immigrazione' in A. Panaccioni e R. Taddeo (eds), *Migranti in Italia e italiani migranti: esperienze a confronto tra passato e presente*, Atti convegno, Milano, 8 Giugno 1998, Provincia di Milano: 20–37.

Petruccioli, C. (1992), 'Hanno spinto Milano lontano dall'Europa', *L'Unità*, 30 March.

Piccardi, A. (1999), 'Elogio del momento laterale', *Cineforum*, 389: 70–1.

Piccoli, I. (1996), 'I comportamenti di consumo negli anni '90', *Sociologia del Lavoro,* 63: 191–209.

Piccone Stella, S. (1993), *La prima generazione. Ragazze e ragazzi nel miracolo economico italiano*, Franco Angeli.

Pieroni, A. (2000), 'Ma la classe operaia è andata in paradiso', *Corriere della Sera*, 30 May.

Pietro Gennaro e Associati (1964), *Risultati dell'indagine sulle aspettative dei quartieri periferici: 3. Rapporto sul quartiere Comasina*, ILSES.

Piva, A. (ed.), (1982), *BBPR a Milano*, Electa.

Pivetta, O. (1995), 'Milano, Il "blob" sulla città', *La Repubblica*, 13 February.

Pizzorno, A. (1960), *Comunità e razionalizzazione. Ricerca sociologia su un caso di sviluppo industriale*, Turin: Einaudi.

—— (1980), 'I ceti medi nei meccanismi del consenso', in ibid., *I soggetti del pluralismo. Classi, partiti, sindacati*, Bologna: Il Mulino: 67–98

Ponti, G. (1952), 'Senza aggettivi', *Domus*, 268: 1.

—— (1956), '"Espressione" dell'edificio Pirelli in costruzione a Milano', *Domus*, 316: 1–13.

Ponti, L. L. (1990), *Giò Ponti. The Complete Work 1923–1978*, London: Thames & Hudson.

Ponziani, L. (1977), 'Com'è triste Milano. Paralisi economica e crisi d'identità all'ombra del Pirellone', *Il Messagero*, 31 December.

Portelli, A. (1985), *Biografia di una città. Storia e racconto: Terni 1830–1985*, Turin: Einaudi.

—— (1991), *The Death of Luigi Trastulli and Other Stories. Form and Meaning in Oral History*, New York: State University of New York Press.

—— (1997), *The Battle of Valle Giulia. Oral History and the Art of Dialogue*, Wisconsin: The University of Wisconsin.

—— (1999), *L'ordine è già stato eseguito. Roma, le Fosse Ardeatine, la memoria*, Rome: Donzelli.

Progetto Bicocca. 1985–1998, (1999), Skira.

Pugliese, E. (1996), 'L'immigrazione', *Storia dell'Italia repubblicana*, 3*, *L'Italia nella crisi mondiale. L'ultimo ventennio*. 1. *Economia e società*: 933–84.

Putnam, R. Leonardi, R. and Nanetti, R. Y. (1993), *Making Democracy Work. Civic Traditions in Modern Italy*, Princeton: Princeton University Press.

Quagliata, L. (1999), 'Stessa strada: dall'accoglienza alla detenzione', *Il manifesto*, 25 November.

Ramona, J. (1992), 'Perifèria', *Urbanisme revista*, 9–10: 1.

Ravelli, F. (1994), 'C'era una volta la Stalingrado d'Italia', *La Repubblica*, 28 April.

Renzi, E. (1975), 'Milano nell'ultimo decennio: I grandi interventi nella periferia, le battaglie per la casa e nei quartieri' in Dragone (ed.): 22–31.

Revelli, M. (1989), *Lavorare in FIAT*, Garzanti.

Revelli, M. (1997), 'Crisi dello stato-nazione, territorio, nuove forme del conflitto e della convivenza', *Il ponte della Lombardia*, VI: 7–13.

Reyneri, E. (1993), 'La ritardata creazione e il rapido declino della classe operaia centrale in Italia', in Antonioli, *et al.* (eds): 499–507.

Riccardi, C. (ed.), (1991), *Milano 1881*, Palermo: Sellerio.

Rigoldi, G. (1978), 'Milano: devianza e territorio', *Hinterland*, 3: 50–1.

Rizza, N. (1986), *Costruire palinsesti. Modalità, logiche e stili della programmazione televisiva tra pubblico e privato*, Rome: Rai.

Rogers, E. (1946), 'Editorial', *Domus*, 205: 1–4.

—— (1947), 'Esperienza dell'Ottava Triennale', *Domus*, July.

Rogers, R. (1997), *Cities for a Small Planet*, London: Faber & Faber.

Ronzoni, D. F. (1994), *Dai campi alla fabbrica. Alle origini della Brianza industriale*, Missaglia: Bellavite Editore.

Rosa, G. (1982), *Il mito della capitale morale. Letteratura e pubblicistica a Milano fra Otto e Novecento*, Edizioni di Comunità.

Rosso, M. (1998), 'La crescita della città' in N. Tranfaglia (ed.), *Storia di Torino. Dalla Grande Guerra alla Liberazione (1915–1945)*, Einaudi: 427–500.

Rota, E. (1997), 'Ambiente e territorio', *Il ponte della Lombardia*, VI, 1: 21–2.

Rovati, G. (2000), *Le imprese culturali e gli imprenditori: i risultati di una survey di quartiere*, (unpublished conference paper: Imprese culturali e futuro della città, Università Cattolica, Milan, 7 March).

Ruggeri, G. (1995), *Berlusconi. Gli affari del presidente*, Kaos.

—— and Guarino, M. (1994), *Berlusconi. Inchiesta sul signor Tv*, Kaos.

Sacconi, A. and Valtorta, R. (eds), (1997), 1987–97 *Archivio dello Spazio. Dieci anni di fotografia italiana sul territorio della provincia di Milano*, Udinese: Arte e Editore.

Samuel, R. (1994), *Theatres of Memory. Vol. 1, Past and Present in Contemporary Culture*, London: Verso.

—— and Thompson, P. (eds), (1990), *The Myths We Live By,* London: Routledge.

Santini, P. C. (1981), *Gli anni del design italiano: ritratto di Cesare Cassina,* Electa.

Sapelli, G. (1987), 'La cultura della produzione: "autorità tecnica" e "autonomia morale"' in Bottiglieri and Ceri (eds): 23–51.

—— (1989), *L'Italia inafferrabile,* Venice: Marsilio.

—— (1991), 'Dalla periferia all'integrazione europea' in R. Romano (ed.), *Storia dell'economia italiana, III, L'età contemporanea: un paese nuovo,* Turin: 59–141.

—— (1994), *Cleptocrazia. Il "meccanismo unico" della corruzione tra economia e politca,* Feltrinelli.

—— (1996), 'Dal "miracolo economico" alla "neoindustria": grandi famiglie e nuova borghesia' in *Storia di Milano,* vol. XVIII, *Il Novecento,* Rome: Treccani: 147–81.

Saraceno, C. (1976), *Anatomia della famiglia. Strutture sociali e forme familiari,* Bari: De Donato.

—— (1981), 'La famiglia operaia sotto il fascismo', in G. Sapelli, (ed.), *La classe operaia durante il fascismo,* Annali Fondazione G. Feltrinelli, XX, 1979/80, Feltrinclli.

—— (1988), 'La famiglia: i paradossi della costruzione del privato', in Ariès, P. and Duby, G. (eds), *La vita privata,* vol. V: *Il Novecento,* Bari: Laterza: 185–227.

—— (1988), *Sociologia della famiglia,* Bologna: Il Mulino.

Scerbanenco, G. (1993), *Milano calibro 9,* Garzanti.

Sciolla, L. (1997), *Italiani stereotipi di casa nostra,* Bologna: Il Mulino.

Scramaglia, R. (1993), 'Considerazioni sociologiche sugli abitanti di una periferia milanese. Indagine qualitativa e ricerche documentarie-bibliografiche come verifiche di uno studio quantitativo' in Guiducci (ed.): 27–119.

Seabrook, J. (1984), *The Idea of Neighbourhood,* London: Pluto.

Secchi, B. (1992), 'La periferia', *Casabella,* 583: 20–2.

—— (1993), 'Un'urbanistica di spazi aperti', *Casabella,* 597/8: 5–9.

Segnocinema (1988), 'Il cinema e la città', 33.

—— (1996), 'I luoghi del cinema', 78.

—— (1996), 'I nonluoghi del cinema', 79.

Selvafolta, O. (1990), 'Milano operaia' in *Guide di architettura. Milano,* U. Allemandi: 200–2.

Sennett, R. (1990), *The Conscience of the Eye: The Design and Social Life of Cities,* London: Faber & Faber.

Serra. M. (1993), 'Che tempo fa', *L'Unità,* 29 July.

Servadio, G. (1981), *Luchino Visconti: A Biography,* London: Weidenfeld & Nicolson.

Shopping Milano (2000), 12, 37.

Signorelli, A. (1996), *Antropologia urbana. Introduzione alla ricerca in Italia*, Guerini Studio.

Silverstone, R. (1994), *Television and Everyday Life*, London: Routledge.

Simon, D. (1991), *Homicide. A Year on the Killing Streets*, New York: Ivy Books.

Sistema Design Milano (1999), Abitare Segesta.

Sisti, L. and Gomez, P. (1997), *L'intoccabile. Berlusconi e Cosa Nostra*, Kaos Edizioni.

Sollazzo, L. (1999), 'Giorgio Armani' in Vergani: 30–4.

Sorlin, P. (1991), *European Cinemas, European Societies*, London: Routledge.

Sparke, P. (1988), *Italian Design: 1870 to the Present*, London: Thames & Hudson.

—— (1990), 'A Home for Everybody?'. Design, Ideology and the Culture of the Home in Italy, 1945–72' in Z. Baranski and R. Lumley (eds), *Culture and Conflict in Postwar Italy*, New York: St Martins: 225–41.

—— (1998), *An Introduction to Design and Culture in the Twentieth Century*, Routledge, London, 1998.

—— (1999), 'Nature, Craft, Domesticity, and the Culture of Consumption: the Feminine Face of Design in Italy, 1945–70', *Modern Italy*, 4, 1: 59–78.

Spinazzola, V. (1981), 'La "capitale morale". Cultura milanese e mitologia urbana', *Belfagor*, XXXVI: 317–27.

Spriano, P. (1972), *Storia di Torino operaia e socialista. Da De Amicis a Gramsci* Turin: Einaudi.

Squarcina, E. (1987), *Il paesaggio dell'espansione metropolitana. Il caso di Segrate*, Circolo culturale Janus di Segrate.

Stajano, C. (1993), *Il disordine*, Turin: Einaudi.

Stearns, P. (1997), 'Stages of consumerism. Recent Work on the Issues of Periodization', *Journal of Modern History*, 69, 1: 102–17.

Stedman-Jones, G. (1971), *Outcast London. A Study in the Relationship between Classes in Victorian Society*, Oxford: Clarendon.

Tadini, E. (1993), *La tempesta*, Turin: Einaudi.

—— (1996), 'Falck, nella Terra desolata', *Corriere della Sera*, 13 January.

Tavolato, V. and Zanuso, L. (1974), 'Le condizioni di vita nella società', *Classe*, 10: 153–81.

Tentori, T. (1977), *Antropologia culturale*, Rome: Studium.

Tessera, V. (1995), *Innocenti Lambretta*, Nada Editore.

Testori, G. (1961), *Il fabbricone*, Feltrinelli.

—— (1985), *Il ponte della Ghisolfa*, Garzanti.

—— (1996), *Opere, 1943–1961*, Bompiani.

—— (1998), *Opere, 1965–1977*, Bompiani.

Thrändhardt, D. and Miles, R. (1995), *Migration and European Integration. The Dynamics of Inclusion and Exclusion*, London: Pinter.

Tognoli, C. (1983), 'Prefazione', in P. Caputo (ed.), *Il ghetto diffuso. L'immigrazione straniera a Milano*, Franco Angeli: 9–10.

Tonetti, C. (1983), *Luchino Visconti,* Boston: Twayne Publishers.

Tonon, G. and Consonni, G. (1976), 'Aspetti della questione urbana a Milano dal fascismo alla ricostruzione', *Classe*, 12: 43–101.

Tosi, A. (1993), *Immigrati e senza casa. I problemi, i progetti, le politiche*, Franco Angeli.

—— (ed.), (1998), 'Lo spazio urbano dell'immigrazione', *Urbanistica*, 111: 7–46.

Tredicesima Triennale di Milano, (1964), *Tempo Libero, 12.6–27.9.1964.*

Triani, G. (1994), *Bar Sport Italia. Quando la politica va nel pallone*, Elèuthera.

Tullio-Altan, C. (1996), *Antropologia. Storia e problemi*, Feltrinelli.

Turani, G. (1988),'I milanesi senza Milano', *La Repubblica*, 30 December.

—— and Sasso, C. (1992), *I saccheggiatori: Milano: facevano i politici ma erano dei ladri*, Sperling & Kupfer.

Turone, S. (1993), *Politica ladra. Storia della corruzione in Italia. 1861–1992*, Laterza: Bari.

Valera, P. (1996), *Milano sconosciuta*, Greco & Greco.

Vargiù, A. (1997), *La città di carta. Milano nell'immaginario dei corrispondenti della stampa estera*, Franco Angeli.

Veltroni, W. (1992), *I programmi che hanno cambiato l'Italia. Quarant'anni di televisione*, Feltrinelli.

Vercelloni, I. T. (1999), 'Walter Albini' in Vergani: 14–17.

Vercelloni, V. (1989), *La storia del paesaggio urbano a Milano*, L'archivolto.

Vergani, G. (ed.), (1999), *Dizionario della moda*, Baldini & Castoldi.

Viale, G. (1996), *Tutti in taxi*, Feltrinelli.

Virciglio, G. (1991), *Milocca al nord. Una comunità di immigrati siciliani ad Asti,* Franco Angeli.

Visco, V. (1976), 'Il consumo dei beni durevoli in Italia nel 1969: Appunti per una analisi' in Campa, (ed.): 163–232.

Vitone, L. (1998), *Milano, Wide City. Mappa delle presenze straniere a Milano*, Comune di Milano, Progetto Giovani.

Volli, U. (1988), *Contro la moda*, Feltrinelli.

Vuillamy, E. (1993), 'The Kickback Culture', *The Guardian*, 8 April.

Wacquant, L. (1993), 'Urban Outcasts: Stigma and Division in the Black American Ghetto and the French Urban Periphery', *International Journal of Urban and Regional Research*, 17, 3: 366–83.

White, J. (1986), *The Worst Street in North London. Campbell Bunk, Islington Between the Wars*, London: Routledge.

White, N. (2000), *Reconstructing Italian Fashion. America and the Development of the Italian Fashion Industry*, Oxford: Berg.

Willmott P. and Young M. (1962), *Family and Kinship in East London*, London: Penguin.

Wolf, M. (1992), *Gli effetti sociali dei media*, Bompiani.

Wolfe, T. (1987), *The Bonfire of the Vanities*, New York: Straus.

Zannier, I. (1994), 'Reality and Italian Photography' in G. Celant, (ed.), *The Italian Metamorphosis, 1943–1968*, Guggenheim Museum, New York: 316–23.

Zardini M. (1996), (ed.), *Paesaggi ibridi. Un viaggio nella città contemporanea*, SKIRA editore.

Zenoni, P. (ed.), (1994), *Dizionario cinematografico di Milano*, Comune di Milano.

Zucchetti, E. 'Introduzione' (1995), Fondazione Ambrosianeum, *Milano '94. Rapporto sulla città*, Franco Angeli: 13–29.

Index

Abatantuono, Diego, 72
Abitare, 123
AC Milan, 12–13, 104
Accidental Death of an Anarchist, The see Fo,
   Dario
Advertising, 4, 166
   and film, 72
   and politics, 183
   as service industry, 2
   during boom years, 122
   links to Berlusconi, 99, 101
   links to Socialists, 81
   symbol of Milan, 175–6, 181
aerials *see* TV aerials
albanesi see Albanians
Albania, 37
Albanians, 13–4
Alberoni, Francesco, 38, 45
Albertini, Gabriele, 130n16, 157, 173
   and Berlusconi, 105n22
   and the fashion industry, 130n16
   elected Mayor (1997), 16, 157, 173
   on immigration, 67
Albertini, Luigi, 15
Albini, Franco, 119–20
Albini, Walter, 131
Alessi, 118
Alfa Romeo
   and snake symbol, 101
   and urban immigrant workers, 57
   as periphery, 78
   closure, 2
   founders' graves, 174
   location in *Rocco and his Brothers*, 75
   old identity of Milan, 175
   set for Nirvana, 83–4
Alleanza Nazionale, 16, 173
Alto-Adige terrorists, 7
Amaro Ramazzotti, 165
Amelio, Gianni, 72, 75–6, 79

American Gigolo, 132
Andreotti, Giulio, 171
anima divisa in due, Un', 75, 82
anni di piombo see lead, years of
Ansaldo factory complex, 130
   hosts Socialist Party Congress 1989, 166
Antonioni, Michelangelo, 10, 71, 77, 79, 81
Apulia, 7, 59, 85
architecture, 15, 109, 109n1, 110, 149
   University Faculty of, 5, 17
architects, 116
Archivio Fiom, 48
Archizoom, 123
Arcore, 105
aree dismesse (ex-industrial areas), 2, 173
Arflex, 114
aria serena dell'ovest, L', 75–6, 80–3
Arialda, L', 78
Armani *see* Armani, Giorgio
Armani, Giorgio
   as boss of Milan, 3, 176
   and 'Block of Gold', 127–8
   career, 122, 132
   importance, 125
Artemide, 114
Associazione per il Disegno Industriale
   Italiano (ADI), 123
Asti, 138
Auschwitz, 7
Avanti!, 78
Aymonino, Carlo, 145
Azione Cattolica, 46

Baggio (zone of Milan), 30, 43, 46, 54–7
Baggio Vecchio, 29, 56
Baglioni, Guido, 38, 45
balcony *see ringhiera, case di*
Baldessari, Luciano, 121
Baldoni, Sandro, 72
Banditi a Milano, 72

Index

Banfi, Gian Luigi see BBPR
banks, 3–5, 17, 176
Bar Skirrat, 67–9
Barcelona, 104, 161
Baresi, Franco, 104
Barona (zone of Milan), 29, 43, 46, 55–6
bars, 8,
Basili, Giancarlo, 83
Basilicata, 85
Basilico, Gabriele, 146, 153
BBPR (architectural group), 10
Beccaria, Il (youth prison), 11
Belgiojoso, Lodovico see BBPR
Bellocchio, Marco, 72
Bentivoglio, Fabrizio, 72, 75
Bergamo, 161
Berlusconi, Silvio
    and AC Milan
    and Craxi, 101, 103
    and *Forza Italia!*, 2, 35, 157, 161, 175, 183
    and *Milano 2*, 92n7, 99, 126
    as President of the Council of Ministers, 107
    as symbol of Milan, 81
    career of, 99–106, 173
    television entrepreneur, 3, 86, 89, 176
Bertolucci, Giuseppe, 8
Bethnal Green (zone of London), 24
    model of family, 24
Bianciardi, Luciano, 1, 8, 80, 119
Bicocca University, 176
Bicocca (zone of Milan), 173
bicycles, 19
Big Pirelli see Pirelli Tower
Bigazzi, Luca, 77, 82
Birmingham, 159
birth rate, 176
Blade Runner, 159
Boeri, Stefano, 149, 152–5
'block of gold' see 'Fashion block'
Bollate, 142
bomb, Via Palestro (1993), 63–4, 66
Bompiani, 15
Bonasia, Aldo, 79
Bonfire of the Vanities, The, 159
Bongiorno, Mike, 94 and n8, 97 and n12, 102
boom (1950s and 1960s), 1, 4, 19, 38, 110,
    157, 176, 182
    and cars, 6, 95

and film, 72, 83
and design, 124
and Pirelli Tower, 118–9
and television, 107
immigration during, 42, 44, 47
Milan as capital of, 53, 157
pre-, 143
boom (1980s), 118, 131, 157, 166, 176
boom (1990s), 131
Booth, Charles, 138
Borrelli, Francesco Saverio, 15
Borghini, Gian Piero, 164
Borgo San Paolo (zone of Turin), 24
Borletti, 122
Bossi, Umberto, 173
Bottoni, Piero, 116
Bovisa (zone of Milan), 1, 5
    as historic microcosm, 16–17
    as periphery, 25, 139
    factory closures in, 174, 176
    immigration to, 43, 46, 48
    old neighbourhood, 53–57
    open space in, 58
    riot, 51
    site of design museum, 118
    working class in, 24
    station, 17
box (garage), 6, 146
Branzi, Andrea, 119, 123
Brazilians, 13
Breda, 2–3, 24, 162,174–5, 181
Brera (zone of Milan), 129
Brera courtyard, 76
Brescia, 161
Brianza (zone north of Milan), 111, 114, 126–7
Bribesville see *Tangentopoli*
Bronx, The, 138n1, 139, 158
Brussels, 163
Brustio, Cesare, 123
Buccinasco (zone of Milan), 11
Bullring (Birmingham), 159
business users, 134, 151–2
Buy, Margherita, 83

Calabresi, Luigi, 10
Calabria, 7
Callas, Maria, 14
Camera di Commercio, 126

Campania, 7
canals, 8, 17, 53, 76, 145, 182
Canary Wharf, 158
Canella, Guido, 117, 145
Cannibali, I, 72
Capanna, Mario, 14
car *see* cars
car workers, 35
Carimate chair, 114
golf club house, 115
Carosello, 29, 106
cars
  and families, 33
  and public transport, 12
  and the ring road, 13
  as city boss, 7, 9, 179, 182–3
  factories *see* Alfa Romeo, Fiat, Innocenti
  private, 179
  replaces scooter, 19
  theft, 6
Casa Vogue, 123
Casabella, 10, 123
Caserta, 51
Cassina company, 113–4
Cassina, Cesare, 113
Catanzaro, 11
catenaccio (football tactics), 104
Cathedral see *Duomo di Milano*
Cathedral Square *see Piazza del Duomo*
Catholic Church, 39, 93, 103, 158
Catholic parties, 161
Cavaliere, Il see Berlusconi, Silvio
Cavani, Liliana, 72
Cederna, Camilla, 15, 72
Cemetery, Lambrate, 64
  Monumental, 174
  Musocco, 15
Central Station *see Stazione Centrale*
centre, historic, 1
Centri di prima accoglienza (Cpas), 60–3, 66
Cerruti, 132
Cervi, Mario, 67
CGE, 93
CGIL (Trade Union Federation), 175
chairs, 113
Chanel, 128
Chiavari, 113
Chicago (Milan as), 72

Chiesa, Mario, 16, 167
children, 6, 9, 55, 177, 180
Chinese (in Milan), 39, 41
Christian Democrats, 2, 93, 98, 167, 171–2
Church see Catholic Church
Cimitero monumentale see Cemetery,
  Monumental
Cinecittà, 71
cinema, 71–84
cinemas, 178
Cinquecento (car) *see* Fiat 500
Circonvallazione, 13, 16, 145
citizenship, 39
city administration see *Comune di Milano*
city users, 134, 150–3
clandestini, 42, 68–9
classe operaia va in paradiso, La, 72, 77,
  79–80
Clean Hands (Judicial inquiry) *see Mani pulite*
clearances see *sgomberi*
Colpire al cuore, 72, 76
Comasina (zone of Milan)
  and television, 29, 89
  as neighbourhood, 46–7
  as periphery, 136
  housing, 69
  immigration to, 5, 40, 43, 69
  new quarter, 57
Comune di Milano, 5, 45, 54, 160, 174
communism, 24
communism, anti-, 103
Communist Party, Italian, 10, 35, 167
commuters, 6, 135, 150–1, 176–7
commuting, 8, 37, 121, 181
Como, 127, 161
  Cathedral, 113
Compasso d'oro, 122
consumerism, 46
Coree (immigrant housing), 27, 31, 40, 44 and
  ns6–7, 63
Corriere della Sera, Il, 15, 21, 168
Corsico, 11
Corso Buenos Aires, 40
Corso Sempione, 92–3
courtyards, 76, 177–9
Cpas *see Centri di prima accoglienza*
Craxi, Bettino, 105n22, 164
  and Berlusconi, 101, 103

and corruption, 157, 170
authoritarian, 165
Milanese socialist, 2, 129–30, 161
opera-goer, 15
project, 167
Crespi (family), 15
crime, 178
Cronaca di un amore, 71
culture, 19–36 and passim
definitions of, 20
consumerist, 32–4
mass, 19–36, 106
see also Pasolini, cinema, television

Dalla Chiesa, Nando, 170–1
Dallas, 102
Damiani, Damiano, 72
DC see Christian Democrats
de-industrialization, 1, 3, 42, 174
De Corato, Riccardo, 67
De Lorenzo, Francesco, 171
De Sica, Vittorio, 14, 44, 76, 78, 80–1
design, 3, 15, 109–24, 181
designers, 109–24
Detroit, 179
Dicembre, 22 (film company), 72
Dickens, Charles, 138
Di Pietro, Antonio, 167, 170
Dolce & Gabbana, 125, 127, 131, 176
Domus, 123
Domus Academy, 123
Double or Quit? see Lascia o raddoppia?
drugs, 178
Duomo di Milano, Il (Cathedral)
and architecture, 10
and canals, 8
and fashion, 134
in film, 76, 78
Piazza del, 64, 76, 145, 159
Versace's funeral in, 133

economic miracle see boom (1950s and
1960s)
Edipo Re, 71
Egypt, 5, 37
Egyptians, 68, 177
elections, local, 167
emigration, 70
engineering, university faculty of, 5

engineers, 168
European Union, 42
EU see European Union
European Cup, 104
ex-barraccati (ex-shack dwellers), 47
extra-comunitari, 42, 65
Expo, 15, 168
expulsion orders, 60

FACE factory, Bovisa, 51, 78
paternalism, 48
factories, 5, 17, 174, 176
factory, the, 8, 42, 47, 173
factory closures, 175
Falck, 2, 3, 16, 163, 174
fascism
and the periphery, 142
bomb, 7
in Milan, 3, 14–15, 183
defeat of, 25
moves to Rome, 169
fascists, 7, 8, 14–5
fashion, 2, 125–34
and publishing, 15
and ready-to-wear, 33
as engine of economic change, 3, 4, 176, 181
as new industry, 166
at *La Rinascente*, 122
links with Socialists, 81
Milan as capital of, 125–6, 173
weeks, 125, 134, 151
Fashion block, 127–9, 162
fashion district see fashion block
FC Internazionale see Inter Milan
Fellini, Federico, 71
Feltrinelli (publishers), 15
Ferrè, Gianfranco, 81, 125, 176
Ferrovie Nord, 5, 8, 75
Fiat, 24, 27, 34–5, 52, 58, 121, 175
Fiat 500 (car), 19, 122
Fiat 600 (car), 95–6, 106
Fiera (Trade Fair), 4–5, 121–2
and fashion, 126, 133
and radical design, 117–8
Fiera Campionaria (annual trade fair), 4–5, 95,
121–2
Fiera di Milano (institution), 4–5, 118, 126
Fiera di Milano (new location, Portello), 179,
182

film-makers, 7, 71–84
film-making
  experimental, 72n2
  political, 72
financial capital (Milan as), 1
Fininvest, 103–4, 106–7
Fiom (Metalworkers' trade union), 48–50
Fiorucci, Elio, 131–2
Florence, 123, 131
Fo, Dario, 10
fog, 3, 77, 81, 146, 159
football, 104
  see AC Milan
  see Inter Milan
  see San Siro
Fordism, 175
  Fordist techniques, 120
Forlanini (zone of Milan), 29
Formentini, Marco, 61, 172
Formigoni, Roberto, 105
Fortini, Franco, 22
Forza Italia!, 35, 105, 157, 161, 175,
  and Berlusconi, 103
  and Milanese politics, 2, 167, 183
Fumagalli, Aldo, 173
Fuori dal mondo, 82
furniture, 111, 118, 122–3

Gallaratese (zone of Milan), 5
Galleria, La, 181
  and cinema, 83
  and fashion, 128, 133–4
  and urban space, 145, 159
gangster movies, 72
garage *see* box
Gardella, Ignazio, 122
Gargano, 85
Garibaldi, Stazione (Station) see *Stazione*
  Garibaldi
Garzanti, 15
gasometers, 5, 174
Gazzetta dello Sport, La, 15
Geloso, 93
Genoa, 38, 66, 155, 161
Giacosa, Dante, 122
Giambellino (zone of Milan), 1
Giorno, Il, 15
Giustizia, Palazzo di see *Palazzo di Giustizia*

Gramsci, Antonio, 11
Gratosoglio (zone of Milan), 5
green movement, 180
green space, 9, 58, 115, 180
Gregotti, Vittorio, 115
Guggenheim Museum (New York), 119
Guiducci, Roberto, 140–1
gypsies, 73, 79

Hamburg, 163
Hendel, Paolo, 165
Herg, Franca, 119
Hitler, Adolf, 7
Hotel Paura, 8
housing
  and integration, 39–40, 53
  and *Rocco and his Brothers*, 53
  and *Tangentopoli*, 165
  Bicocca project, 176
  immigrant, 60–3, 66, 177
  in Asti, 138
  in Bovisa, 16, 176
  in Comasina, 47
  in Turin, 138
  occupations, 68
  Piazzale Lugano, 22, 177
  post-war, 5, 47, 110, 115
  public, 165
  ringhiera, case di, 9, 24, 137
  see Coree
  see Milano 2
  see Milano 3
  see periphery

Ile de France, 163
immigrants, 1–2, 5, 14, 37–70, 173, 177
  and cinema, 81
  and Pirelli Tower, 10, 118
  and San Vittore prison, 11
  and shopping, 122n9
  and the Central Station, 7
  as basis of the modern city, 181
  see also integration, *Rocco and his*
    Brothers
immigration, 37–70
  concepts, 40–2
  internal, 40–59
  foreign, 59–70

lack of comparison between internal and foreign, 37–40
industrial capital, Milan as, 1
Innocenti, 2, 120, 174
  dispute at, 175
integration, 69
  Alberoni, Francesco, theory of, 45
  and foreign immigrants, 59–70
  and housing, 53–8
  conservative, 47–53
  definition, 40–2
  radical, 48–53, 59
  social, 46
  workplace, 46, 47–53
Inter Milan, 12–13, 104
irregolari (undocumented/illegal immigrants), 42
Italian Metamorphosis, The, 119
ITT, 48

Japan, 133
Japanese, 127, 151
Jews
  deportation of, 11
  Italian, 7
  Milanese, 39
Juventus, 104

Kamikazen, 80–1
Kartell, 114
Katznelson, Ira, 53
King of Italy, The, 4
Korean war, 40
Kurds, Kurdish, 177
Kusturica, Emir, 76, 79

La Galleria see Galleria, La
Lambrate (zone of Milan), 120
Lambretta scooter, 120
La Repubblica, 15, 170
La Rete, 161
La Rinascente, 122, 132
La Scala, 15, 74, 129
Lascia o raddoppia?, 94–8
  and boom, 106
  and language, 85
  and Mike Bongiorno, 102
  and schools, 93

success of, 3, 29
Lattuada, Alberto, 7, 79, 83
Lavoro, Il, 77, 79
lead, years of, 1, 11, 14, 79
left, intellectual, 2
left, traditional, 2
Lega see Northern Leagues
Lerner, Gad, 35
Leopard, The, 92
Leopardi, Giorgio, 8
Levi, Primo, 59
Ligresti, Salvatore, 164n3, 170
living room see salotto
Lizzani, Carlo, 72, 119
local administrations, 39
Lombard region see Lombardy (Region)
Lombard Regional Government, 10, 160, 162
  and Pirelli Tower, 119
  elections, 2000, 105
Lombardy (Region),
  and de-industrialization, 166–7
  and design industry, 110–1, 123–4
  and internal immigration, 37, 43
  and MM, 12
  and Pirelli Tower, 118
  and private transport, 155
  and strikes, 175n17
  as economic powerhouse, 163
  economy, 4
  industrial revolution, 9
  origins of fashion and textile industries, 126
London, 66, 125, 138, 158, 161
Los Angeles, 159
Lotta Continua, 10
Luchetti, Daniele, 73
L'Unità, 78

Maddaloni, 51
Madonnina, La, 9
Madonna, 133
Mafia, 171, 179
Mafioso, Il, 8, 79
Mani pulite (Judicial inquiry), 11, 16, 157
Magistretti, Vico, 109n1, 110, 113–5, 117
Magneti Marelli, 93
Malatesta, Errico, 11
Maldini, Paolo, 104
Malpensa airport, 127

Mantua, 73
Maralunga sofa (Magistretti), 114
marketing, 183
marocchini see Moroccans
Marrakech Express, 81
Martinotti, Guido, 150–2, 155, 163
mass media, 176
mass worker, 27
Massa, Lulù, 80
Mastroianni, Marcello, 75–6, 81
Mauthausen, 10
Mean Streets, parody of, 76
Mediaset, 103
Mediolanum, 168
migrants *see* immigrants
migration *see* immigration
Milan Cathedral see *Duomo di Milano*
Milan Football Club *see* AC Milan
miracolo economico see boom (1950s and
    1960s)
Milano 2, 99–101
    and Berlusconi, 2, 101n18
    and fashion industry, 126
    and 1968, 107
    and TV aerials, 92n7
Milano Films, 71
Milano nera, 71, 77
Milano '83, 79
Milano San Felice, 115
Milan, Province of, 174
Milanese metro (underground) *see* MM
Milano da bere, 178
    and cinema, 72, 81–2
    and Craxi project, 165–7
    and fashion, 129–30
    and *Tangentopoli*, 169
    as image of Milan, 165–7
    as reflection of 1980s, 2, 172, 178
miracle *see* boom (1950s and 1960s)
Miracolo a Milano, 14, 44, 74, 76, 78–9
miracolo economico, il see boom (1950s and
    1960s)
Miracle in Milan see *Miracolo a Milano*
Mirafiori Sud, 35
MM (*Metropolitana Milanese*), 8, 12, 75, 119,
    180
    signs, graphics, 119
Mondadori, 15, 101n18

Monicelli, Mario, 77, 79
Monte Stella, 3, 116, 159
Monza, 5
Monza, Royal Villa, 112
Moreau, Jeanne, 75, 79
Moroccans, 14, 63, 67–8
Morocco, 5, 64
Mobile italiano, Il, 123
Modenese, Beppe, 126
Modo, 123
Momi-Modit-Milano *see Modit*
Modit, 126
Montecatini, 162
mosque (Segrate), 64
motorways, 76
Motta, Giancarlo, 147–8, 153–4
Mousaffir, Driss, 14, 63–6
MSI *see* neo-fascists
Munari, Bruno, 122–3
Mundialito, 102
Munich, 161
Musocco cemetery *see* cemetery, Musocco
Mussolini, Benito, 7, 11, 15, 22, 183
Muzio, Giovanni, 116

Naples, 26, 38, 104, 141, 158, 170
Napoletani a Milano, 76
Napoli *see* Naples
Natali, Antonio 164n3
Navigli *see* canals
nebbia, la *see* fog
Nebbiosa, La, 77
neo-fascists, 61
neo-realism, 72
Nervi, Pier Luigi, 118–9
New York, 119, 159
Nichetti, Maurizio, 72
Nigerians, 13
Nirvana, 81–4
non-places, 143–4
Noorda, Bob, 119
North Africa, 37, 42
Northern Leagues,
    and administration after 1993, 172–3
    and foreign immigrants, 61
    and 1993 elections, 157
    and *Padania*, 160–1
    and *Tangentopoli*, 167–8, 171

in 1990s, 2
Northern Railways *see Ferrovie Nord*
Notte, La, 10, 71–2, 75–7, 81
Novara, 79
Novate Milanese, 1

Olmi, Ermanno, 8, 72, 75, 77, 79
  and Bovisa, 25–6
  image of Milan, 81–2
  see Il Posto
  see The Tree of the Wooden Clogs
Oggetti smarriti, 8
OM, 2, 174
open spaces, 58
Orlando, Silvio, 72
Ortese, Anna Maria, 7
Ottagono, 123
Ottone, Piero, 15

Paci, Enzo, 109
Padania, 161, 163
Pallavicino, Cesare, 120
Palazzo dell'Arte, 116
Palazzo degli Affari, 4
Palazzo di Giustizia (Law courts), 10, 171
Palazzo Pitti (Florence), 131
Panseca, Filippo, 130
Parco Nord, 173
Parco Sempione, 76, 116
Paris, 125
parking, 120, 179
parks, 58
Parondi family *see Rocco and his Brothers*
partisans, 15
partitocrazia (partitocracy), 54
Pasolini, Pier Paolo
  and cinema, 8, 71–2, 77, 79
  and debates over culture, cultural change,
    21–3
  and television, 29, 92–3
  and the urban periphery, 35
  and working class culture, 28–9
  nostalgia of, 26
  see also Teorema
  writes for *Il Corriere della Sera*, 15
Pavia, 5
PCI *see* Communist Party, Italian
peasant world, 21

pensioners, 176, 180
Peressutti, Enrico *see* BBPR
periferia urbana see periphery, urban
peripheries, 76
periphery, urban, 135–55
  and cinema, 73, 77–8, 80–1
  and crisis of the city, 178
  and fashion industry, 127
  and foreign immigration, 40, 60
  and internal immigration, 39–40
  and the scooter, 121
  movement of working class to, 53
  spread of, 1, 5
  see also Bovisa, Comasina, Pasolini, Via
    Bianchi
Perrucchetti (zone of Milan), 29
Petri, Elio, 72, 77, 79–80
Philips, 93
photographers, 7
Piacenza, 132
Piaggio, 120
Piazza del Duomo, La, 64, 122, 145, 159, 171,
  181
Piazza Fontana bomb/massacre, 1, 11, 13–4,
  16, 73
Piazzale Loreto, 15
Piazzale Lugano, 16
Piazza San Sepolcro, 15
Piazza Santo Stefano, 8
Piccioni, Giuseppe, 82
Piccolo Teatro, 159, 166
Piccolo Teatro, Nuovo, 178
Pillitteri, Paolo, 164, 170
Pinelli, Giuseppe 'Pino', 1
Pinelli case, 14
Pirelli, 2, 162
  and cemetery, 174
  and cinema, 73
  and Italian immigrants, 181
  Bicocca project, 176
  closure, 175
  growth, 168
  neighbourhood, 115
  workers, 10, 52
Pirelli Tower
  and cinema, 76–7, 83
  and fashion, 134
  and immigrants, 10

and private television, 101
as seat of Lombard Regional Government, 160
as symbol of the boom, 9–10
as urban design, 118–9
Pirellone see Pirelli Tower
planning, 109, 168
plastics, 114
Poggiolini, Duilio, 171
Politecnico di Milano, 10, 115, 117
pollution, 123
Ponti, Giò,
  and Pirelli Tower, 9, 118–9
  and *Superleggera* chair design, 113–4
  as architect-designer, 109n1
  designs Rai offices, 93
Portaborse, Il, 73
Porta Ticinese, 8, 125
Porta Venezia, 66
post-fascists, 157
post-industrial city, 2
post-industrial revolution, 4
Posto, Il, 8, 72, 74–6, 79
Prada
  and the 'Fashion block', 127
  as Milanese ruling class, 3
  history and origins, 133–4
  importance, 125
private television see television, private
prostitutes, 13, 151
prostitution, 41
Province of Milan see Milan, Province of
PSI see Socialist Party, Italian
public transport, 180
publishing, 4
Publitalia, 101

Quartiere Triennale Ottava (QT8), 116
Quarto Oggiaro (zone of Milan), 5, 27, 40, 138–9

Radical design, 123
Radice Fossati, Carlo, 165
RAI (Italian State Television company), 93
aerial, Milan, 92
Re, Luigi, 93–4
ready-to-wear, 127
reconstruction, 110

red belt, 142, 161
around Paris, 24
Reggio Calabria, 132
regolari see immigrants
Renzo e Luciana, 79
Repubblica, La see *La Repubblica*
residents, 42, 150–2
Resistance, The, 2–3, 16, 169
Rete, La see *La Rete*
Rhine Valley, 161
Rizzoli, 15
Rifondazione Comunista, 161, 173
Rimpatriata, La, 72
Rinascente, La see *La Rinascente*
ring road see Circonvallazione
ringhiera see housing, ringhiera, case di
*Rocco and his Brother*s, 74–81
  as symbol of the boom in Milan, 1, 78
  and Central Station, 7
  and fog, 80–1
  and housing, 9
  and immigrants, 74–6
  and Milanese locations, 75, 79
  and periphery, 140
  and trams, 74
  and Visconti, Luchino, 71–2
  shot in black-and-white, 53, 146
Rogers, Ernesto , 109, 123
  see also BBPR
Romanzo popolare, 77
Rome,
  and cinema industry, 71
  and Craxi, 161
  and internal immigration, 38
  and moral capital myth, 168–9
  and Northern Leagues, 172
  and state television, 96
  and Tangentopoli, 169–72
  shift of power away from, 102
Rossi, Aldo, 109n1, 145
Rotunno, Giuseppe, 78
rubbish, 178
rural traditions, 21

Sacchi, Arrigo, 104
salotto, 90
Salò, Republic of, 16
Salvatores, Gabriele, 72, 75, 80–1, 84

San Babila, 120, 134
San Francisco, 158
San Salvario (zone of Turin), 66–7
San Siro stadium, 12–13, 104
Salone del Mobile, 121, 124
San Vittore (prison), 10, 170
Sbatti il mostro in prima pagina, 72
Scala, La, 14, 78, 129
Scerbanenco, Giorgio, 7, 11
schools, 177
scooter, 19, 33
second miracle *see* boom (1980s)
Secrets of Milan, The, 1
Segrate, 64, 100
senza-tetto (homeless), 47
Sesto San Giovanni,
  and cinema, 79
  and deindustrialisation, 16, 174–5
  and the mass worker, 27
  as periphery, 5, 11
sfrattati (evicted), 47
sgomberi, 60
Sicily, 7, 79, 92, 181
silkworm farming, 112
Sinatra, Frank, 129
Sit-Siemens, 93
socialism, 24, 183
Socialist Party, Italian
  and cinema, 81
  and fashion industry, 125, 129–31
  and 1980s, 2
  and *Tangentopoli*, 2, 16, 157, 164–8, 171–2
  1989 Congress, 130
  reformist tradition, 3
  strength in 1919, 5
  see also Craxi, *Milano da bere*, Pillitteri,
    Tangentopoli, Tognoli
Società Civile, 161, 164, 171
Società Umanitaria, 168
Soldini, Silvio, 72, 75, 77, 80–82
Sole-24 ore, Il, 15, 166
Somalians
  refugees, 39
Sordi, Alberto, 7, 79
Sotto il vestito niente, 72
south, the,
  and FACE factory, 51
  and moral capital myth, 168

and Northern Leagues, 160, 171
and *Tangentopoli*, 171
and San Vittore prison, 11
and the mass worker, 27
immigrants, 5
immigration from, 38–9
southerners, 38, 43–7, 49–59 passim,
  68–70
and cinema, 78
Stadera (zone of Milan), 66, 68
Stajano, Corrado, 166
Stalingrad of Italy *see* Sesto San Giovanni
Stazione Centrale (Milan)
  and cinema, 73–4, 76
  and fashion industry, 129
  and immigration, 53, 66, 70
  and Pirelli Tower, 10, 118
  as 'non-place', 143
  history, 7
  MM stop, 120
Stazione Garibaldi, 8, 53, 83
Stendhal, 8
Stile industria, 123
Stock exchange, 4, 82, 121, 129
Stock market, 2
Stoke Newington, 66
Storia Milanese, Una, 72
Strane storie, 72
'strategy of tension', 16
street signs, 175
student movement (1968), 1, 2, 53, 72
students, 14
Superleggera, 114

Tadini, Emilio, 16
Tangentopoli, 2, 16, 164–73, 178
  and Law Courts, 11
  and Piccolo Teatro, 159
  and San Vittore prison, 11
  lack of films about, 73
  political effects, 161
Teatro della Fiera, 95
TeleMilano, 101, 107
Television, 85–107
  and Comasina, 58
  and cinema, 77, 81
  and cultural change, 1950s and 1960s,
    19–20, 22, 29, 31–3, 58

Index

and Fiera, 4, 15
and internal immigration, 48
and reporting of foreign immigration, 1990s,
	67–8
and the home, 89
ownership, 30
private, 2–3, 86, 88, 93, 101–2, 106, 166
state, 1
see also Berlusconi, Bongiorno, *Lascia o
	raddoppia?*, Pasolini, Rai
Il tempo dei gitani, 76
Teorema, 8, 71–2, 74–5
terrorism, 14
terrorists, 7
Testori, Giovanni, 1, 78
textile manufacture, 112
Thatcher era, 159
Time, 132–3
Tognazzi, Ugo, 76–7
Tognoli, Carlo, 164, 170
Torre Velasca, 10, 76
Toscanini, Arturo, 14
Totò,
	character in *Miracle in Milan*, 14, 78
	comic actor, 71, 75, 76, 81
Trade Fair see *Fiera, Fiera di Milano*
Trade Unions, 3, 161
	see also CGIL
Trams, 24
Tree of the Wooden Clogs, 79
trees, 120
Triennale, La, 116–8
	and *Compasso d'oro*, 122
	and design, 110
	and chair exhibition, 2000, 113
	and fashion, 126, 129, 134
Trussardi company *see* Trussardi, Nicola
Trussardi, Nicola, 129, 132
Turin,
	and Fiat, 121
	and foreign immigration, 66
	and *Tangentopoli*, 170
	and urban sprawl, 1, 5, 155, 161
	and working-class culture, 25, 28
	and 1980s, 34–5
	housing in, 44n6, 138
	in comparison with Milan, 52
	internal immigration to, 38, 40, 52, 59

see also Fiat
Turkey, 5
Tuscany, 120
Tutto a posto, niente in ordine, 74
TV aerials, 92, 101

underground system *see* MM
Unification of Italy, 169
union movement, 2
universities, 168
UPIM stores, 122
urbanization, 21
Urso, Ubaldo, 175

vacuum cleaners, 33
Valentino, 81
Valera, Paolo, 11
Valpreda, Pietro, 1, 14
Veneto, 7
Venice, 1, 155, 161
Verona, 161
Versace
	as Milanese ruling class, 3, 176
	history, 131–2
	importance, 125
Versace, Gianni
	career, 131–2
	funeral, 132
Vespa, 120
Via Artom (Turin), 138
Via Bianchi, 138–9, 178
Via Corelli, 40, 60–3
Via Fatebenefratelli, 13
Via MacMahon, 1
Via Meda, 66, 68
Via Montenapoleone, 72, 128
Via Palestro, 63
Via Solferino, 15
Via Spaventa, 66
Villa Reale (Monza) see Monza, Royal
	Villa
Virzí, Paolo, 174
Visconti, Eriprando, 72
Visconti family, 16, 106
	Visconti, Luchino, 1, 16, 53, 71, 73, 75–81,
		140, 146
	making of *The Leopard*, 92
	see also Rocco and his Brothers

Index

Vitti, Monica, 81
vita agra, La, 1, 76, 80, 119
voluntary sector, 39

Wertmüller, Lina, 74

wood-based manufacture, 112
workers, 5, 28
movement, 53
working-class culture *see* culture, working
class